P9-DMG-370

Life Moves Pretty Fast

The Lessons We Learned from Eighties Movies
(and Why We Don't Learn Them from Movies Anymore)

Hadley Freeman

POQUOSON PUBLIC LIBRARY
500 CITY HALL AVENUE
POQUOSON, VA 23662

Simon & Schuster Paperbacks

New York   London   Toronto   Sydney   New Delhi

Simon & Schuster Paperbacks
An Imprint of Simon & Schuster, Inc.
1230 Avenue of the Americas
New York, NY 10020

Copyright © 2015, 2016 by Hadley Freeman

An earlier edition of this work was published in Great Britain in 2015.

All rights reserved, including the right to reproduce this book or portions
thereof in any form whatsoever. For information, address
Simon & Schuster Subsidiary Rights Department,
1230 Avenue of the Americas, New York, NY 10020.

First Simon & Schuster trade paperback edition June 2016

SIMON & SCHUSTER PAPERBACKS and colophon are
registered trademarks of Simon & Schuster, Inc.

For information about special discounts for bulk purchases,
please contact Simon & Schuster Special Sales
at 1-866-506-1949 or business@simonandschuster.com.

The Simon & Schuster Speakers Bureau can bring authors to your live event.
For more information or to book an event, contact the
Simon & Schuster Speakers Bureau at 1-866-248-3049 or
visit our website at www.simonspeakers.com.

Interior design by Ruth Lee-Mui

Manufactured in the United States of America

1   3   5   7   9   10   8   6   4   2

Library of Congress Cataloging-in-Publication Data

Names: Freeman, Hadley.
Title: Life moves pretty fast : the lessons we learned from eighties movies
(and why we don't learn them from movies anymore) / Hadley Freeman.
Description: First Simon & Schuster trade paperback edition. | New York :
Simon & Schuster, 2016. | Includes bibliographical references and index.
Identifiers: LCCN 2015048387 (print) | LCCN 2016000145 (ebook)
Subjects: LCSH: Motion pictures—United States—History—20th century. |
Motion pictures—Social aspects—United States—History—20th century. |
BISAC: PERFORMING ARTS / Film & Video /
History & Criticism. | BIOGRAPHY &
AUTOBIOGRAPHY / Personal Memoirs. | HISTORY / North America. |
Classification: LCC PN1993.5.U6 F75 2016 (print) | LCC PN1993.5.U6 (ebook) |
DDC 791.430973/09048—dc23
LC record available at http://lccn.loc.gov/2015048387

ISBN 978-1-5011-3045-8
ISBN 978-1-5011-3066-3 (ebook)

*For Andy, who is even better than Andrew McCarthy,
Michael J. Fox, Matthew Broderick, Eddie Murphy,
Bill Murray, and Dan Aykroyd.*

Combined.

Contents

Life

Moves

Pretty

Fast

Introduction

"Whatever happened to chivalry? Does it only happen in eighties movies? I want John Cusack holding a boom box outside my window. I wanna ride off on a lawn mower with Patrick Dempsey. I want Jake from *Sixteen Candles* waiting outside the church for me. I want Judd Nelson thrusting his fist into the air because he knows he just got me. Just once, I want my life to be like an eighties movie, preferably one with a really awesome musical number for no apparent reason. But no, no, John Hughes did not direct my life."

I am not actually quoting myself here, though heaven knows I could be (except for the part about wanting the moronic Jake from *Sixteen Candles*, for reasons that shall be explained soon enough). That monologue comes from the film *Easy A*, which was released in 2010, and is spoken by Olive, played by Emma Stone, an actress who was born years after most of the movies her character mentions came out. Two years after *Easy A* was released, *Pitch Perfect* arrived and, once again, a film made thirty years earlier was the inspiration and crucial plot point for a twenty-first-century teen film:

"*The Breakfast Club*, 1985, the greatest ending to any movie ever. [The Simple Minds'] song perfectly sums up the movie in that it's equally beautiful and sad," Jesse (Skylar Astin) tells a skeptical Beca (Anna Kendrick). But, of course, Beca's skepticism is as misplaced as the assistant principal's mistrust in Molly Ringwald, Judd Nelson, and the rest of the kids in the 1985 film, because it is only when she watches John Hughes's *The Breakfast Club* that Beca learns to open up emotionally (moviespeak for "get over yourself, you frigid moose, and make out with the dude") and, more important, win the a cappella competition. (Winning an a cappella competition. That is what teens have to live for today. To quote the greatest of all eighties teen films,* "I weep for the future.") Every week, it seems, it's announced that another eighties film is being remade, sequelized, or turned into a stage musical, from *Top Gun* to *The Goonies* to *Dirty Dancing*, invariably starring actors who weren't even born when the originals came out. In 2013 the pop band The 1975 said of their newly released eponymous debut album, "We're massive fans of John Hughes. We wanted to make a record [that] was almost a soundtrack to our teenage years. If he made a movie about us, this would be the soundtrack." Their lead singer was born in the nineties.

I was born in New York City in 1978, meaning that, while I did exist in the eighties as more than a zygote, I wasn't yet a teenager, either. Instead, actual teenagehood for me felt as distant and desirable as the moon. I was a typical older child from a middle-class Jewish family: well behaved, anxious, bookish, and therefore especially curious about the vaguely imagined freedoms I imagined being a teenager would bring. My little sister and I weren't allowed to watch television stations that showed commercials—yes, I come from one of those families—meaning that our viewing options were limited to

---

* *Ferris Bueller's Day Off*, of course.

Sesame Street and whatever our mother allowed us to rent from East 86th Street Video. When I was nine years old, she, for the first time, allowed me to rent something that neither featured animation nor starred Gene Kelly: *Ferris Bueller's Day Off*. I couldn't believe it. How on earth could she—the dorkiest mother EVER, who only ever gave us FRUIT for dessert, I mean I ask you—let me watch such a film? This movie featured BOYS, actual real-life BOYS! Kissing girls—with their tongues! Within the extremely limited framework of my life experience on the Upper East Side in Manhattan, my mother had basically allowed me to rent hard-core porn (tongues!).

Ferris proved to be a mere gateway drug, and I became such a heavy user of East 86th Street Video that for my tenth birthday my parents gave me my own membership card. I was soon mainlining the classics: *Mannequin*; *Romancing the Stone*; *Good Morning, Vietnam*; *The Breakfast Club*; *Short Circuit*; *Indiana Jones*; *E.T.*; *Spaceballs*; *Coming to America*; *Three Amigos!*; *Planes, Trains and Automobiles*; anything produced by Touchstone Pictures, and absolutely everything featuring the two actors who I assured my little sister were the real talents of our era: Steve Guttenberg and Rick Moranis. My highbrow taste, which has lasted all my life, was forged then.

These movies, which were largely seen as junk when they came out, were deeply formative, and everyone I know in my generation feels exactly the same way. They provided the lifelong template for my perceptions of funniness (Eddie Murphy), coolness (Bill Murray), and sexiness (Kathleen Turner). They also taught me more about life than any library or teacher ever would. My parents could have saved literally thousands of dollars, jacked in the schools, and kept the membership to East 86th Street Video and I'd still be essentially the same person today.

•   •   •

But for a long time, these films had a terrible reputation, critically speaking. They were—and largely still are—dismissed as being as drecky as Ray, Egon, Winston, and Peter at the beginning of the *Ghostbusters* sequel. Sold out and bloated, something faintly embarrassing from the past that has left an ugly legacy of franchises and superheroes. Eighties Hollywood, goes the popular critical thought, is when movies started to go wrong: they became obsessed with money and sequels and explosions and cheap gags as opposed to Art. Whereas the far more respected 1970s was the era of the auteur, when Hollywood directors like Robert Altman and Michael Cimino were allowed to pursue their creativity unhindered by studio meddling, the 1980s was the era of the producer, when entertainment took precedence and cartoonish figures like creepy Don Simpson and Jon Peters—who started his career as Barbra Streisand's hairdresser—were the ones with the power.

Many have bemoaned this shift in power from the seventies to the eighties, aghast that the man who once permed *Yentl*'s hair commanded the kind of industry respect once accorded to Altman. But my personal feeling is, when working in the entertainment business, an emphasis on actual entertainment is not necessarily a bad thing, especially if it means producing something like *Top Gun* instead of *Heaven's Gate*. After all, pretty much everyone, if they're honest, is happy to watch some eighties Cruise on a Friday night, but only a very special few would kick off the weekend by cracking open a Cimino DVD.*

---

* And eighties Cruise is, for me, Ultimate Cruise. Nineties Cruise is Actorly Cruise, when he started to take himself awfully seriously, with actorly performances in *A Few Good Men*, *Jerry Maguire*, and *Magnolia* (a film that holds up so much worse than you probably think). (I'm such a nice person I'm not even mentioning nineties films *Far and Away*, *Days of Thunder*, or *Interview with the Vampire* here.) Twenty-first-century

Yet snooty critics aside, eighties movies have maintained an astonishing level of popularity among actual audiences, now, it feels, more than ever. It is taken as a given that mainstream American films from the 1980s have a kind of ironic appeal—everyone wants to watch *Trading Places*, *Scrooged*, and *Die Hard* at Christmas—to the point that to use a photo from an eighties movie as your Facebook avatar is pretty much a hopeless cliché. Partly this veneration comes from what I call the thirty-year rule. This is when movies—and fashions, and TV shows, and pop music—that were dismissed as trash in their day are given their overdue status when their original fans grow up and insist that the culture of their youth was ACTUALLY really important and ACTUALLY nothing's been as good since. But adults today who saw those eighties movies as kids still adore them in a way that those who came of age in, say, the sixties most definitely do not of the Beach Party franchise, the teen movies of their youth. If anything, I love these eighties movies even more than when I first saw them, which is not something I'd say about most other things that I considered cool in the eighties. (Sorry, Milli Vanilli. Although if it's any consolation, you're still on my iPod and I'm not ashamed of that.) More strikingly, teenagers today who were born long after the decade itself love eighties

---

Cruise is Generic Action Cruise, with the endless *Mission: Impossible* franchise and identikit twaddle like *Knight and Day* and *Jack Reacher*. Eighties Cruise, by contrast, is Fun Cruise: *Risky Business*, *All the Right Moves*, *Top Gun*, *The Color of Money*, *Cocktail*. Even his more actorly eighties performances, such as in *Rain Man* and *Born on the Fourth of July*, were Fun because it was fun (and somewhat surprising) to see that the dude really can act. (And Cruise totally deserved the Oscar for *Rain Man* more than Dustin Hoffman. Yeah, I said it.) Eighties Cruise was also pre–Scientology Scary Cruise, in that his allegiance to the Church was not widely known and he hadn't jumped on any sofas yet, meaning we could all watch him without Complicated Feelings. So all in all, eighties Cruise wins.

movies in a way I certainly never did love the movies my parents grew up with.

"Some of the people who come up to me were teenagers when the movies originally came out, but the vast majority of the approaches I get on a daily basis come from eleven- to fifteen-year-old kids," says Alex Winter, who appeared in two of the most fun eighties teen films, *The Lost Boys* and, of course, *Bill and Ted's Excellent Adventure*. "They come up to me and are like, 'Hey, you're Bill!' It's amazing."

I should probably pause here and explain what, precisely, I mean by "eighties movies." When I started to think about writing this book, I spoke to a few film critics for their thoughts on eighties movies, including Peter Biskind, whose excellent book *Easy Riders, Raging Bulls* is probably the best-known example of the kind of dichotomy I just described: 1970s Hollywood good, 1980s Hollywood tacky hell. To his enormous credit, he didn't slam the phone down on me when I told him my idea.

"It's true, I haven't been very kind about eighties films, but they are ripe for revisionism," Biskind said.

I took a deep breath, gearing up to explain my deeply involved critical theory about *Three Men and a Baby*.

But Biskind spoke first: "Take *Salvador*, for example," he said, referring to Oliver Stone's 1986 movie about leftist guerrillas in the Salvadoran civil war. "That's a fascinating film. You should really write about *Salvador*."

Dear reader, I have not written about *Salvador*. As you might have gathered by now, my tastes lie in a different direction: an unabashedly, unremittingly mainstream direction. I'm sure there are plenty of eighties film aficionados out there who, when they think of the eighties, think of James Woods being terrorized by death squads in Central America. But when I think of the eighties, I think of the giant Stay Puft Marshmallow Man crushing New York cabs underfoot. I'm not saying one take is better than the other,* but I am saying, when was the last time you fancied watching *Salvador*? At ten past never, probably. And when did you last want to watch *Ghostbusters*? Two seconds ago, when I mentioned Mr. Stay Puft, right? Popularity is never a guarantee of quality (just look at *Two and a Half Men*), but it is a sign of something when a movie made more than thirty years ago is still regarded as one of the best comedies of all time (something, I guarantee, will not happen to *Two and a Half Men*). Anyway, no one needs telling that *Salvador*—or *Blade Runner*, or *Aliens*, or *Scarface*, or *Full Metal Jacket*—are Good Eighties Movies. Everyone knows that. I wanted to write about why the Fun Eighties Movies—like *Die Hard*, *Steel Magnolias*, *Pretty in Pink*, and *Adventures in Babysitting*—are also Good Eighties Movies.

The eighties movies I watched as a kid are still the eighties movies I love today, and, yes, there is, inevitably, some sentimentality going on here. But there is something else, too, that lies behind my love of them and everyone else's love of them: these movies offer something that equivalent movies today don't.

Obviously, good movies get made today. Classics, even.

Hell, I can name loads of movies† that I love that were made after 1990, so I'm certainly not saying that only in the eighties were good films forged, or that all films made in the eighties were stone-cold classics. (*Mannequin*, for a start, is absolute crud.) There were loads of things that were completely awful about eighties movies, but not the things that people generally talk about when they complain about eighties movies.

For a start, the social attitudes occasionally leave more than

---

* Mine is better.
† Well, maybe seven.

something to be desired. There was a weird tendency in some eighties films to treat rape as a comedic plot device. Tedious Jake* in *Sixteen Candles* hoots about how his girlfriend, Caroline, is so drunk he "could violate her ten ways if I wanted to." Did I mention this is the film's romantic lead, the one we're supposed to cheer on? I don't think so, John Hughes. And then, just to prove Jake's theory, the school geek (played by Anthony Michael Hall) has sex with Caroline when she's pretty much comatose. There's a similarly gruesome moment in *Revenge of the Nerds*, when one of the nerds tricks a girl into having sex with him by pretending he's someone else. Finally, in *Overboard*—a movie I enjoy way more than I know I should— a handyman (Kurt Russell) convinces a rich lady with amnesia (Goldie Hawn) that she's his wife and has sex with her accordingly. In all these films, the women end up happily partnered with their rapists, which is just what happens in all rape scenarios, right?

Then there are the casual racist epithets, homophobic slurs (it is deeply depressing to see actors as lovely as Michael J. Fox and Molly Ringwald using words like *faggot* with gleeful abandon), and the forays into faintly deranged American patriotism. But, in the main, I'll defend eighties movies with the ferocity of Crocodile Dundee protecting his mullet-haired woman. THAT'S a knife.[†]

"I still get stopped in the street by people who ask, 'Why don't they make movies like they did in the eighties?' And I don't really know the answer," muses my thespian eighties icon, Rick Moranis.

The reason it feels as if they just don't make fun movies today

---

[*] Played by Michael Schoeffling, later spotted in nineties teen classic *Mermaids* toying with Winona Ryder's heart. Talk to the hand, Michael Schoeffling.
[†] And in any case, it's not as though movies today are exactly perfect in their social attitudes. After all, Will Ferrell, who presumably has some say over his career choices, made a 2015 comedy, *Get Hard*, in which the entire premise is that white and black people are from different species, and gay men are gross.

like they did in the 1980s is that they don't, and this is down to three specific factors: economics, shifting social attitudes, and (the following should be said in your deepest James Earl Jones voice, either as Darth Vader or as the angry author in *Field of Dreams*) the changing world order. When people talk about eighties movies, by which I mean the eighties movies I love, they tend to focus on the kitschiness of them: the outfits, the anachronistic jokes, the endlessly quotable quotes. And I do, too (I've tried to limit myself to just one quote in each chapter since otherwise this book would have become a massive quote-a-thon). I love the silliness of eighties movies, their sweetness, the stirring music (the theme music for *Back to the Future*, *Top Gun*, *Beverly Hills Cop*, and *Indiana Jones* all very much feature in my mental greatest hits of all time), the power ballads, the formulae. Even if you don't think the eighties made the best movies,* it's hard to argue against the theory that the eighties produced the most fun movies. And, hell, there is nothing wrong with fun.

But there is more to these movies than kitsch.

Kitsch is fine but it tends not to have longevity. These movies have certain qualities and feature particular lessons that you simply don't see in films made today. That, for me at least, is a large part of what makes them feel so special.

To divide up anything by decade is, by nature, totally spurious—best nineties dance music! best seventies hair styles!—but in the case of eighties movies there is a point because movies made in Hollywood in the 1980s marked the beginning of a new era (the Producer Era) and, by 1989, the start of another (the corporate buyouts of the studios). As anyone who has ever watched an eighties film—or who even is (gasp!) old enough to remember the

---

* And you'd be wrong if you don't.

eighties—knows, life has changed a lot in the past thirty years: cell phones aren't the size of cars and men don't tend to sport eighties Michael Douglas–style bouffant hair; more's the pity. Moviemaking in Hollywood has changed a lot in those years, too. The big studios are now owned by international conglomerates: Columbia has been owned by the Sony Corporation since 1989; Warner Bros. merged with Time Inc. and became Time Warner, also in 1989; 20th Century Fox has been owned by Rupert Murdoch's News Corporation since the mid-1980s; Universal has gone through a series of owners in the past twenty years, including a French water and media company and General Electric, and is now owned by cable provider Comcast; Paramount is owned by Viacom. Whereas once moviemaking was the sole business of the studios, now it is a relatively tiny part of a big company.*

"There are a million reasons why moviemaking is different now, but a big one is the conglomerates," says John Landis, who in the eighties alone directed *An American Werewolf in London*, *The Blues Brothers*, *Trading Places*, *Three Amigos!*, and *Coming to America*. "Between Disney and Rupert Murdoch, only four or five companies own the media now, and they own everything. This means that management has become much more corporate. I had final cut on my movies for twenty years—now they never give you final cut. Of course we had arguments [with studios in the eighties], but not like it is now. Now if you make a studio picture it's like—uh oh . . ."

"The studios had been individually held entities that were focused on making movies. But when they were sold off and bought by multinational corporations, they became cogs in the wheels

---

* Edward Jay Epstein, *The Big Picture: The New Logic of Money and Power in Hollywood* (New York: Random House, 2005). A very good primer if you're interested in this wonky sort of stuff.

of these big corporations and the priority is never about making movies—the priority is about making money," says film writer Melissa Silverstein. "So those pressures took over and the people who were executives were more focused on the financial bottom line, not the artistic bottom line."

"The eighties," adds Landis, "is the last era of the studio system."

The world has changed, too. Back in the mid-eighties, the international market would make up about 20 percent of a film's revenue. Now it's 80 percent because, while U.S. audiences have gently fallen (although box-office takings have generally remained steady due to rising ticket prices), the international market has grown exponentially, led by China. On the one hand it's great that America—or Hollywood, at least—is acknowledging the importance of audiences outside its borders. But it's less brilliant if that means it just makes more films like 2014's mind-numbing *Transformers: Age of Extinction*, a film that was expressly made with the Chinese market in mind. If you wondered why there are so many big dumb franchises and mind-numbing blockbusters around these days, the answer is simply that they make an enormous amount of money overseas, even when they lose money in the United States, as they increasingly do.* Conversely, it has never been harder for smaller, original movies with good storylines to get made in today's Hollywood studios.

"I doubt very much I could get a studio to make *Cocoon* today— it would be seen too much as an oddity and too eccentric," says the not-exactly-cloutless Ron Howard. "I could probably get it made as an independent, but then it wouldn't get the kind of distribution

---

* In 1993, twenty-two blockbusters opened on U.S. screens in the summer. In 2013, it was thirty-one, all costing more than $100 million to make, and most of them flopped. Catherine Rampell, "Hollywood's Tanking Business Model," *New York Times*, September 3, 2013.

that made it a top ten box-office hit [back in the eighties]. I think in a lot of ways, the system is less flexible and less open today."

"Half of my movies wouldn't have been made today. Not in a million years would a studio make *The Blues Brothers*," says John Landis.

"Back in the 1980s, you could make something like *Back to the Future* that was a little wacky. You could try things. The world was a completely different place. Now there's no room for that. It's hard to get something made that isn't derivative. *Back to the Future* would be impossible to do," says Robert Zemeckis.*

Instead, studios focus almost solely on big movies—or "tent-poles," so called because they are intended to act as financial support for a whole studio—like *Twilight*, *Transformers*, *X-Men*, *Hunger Games*, and superheroes that will work around the world. (It's easy to translate explosions for foreign markets; long dialogue about old people traveling to other planets? Not so much.) Obviously big movies and blockbusters existed in the eighties—the seventies and eighties damn near invented them—but they were seen as annual one-offs by studios rather than the only interest. The ridiculous irony now is that the very filmmakers who coined the seventies and eighties blockbuster, Steven Spielberg and George Lucas, can't get studios to back their films. In June 2013 the directors gave a talk at the University of Southern California School of Cinematic Arts and discussed how studios "would rather spend $250m on a single film [rather] than make several, personal quirky projects." "The studios are going for the gold," said Lucas. "But that isn't going to work forever. And as a result they're getting narrower and narrower in their focus. People are going to get tired of it. They're not going to know

---

* Ryan Gilbey, "*The Walk*: Interview with Robert Zemeckis," *Guardian*, September 24, 2015.

how to do anything else . . . [Spielberg's] *Lincoln* and [Lucas's] *Red Tails* barely got into theaters. You're talking about Steven Spielberg and George Lucas can't get their movies into theaters."

The movie business itself is in what one producer describes as "chaos," flummoxed by how to compete with the Internet and on-demand TV, and how to make the most money possible from streaming. "It's very much like when television started and the studios went reeling. We're seeing that seismic shift again," says Landis.

Also, movies and the marketing of movies have become insanely expensive (in 2012 the Motion Picture Association of America, MPAA, stopped revealing how much they spend on marketing movies but one studio chief told *Variety* that "$150–175m for global marketing costs" is pretty standard). So now studios will only back films that are easy to sell and will work around the world because this then guarantees they will make their money back. This also means that they want movies that appeal to as many demographics as possible, or "quadrants," as film marketing staff refer to people: men, women, old people, and young people. This in turn has led to the demise of traditional women's movies, because they wouldn't appeal to enough quadrants (according to a Hollywood theory that has been around only for the past thirty years, women will see movies starring men and women, but men will see only movies starring men). It also means that films become less interesting because whenever anyone says they want to make something appeal to everybody, they inevitably blandify it to such a degree that it is loved by nobody.

What studios don't want anymore is the kind of mid-budget movies that were made alongside the blockbusters and blockbuster franchises in the eighties, which is what John Hughes's films were. *The Breakfast Club*, let alone *Ferris Bueller's Day Off*, would simply not get made today by a studio. The eighties invented the film franchise, and now it's film franchises that are killing the best sort of movies that were made in the eighties. Teen actors who would have made for perfect sensitive teen stars—Elijah Wood, Tobey Maguire, Shia LaBeouf—instead get shuffled into blockbuster action McFranchises.

"Without a film that can work on thousands of screens and draw in big audiences based upon a presold property, i.e., a remake, sequel, bestseller, major star vehicle, no one will commit the money to marketing the film. So we're getting a certain kind of film, the McMovie, and there's a growing sameness to what works in these big mainstream releases. Thirty years ago in 1984 films like *Amadeus* and *The Natural* were all top hits. Would they get green lights today? I doubt it," says Steven Gaydos, editor of *Variety*. "*Field of Dreams*? *The Big Chill*? *Moonstruck*? No way, not today," says film producer Lynda Obst. Comedy, too, has suffered because of this. But wait! you cry. Surely this is the golden age of comedy! *The Hangover*! *Bridesmaids*! APATOW. Ah, but those are gross-out comedies, and raunch is funny in all languages. What is less easy to translate is Nora Ephron–style comedy, the kind of comedy you quote forever and live and die by. No one will ever live and die by anything that is said or happens in *The Hangover*. But I know people who have changed their entire lives because of a line of dialogue from *When Harry Met Sally . . .* and when I say "people" I obviously mean "me."

But this is not just about studio system shenanigans. It's also about how Western culture and politics have changed. American culture has become increasingly conservative since the 1980s. This might seem counterintuitive, considering the legalization of gay marriage and the election of a two-term mixed-race president. But the fightback from these and other developments has been vicious, and this and the growth of pressure groups have impacted on what studios feel able to show now in movies, especially when it comes to young women's stories, sexuality, and abortion. "What happens in movies always reflects what's happening in the culture and what we're seeing on-screen is an American culture trying to put women back in their place," says Melissa Silverstein.

Then there are the increasingly screwy ideas about beauty, desirability, and maturity that come from Western pop culture. It is impossible to imagine a young woman playing the romantic lead in a movie today without perfectly blow-dried hair, a size 0 body, and body-clinging clothes—or if she did go without any of those, it would be some kind of statement about her (and she'd certainly remedy her oversight by the end of the film). But this was simply not the case back in the 1980s. Molly Ringwald, Jennifer Grey, Ally Sheedy, Jennifer Jason Leigh, Elisabeth Shue, Annie Potts, Susan Ursitti: the reason young women loved those actresses so much is that they felt recognizable to them. They still do. The sight of Melanie Griffith's gorgeously curvaceous and pale body in *Working Girl* when she's dolled up in her lingerie feels downright subversive compared with nowadays, when actresses' bodies are tanned and toned to an occasionally painful fault. That movies from the eighties—the eighties!—look so much more innocent and politically engaged and female-friendly and even moral than many of today's mainstream films says quite a lot about how things have changed since, and without many of us really noticing because these changes happen incrementally.

Now, a word of warning: there is an excellent chance that your favorite eighties movies are not discussed in this book. That is because this book features my favorite eighties films and, as such, is faintly autobiographical and deeply subjective. To spare you the shock and disappointment, here are some of the eighties movies that are pretty much ignored in this book:

The Empire Strikes Back

The Return of the Jedi (fine, I admit it: I never got into *Star Wars*)

Star Trek (ditto)

Most films starring Arnold Schwarzenegger

Ditto Sylvester Stallone

Friday the 13th and *Nightmare on Elm Street* (I find the opening scene of *Ghostbusters* terrifying enough, thanks)

Anything horror, in fact

Iron Eagle (apparently guys really love this movie)

Salvador (sorry, Peter Biskind)

Many, many more that I love but just couldn't fit in

This is not an encyclopedia of eighties movies. If you want that, buy an encyclopedia (although probably the last time you saw an encyclopedia was in the eighties). But I think even if your favorite movie of all time is *The Return of the Jedi* (weirdo), you'll find things here that will go some way to explaining why the *Star Wars* films in the seventies and eighties were great and why the prequel trilogy that George Lucas made twenty years later is absolute garbage.

Another word of warning: I tried to talk to the main people from each of the movies I look at in this book, and that has been one of the real joys of writing it. It took thirty years but I finally found a (vaguely) legitimate excuse to make Molly Ringwald and Ivan Reitman speak to me. But in some cases I was just too late. Three of my favorite filmmakers from the eighties died in the past decade and it is a source of real regret that I didn't get my act together sooner in time to talk to John Hughes, Nora Ephron, and Harold Ramis. They feel like big omissions from this book because they have all been such a huge presence in my life.*

I love these movies because they're hilarious and sweet and smart—because they're fun. They're Good, capital *G*, and it might sound odd to say this of a film behemoth like *Ghostbusters*, but they're also underrated. These films didn't just make us all happy; they teach you more than you learn from movies today. Yes, "the force is in you, Lone Star—it's in you," to quote one particular eighties film† I loved so much as a kid that I watched the videocassette to ribbons. But that force is in me because of these movies. Thanks to them, the true eighties force will always be strong with us.

---

* I also made the decision in the chapter about *Batman* to use an interview I did with Tim Burton for the *Guardian* a few years ago along with my favorite book about the director instead of bothering the poor man again. When I met up with him before, I was so excited I burbled to him for about ten minutes about how much I loved his artwork. "Wow, you really . . . like my drawings," he eventually replied. When Tim Burton pretty much tells you that you're an obsessive nerd, you know you've crossed a line.

† The mighty, mighty *Spaceballs*.

Dirty Dancing

Abortions Happen and That's Just Fine

Few movies have been as underrated and misunderstood as 1987's *Dirty Dancing*. I first saw it when I was ten and I'm afraid that far from appreciating that I was bearing witness to one of the great feminist films of all time, I was so excited to be watching a movie that had the word *dirty* in the title that I spent the whole film waiting for it to finish so I could call my friend Lauren to brag about this achievement.

"Well, I just saw *Can't Buy Me Love*, twice," said Lauren balefully, referring to the Patrick Dempsey teen romcom, "and two viewings of *Can't Buy Me Love* is worth one *Dirty Dancing*."

Out of politeness, I agreed, but we both knew that was totally not true (*Can't Buy Me Love* doesn't have a single sex scene so, like, come on). But just to make sure, I then watched *Dirty Dancing* two more times in a row so that Lauren would definitely not be able to catch up with my coolness. And just to prove how cool I was, I then called Lauren again to tell her that, too.

Adult critics and audiences at the time were just as blind as ten-year-old me when it came to seeing the feminism in *Dirty Dancing* (although presumably most of them didn't immediately brag to their frenemies about having just seen the movie). Partly this comes down to sexism. Partly it's a reflection of how times have changed in the past thirty years. And mainly it's because the film's writer, Eleanor Bergstein, rightly thought the best way to deliver a social message was "to present it in a pleasurable way so that the moral lessons would sneak up on people." But for a long time I was so distracted by the pleasure—specifically, the soundtrack, the sex, the Swayze—that the moral lessons didn't sneak up at all. For years I didn't realize I was watching one of the great feminist tracts of the 1980s, easily up there with Susan Faludi's feminist study of the eighties, *Backlash*. But then, Faludi's book doesn't come with a half-naked Patrick Swayze, so it is easier to recognize it as a contribution to the fight against misogyny.

By the mid-eighties, both *Flashdance* and *Footloose* had been released and studios were desperate for another teen movie that featured dancing and came with a great commercial soundtrack. But one movie they definitely did not want was *Dirty Dancing*.

"I cannot be clear enough about this: everybody thought *Dirty Dancing* was just a piece of teenage junk," says the charmingly chatty Bergstein. "Nobody wanted to make it. Nobody. I would send out the script to studios along with a tape of the soundtrack that I'd made to go with it, that was just recordings of my old forty-fives from the 1960s, and executives would call me and say, 'Oh yeah, Eleanor, we're not going to make the movie, but could you send me another cassette? I wore out the last one.' But not even that convinced them of the movie's potential."

MGM briefly took on the script at the encouragement of several female executives (the men there all hated it), but then dropped it. Not a single other studio would consider it. Eventually a small independent production company looked at it, saw it as an easy quick buck, and offered to make it for $4 million, about a fifth of the average cost of a movie at the time. Bergstein and her producer, Linda Gottlieb, accepted.

Bergstein had already had one screenplay produced, the undeservedly forgotten 1980 film *It's My Turn*, in which Jill Clayburgh plays a mathematics professor who has an affair with an athlete, played by Michael Douglas. The inspiration for that came from Bergstein's observations of female mathematics students at Princeton, where her husband was a professor, and the condescension they had to endure from men, including accusations that their boyfriends did all their work for them ("It made me so mad!" she wails, still just as infuriated today as she was three decades ago). During the making of that film, Bergstein included a dance sequence inspired by the kind of dancing she used to do with her friends when growing up in Brooklyn, but it was ultimately cut. This was fortunate for two reasons: one, just the thought of Michael Douglas *Dirty Dancing* is faintly traumatizing; and, two, this then made her determined to write a movie that foregrounded the dancing. After a few years, she wrote the story of a young woman known as Baby (Jennifer Grey) who goes to a holiday camp in the Catskills with her parents and sister in the summer of 1963 and falls in love with the dance instructor, Johnny (Patrick Swayze).

After having endured so much studio skepticism about the film, Bergstein has become pretty hardened to critics misunderstanding and dismissing her film. Proving author William Goldman's adage that no one knows anything in the film business, one producer said before the film was released that it was so bad they should just burn the negatives and collect the insurance money, and, hundreds of millions of dollars later, Bergstein laughs at the memory. But there are two comments she frequently hears that drive her crazy: "I hate it when people describe Baby as an Ugly Duckling, because Jennifer [Grey]'s beautiful, obviously. I also can't stand it when people describe it as a Cinderella story, because all Cinderella ever did was sit on her rump!"

Baby definitely does a lot more with her rump than just sit on it. When the film opens she is reading a book about economic development because she's going to major in the economics of underdeveloped countries—not English literature, she impatiently corrects a condescending suitor—and join the Peace Corps. "Our Baby's going to save the world!" her proud father, Dr. Houseman (the delightfully eyebrowed Jerry Orbach), boasts to the folk at Kellerman's, the (not very subtly Jewish) holiday camp. (*Dirty Dancing* is easily the most Jewish eighties teen film, which is probably another reason it is so close to my own Jewish heart. As Bergstein says, "You just have to know how to spot the clues."*)

But until she can save the world, Baby sets about saving everyone she meets. Grey is perfect as a naïve and idealistic but likable teenager, one who is determined to help the poor and downtrodden, and yet has no concept of what life is like for anyone who is anything other than Jewish† and middle class (another probable reason why I found it so easy to relate to this film so much). She is repulsed by

---

* The very obviously Jewish Wendy (Mare Winningham) in *St. Elmo's Fire* gets to experience this fantasy, too, when she rejects the nerdy Jewish boy her father picks out for her and loses her virginity instead to Billy (Rob Lowe), which is surely the ultimate fantasy for all eighties girls, Jewish and non. However, seeing as Billy treats Wendy horrendously, and the film suggests he sees this as little more than an intriguing pity shag, I maintain that, in the world of Jewish women's sex fantasies, Baby and Johnny > Wendy and Billy.

† Winona Ryder was originally considered for the role, and she would have been good at conveying Baby's nerviness—and Jewishness—but it would have been much harder to accept her as a wide-eyed sixties teenager. Ryder, even back in the eighties, has always been just that bit too ironic and cool. Grey, on the other hand, was all wide-eyed sweetness.

the disdainful manner with which the holiday camp's bosses treat the (Catholic) working-class entertainment staff, and she is horrified when she realizes her father is just as big a snob. When she learns that the dance instructor Penny (Cynthia Rhodes*) is pregnant with the waiter Robbie's (Max Cantor†) baby, she tells Robbie to pay for Penny's abortion. When he refuses, she gets the money herself. When Johnny needs someone to stand in for Penny for the dance routine, Baby offers herself. When Penny's abortion is botched, she gets her father to step in.

Baby doesn't understand the lower-middle-class world in which Johnny and Penny live, a world in which one can easily lose one's dreams in a snap, but she doesn't judge. Baby is a great film heroine. As Johnny says, Baby looks at the world and thinks she can make it better, and at first he finds this irritating and dismisses her as a "Little Miss Fix-It." But it's also what makes him fall for her: when she messes up the dance and misses the lift, she improvises and they get away with it. "That is when Johnny falls in love with her," says Bergstein. "Because he sees how she always wants to make it better, and she shows him that she can."

She is just as determined when it comes to getting what she wants in her own life, and what she wants in *Dirty Dancing* is to have sex with Johnny, and the film is very, very clear about that. It's

---

* Rather thrillingly, in real life Rhodes was married to eighties pop star Richard Marx. Hard to get more eighties than that.

† Max Cantor had probably the creepiest post-eighties teen movie career of anyone, and that really is saying something. After a privileged New York upbringing and a very brief acting career he became an investigative journalist. He came across a story about a cannibalistic cult in downtown New York and, in order to gain their trust and get the story, he started taking drugs. He soon became addicted and was eventually found dead. Some alleged he was killed by the cannibal, Daniel Rakowitz, but others said he simply overdosed. Whatever the truth, it's hard not to think poor old Robbie should have stuck with Ayn Rand and stayed away from the cannibals.

no surprise that at MGM none of the men liked the script, or that it was ultimately produced by a woman, because *Dirty Dancing* is very much a film about female sexuality. In particular, the physicality of female sexuality, and all the excitement and messiness that entails. It's Baby who makes all the moves on Johnny when she turns up at his cabin at night and then, as he stands stock-still in helpless befuddlement, takes the lead again by asking him to dance. As they dance, her hands pour over his half-naked body, taking real pleasure in his skin, and the camera zooms in on her hand sliding down to feel his butt. The whole film is told from Baby's point of view, which is why there are so many adoring shots of Johnny with his top off and barely any similarly lustful ones of her. There are occasional close-up shots of her pelvis in what is one of the greatest 1980s montage scenes of all, when Johnny is teaching her how to dance while "Hungry Eyes" plays on the soundtrack, but these feel more like a visual nudge about Baby's sexual excitement than the film panting over Grey's slim hips. Instead, it's the man who is objectified by the camera and the woman who gets turned on, in a manner not seen again until Brad Pitt frolicked with a hair dryer for Geena Davis in 1991's *Thelma & Louise*, and hardly seen at all now.˙

"The whole film is told through the female gaze, if I can use that jargon, because I wanted to make a movie about what it's like, as a young woman, moving into the physical world, which means the sexual world," says Bergstein. "So you get those shots of Jennifer

---

˙ One of the reasons—perhaps, in fact, the main reason—the *50 Shades of Cliché* franchise was so successful was that it very specifically told the story from Anastasia's point of view. The big difference between *50 Shades* and *Dirty Dancing*, though, besides the fact that Johnny Castle is a friendly bit of beefcake and Christian Grey is a menacing stalker, is that Anastasia, in distinct contrast to Baby, completely bends herself to Christian's will. James's follow-up, *Grey*, which is written entirely from Christian's point of view because not enough erotica is told from the male gaze, of course, confirmed that Grey is somehow simultaneously a tedious and repulsive character.

looking up with her big eyes and then about a hundred shots of Patrick. I remember when we were in the editing suite and people were saying, 'Why do you have all those shots of Patrick?' I'd say, 'It's because that's what she sees.' The film is through the female gaze and most movies are not."

Johnny is no cipher—and no one other than Swayze, the son of a cowboy and ballet dancer, could have captured Johnny's feminized masculinity—but other eighties teen films such as *Pretty in Pink* and *Say Anything* at least offered male characters whom young straight male audiences might empathize with. Johnny, however, is a character for the girls. *Dirty Dancing* is wholly a film for female audiences, and, lo, male critics gave it terrible reviews. Roger Ebert dismissed it as "relentlessly predictable" and *Time* magazine's Richard Schickel was similarly dismissive. The *New Yorker*'s Pauline Kael, on the other hand, wrote that the film left her "giggling happily." The *Philadelphia Inquirer*'s film critic Carrie Rickey wrote decades later: "[The *New York Times*' then film critic] Vincent Canby agreed with me that, as with *Desperately Seeking Susan*, the critical resistance to *Dirty Dancing* might have been because it was a female-centered story." It is nothing new for a women's movie—or book, or TV show—to be dismissed by male film critics as frothy nothingness.* What is more striking is that so many aspects of the film that seem extraordinary now were so overlooked at the time.

Not only does Baby want sex with Johnny, but she loves having sex with Johnny, and the film emphasizes this with the not exactly subtle analogy the film draws between dancing and sex. Her face shines with happiness on the mornings after, her dancing improving

---

* *Sex and the City*, starring Jennifer Grey look-alike Sarah Jessica Parker, would suffer a similar fate two decades later, even though, in its heyday, it was at least as smart and sharp as any critically lauded male TV drama.

as she gains in sexual confidence. Baby's rejection of her father for the sexy staff at Kellerman's Hotel is as symbolic as that of Rose's abandonment of her wealthy life for the Irish-jigging working classes in 1997's *Titanic*. (The poor: there to provide a buttoned-up wealthy girl's sexual awakening. And such good dancers, too!) It's only by losing her virginity that Baby sees the fallibility of her parents and sheds her Baby-ness to become *Frances*, and the film applauds this. (As did audiences: Baby and Johnny's sex scenes were the formative erotic experience for an entire generation; there is still a large part of me that believes I haven't actually had sex yet because none of my sexual encounters has started by lip-synching "Love Is Strange," although God knows not through lack of trying on my part.)

"Baby risks everything for integrity and love, and she doesn't pay the price," says Bergstein. "Most movies make girls pay the price."

Girls in eighties teen movies love sex, and suffer few consequences for it. In the now deservedly little-seen *Valley Girl* (only worth seeing, really, for Nicolas Cage's waistcoat and to hear Modern English's "I Melt with You" on the soundtrack), the teenage girls discuss sex lustfully with one another. In *Mystic Pizza*, Jojo (Lili Taylor) sneaks into bathrooms every spare minute with her fiancé (Vincent D'Onofrio) and they end up happily married, while Daisy (Julia Roberts) seduces her wealthy boyfriend and the two apparently end up contentedly, if improbably, together. (Of the *Mystic Pizza* trio, only Kat—Annabeth Gish—has a bad sexual experience in that she realizes afterward that her lover will never leave his wife. But this plot twist strikes me as more of a comment on the man specifically rather than on sex in general, as Kat seems far more upset by the former than the latter.) In *Say Anything*, Diane (Ione Skye) seems completely unbothered after losing her virginity to Lloyd (John Cusack) in his car. Lloyd, by contrast, is utterly shattered by the encounter and can pull himself together only by listening to a Peter Gabriel ballad, poor boy.[*]

This fairly basic truism—teenage girls enjoy sex—is a lesson gleaned far more rarely from films today. Today a girl in a teen film who has sex—or even just wants to have sex—risks being ravaged by her boyfriend and eaten from within by a vampire baby (Bella in *Twilight*). At the very least, a girl who has sex is certainly emotionally damaged (*The Perks of Being a Wallflower*) and will be universally shamed (*Easy A*). Good, smart, sane girls don't have sex, or at least are extremely reluctant to do so and submit only under sufferance because the boys want it so badly (Dionne in *Clueless*, Vicky in *American Pie*). It's a weird harking back to one of the biggest teen films of the seventies, *Halloween*, in which any teenage girl who has sex is promptly dispatched by a dungaree-wearing psycho. Now, instead, they are destroyed from within. A teen film today can show teens having sex—as long as it's in a raunchy comedy and the sex is presented as extreme or slapstick, such as 1999's *American Pie*, 2007's *Superbad*, 2012's *Project X*, or 2013's *The To Do List* and, from Britain, 2011's *The Inbetweeners Movie*, and is pretty much invariably from the boy's point of view. What you don't see anymore are

---

[*] Boys, too, enjoy their sexual maturity in eighties teen films. In *Risky Business*, Joel (Tom Cruise) enjoys aerobic if somewhat improbable sex with Lana (Rebecca De Mornay) when he loses his virginity. In *Teen Wolf*, as the film's title emphasizes, the old trope about werewolfishness as a symbol for male puberty is employed to its most delightfully ridiculous extent, and in a far sillier way than it was in 1957's *I Was a Teenage Werewolf*. It is almost certainly the best movie ever made about male puberty; what Judy Blume's *Are You There God? It's Me, Margaret* is to girls, *Teen Wolf* should be to boys. When Scott (Michael J. Fox) changes into a wolf, he becomes irresistible to girls in high school, and he enjoys sex with them with a howl. Similarly, the teen vampires in the presciently emo *The Lost Boys* take enormous pleasure in their vampirism. Compared to both these films, the vampire and the werewolf in *Twilight* make sexuality and maturation look a lot less fun.

tender depictions of teen sexuality, or realistic ones.* Instead, teen sex comes with warnings or in the nervily ironic coating of raunch.

"You can have a movie with a wild party and lots of sexual comedy, but you can't have a movie in which a fifteen-year-old girl is teaching her friends about sex," says *Fast Times at Ridgemont High*'s director, Amy Heckerling. "Like in *Borat*, you can have naked men with their dicks swinging around for ten minutes as long as they're not sexual. But you don't see any more young people realistically exploring their sexuality together."

Film producer and director Jon Avnet agrees that one of the biggest differences between today's teen films and those of the eighties is the depiction of sexuality, and, as the producer of *Risky Business*, one of the sexiest and most influential† eighties teen films, he should know.

"The subway scene in *Risky Business* between Rebecca [De Mornay] and Tom [Cruise] is really pretty hot, and I don't think you could have something that hot in a teen film now. Sex as a form of intimacy is tantamount to death in teen films today," he says. Instead, he suggests, sex in teen films is now either nonexistent or "like something out of *Porky's*."

One woman in *Dirty Dancing* very nearly does get punished for having sex: Penny, who almost dies after undergoing an illegal abortion. I'm not sure what I thought was going on with Penny when I was a kid; maybe I thought she was having her appendix taken out, maybe I was so baffled by it that I simply ignored it. But

---

* When I was complaining about this to a friend a year or so ago, she recommended the Shailene Woodley oeuvre to me, specifically *The Spectacular Now* and *The Fault in Our Stars*. As depictions of teen sex go, they're not bad. But they also, respectively, celebrate Manic Pixie Dream Girls and fetishize illness, and thus fail my realism test.
† John Hughes's teen films were clearly and heavily influenced by *Risky Business*, minus the plot about prostitutes (thank God).

when I came back to the film as a teenager, expecting to spend a happy ninety minutes wallowing in sexy dance sequences, familiar one-liners ("I carried a watermelon"), and Jennifer Grey's magnificent original nose (since tragically mutilated), it was something of a shock to realize that what *Dirty Dancing* is really about, at its heart, is the importance of legal abortion. The film is astonishingly open about the brutality of illegal abortions. Penny, we are told, went to "some butcher" who had "a folding table and a dirty knife." This was, we are repeatedly told, "illegal," which is why she can't go to a doctor when it goes wrong and she nearly bleeds to death.

"When I wrote the film, abortion—like feminism—was one of those issues that people thought just wasn't relevant anymore. A lot of young women thought those battles were won, and talking about it was tiresome," says Bergstein. "But I thought *Roe versus Wade* was precarious, and that's why I put in all that purple language about the 'dirty knife' and everything. The film is set in 1963 but came out in 1987 and I wanted young women seeing the film to understand that it wasn't just that she went to Planned Parenthood and it went wrong."

No one—not the studio, not the critics—complained at the time that the movie's entire plot is put into motion by an illegal abortion: "They didn't even notice that it was there," says Bergstein. "The studio thought the script was stupid and bad for so many reasons they scarcely noticed that. Certainly no one suggested that it might be controversial. They thought it was just a stupid teenage dance movie." The first objection raised came from an acne cream company who wanted to sponsor the film—and get their tube of cream on every poster—but they backed away when they saw the film. The studio suggested that the film be reshot but Bergstein pointed out that the abortion is integral to the movie, as it's how Johnny and Baby meet and, most interestingly, prompts them into having sex for the first time, and so the studio backed down.

"I knew that if I put in a social message it had to be carefully plotted in. A lot of movies have social messages but they end up on the cutting room floor. It's true that not many people talked about the abortion plot when it came out, but it meant that I was getting the message to people who wouldn't go see a documentary about abortions, and we were also getting big feminist audiences," says Bergstein.

Just as eighties teen movies didn't shy away from showing how much teenage girls like sex, nor did they avoid discussing one possible result of the activity: getting an abortion. In 1980's *Fame*, wealthy Hilary (Antonia Franceschi) has an abortion after accidentally becoming pregnant (after sleeping with a black student, incidentally, something else that no one comments on). The only one who raises a question about her decision is the nurse, who asks which credit card she is going to use to pay for the operation. In 1982's *Fast Times at Ridgemont High*, Stacy (Jennifer Jason Leigh), who, at fifteen, is underage, loses her virginity and becomes pregnant after a hurried encounter with nineteen-year-old Damone (Robert Romanus). He then fails to help her pay for the abortion and doesn't even turn up to give her the promised lift to the clinic so she has to turn to her dopey brother (Judge Reinhold). The film never judges her, nor does it turn into some terrible morality tale about what happens to loose girls. The only person who is damned by the movie is the feckless Damone for failing to help her. In fact, Stacy ends up completely fine, utterly unaffected by her abortion and dating Rat (Brian Backer), the boy she should have been with all along and who appears similarly untroubled by Stacy's abortion.

"The studio had no problem at all with a fifteen-year-old female character having an abortion. The whole thing was realistic:

teenagers were having sex [off-screen], some teenagers were having abortions, and the film reflected that," says Heckerling. "When [Damone] doesn't give her the check for the abortion, we're saying that these kids aren't ready for kids. He can't even get a check, how's he going to be a father?"

As in *Fast Times*, the woman in need of the abortion in *Dirty Dancing* is not criticized by the film, only the idiot who got her pregnant and then refuses to help. But *Dirty Dancing* is far more vehement in its criticism of feckless men than *Fast Times*, possibly because, unlike *Fast Times*, it was written by a woman. "Some people count and some people don't," sneers the evil impregnator and Ayn Rand fan Robbie, who then heartlessly accuses Penny of sleeping around.

Perhaps the most extraordinary on-screen discussion about abortion comes in *Fatal Attraction*, the ultimate example of the eighties backlash against feminism that Faludi writes about. Yet despite the film's hilarious scaremongering about the risks of feminism, it is strangely, even crazedly, if not strictly speaking pro-choice then certainly pro-abortion. When Alex (Glenn Close) tells Dan (Michael Douglas) that she is pregnant after their affair, he—the good guy—desperately wants her to have an abortion but she—the bad woman—refuses, and this, the film suggests, is proof of his responsible nature and her selfish one. As this is *Fatal Attraction*, and an Adrian Lyne film, there are, inevitably, misogynistic impulses underpinning the film's pro-choice message: namely, that it is unfair that women hold the control when it comes to abortion (I know: ha ha ha) and that the most important thing is that Dan preserves the sanctity of the nuclear family he has at home by making his mistress have an abortion. Still, it's quite something now to see a movie in which a man is good for demanding a woman have an abortion and a woman is bad for refusing to have it.

Obviously, this being the Reaganite 1980s, not all films were jumping up and down and cheering "Yay! Abortion!" Going back to *Backlash*, Faludi details at length the movies that came out in that decade that she feels were explicitly anti-choice, some of which are singled out fairly (Woody Allen's *Another Woman*, in which a woman realizes, too late, that her biggest mistake in life was having an abortion), some less so (Ron Howard's sparkling comedy *Parenthood*, in which an eighteen-year-old, to my mind, credibly decides to have a baby with her deadbeat boyfriend because she is gooey in love). But these predictable voices against abortion make the contemporary movies that endorsed it look all the more extraordinary.

"It's not like movies hadn't talked about abortion before *Fast Times*," says Heckerling. "You can look back to that Steve McQueen film [1963's *Love with the Proper Stranger*] which is all about him trying to find money for an abortion. *Fast Times* was born out of [the film's screenwriter] Cameron Crowe's investigations into modern high schools, and this is what high schools were like. Women were having abortions and the movies then talked about this."

Women still have abortions, but you wouldn't know it from today's mainstream movies, teen or otherwise. Even smart films that are forced to confront the issue dodge it awkwardly. In 2007's *Knocked Up*, which focuses on a couple who conceive after an awkward one-night stand, the only two people who mention the word—her mother, his roommate—are derided as heartless. Whereas *Fame*'s Hilary has an abortion to pursue her dreams as a ballet dancer, twenty-two-year-old Alison in *Knocked Up* recoils in disgust at the thought of putting her burgeoning career ahead of an unexpected, unwanted pregnancy. In the 2007 film *Juno*, the eponymous teenager is dissuaded from having an abortion after an anti-choice protester tells her that her baby will have fingernails, and she then goes into a clinic that appears to have been dreamed up by the Westboro Baptist Church's press office. In 2012's *Bachelorette*, a character reveals that she had an abortion as a teenager and this, the film intimates, is why she's such a promiscuous druggy mess as an adult.

What makes the movie industry's increasing conservatism especially bizarre is that roughly the same percentage of Americans support the legalization of abortion as did in the 1980s. In fact, today's audiences actively like seeing honest depictions of abortion on-screen, in the very few movies that show them. The 2014 indie film *Obvious Child*, about a woman who decides to get an abortion, was released in only 202 theaters in the United States, and yet it made a very impressive $25,772 per theater in its opening weekend. By contrast, the unpleasantly misogynistic 2014 comedy *The Other Woman*, in which the female characters are two-dimensional jealous, sexualized harpies, was released in more than 3,000 theaters and made only $7,727 per theater in its opening weekend. So much for audiences not liking complex female themes.

Teen abortion rates in the United States are at a historic low, having declined by 64 percent between 1990 and 2010 thanks to the commendable work by sex education workers who have so effectively taught young people about the importance of contraception. Therefore why movies should be so fearful of discussing them seems bizarre. Whereas in the eighties there were movies that were both pro- and anti-choice, Hollywood speaks with one voice on the issue today.

"The entertainment industry has elected to silence the discussion on abortion," said Robert Thompson, director of the Bleier Center for Television and Popular Culture at Syracuse University. "It's an issue fraught with moral and ethical challenges and Hollywood has been almost silent on it for the past twenty years. It has been the one controversial subject matter that has not only not progressed, but has totally retreated from popular culture. If you'd watch TV or films in this country, you'd never guess that abortion is such a big issue."

Bergstein says:

I used to say, oh maybe *Dirty Dancing* was ahead of its time and that's why I had to talk about abortion in this covert way. But if you look what's happened since, that's not really true. I would have thought all these movies like *Juno* and *Knocked Up* and *Waitress* would take its place, but in those movies the girls don't have the abortion: at the last minute they take what looks to be the moral choice and they don't do it, and they end up with the guy all happy. So it's presented now as a moral decision not to have the abortion and you have a cute little baby and it's fine. I don't know, maybe that's what you can get financed from studios these days.

When I ask Judd Apatow why there was no discussion of abortion in *Knocked Up*, he replies that there was, originally, but it ended up on the cutting floor. "Anyway, I'm as pro-choice as you can get, but the movie would have been ten minutes long if she'd had an abortion."

Diablo Cody, the writer of *Juno*, is even more dismissive of objections to the depiction of abortion in her movie: "Any feminist out there who doesn't support me gets a big boo because you've got one person out there who is advocating for women in Hollywood and you're going to slag that person? If you're a feminist, you should be up my butt."

But *Juno*'s star, the very thoughtful and engaged Ellen Page, is a little more open to the issue, and less concerned with anyone being in her butt. At first she uses Apatow's argument, saying that if *Juno* "had the abortion it would be a short movie," which is a fair point, but it does provoke the response that the screenwriters should either have written a less improbable scenario in which that particular woman would keep the baby, or they should have been more deft at dealing with the woman's reason for not having the abortion. Page's voice rises a little when she adds, "And at least we say the word *abortion*," suggesting she knows that's a pretty weak argument.

But the problem isn't that *Juno* had the baby, I say. It is that she decides not to have the abortion because of something a pro-life protester said.

"Ohhhh, I see, that's a good point," Page says, sitting back in her chair.

So how does she feel about the film in light of that perspective?

"Well, I feel like we—" she begins gamely, before giving up. "No, that's a good point. But it's funny, I never thought that she responds to the protester but of course you're right."

It would initially seem to make no sense that eighties teen films were so relaxed about sex, especially compared to teen films today. In 1980s America, AIDS was ravaging the country, the anti-abortion movement was emerging, and Republicans were in the White House. If there was ever a time when pop culture might have tried to scare teenage girls off sex, then the eighties was surely it. Yet instead, eighties teen movies generally make sex look, well, great, even (gasp) for women, while teen movies today make sex look absolutely terrifying, especially for women.

It would be easy to see this shift as a reflection of the rise of the Christian right and growing conservatism of America, but there is another way of looking at it. Yes, girls in eighties movies joyfully jump into the sack with everyone from Patrick Swayze to Andrew McCarthy, but this looks less cheering when one considers that, off-screen, teenage pregnancy rates were, for the first time in decades, rocketing in the United States. The *Los Angeles Times* described the eighties as a "greenhouse" for teenage pregnancies due to a combination of the fraying of unions, leading to many teenagers' parents losing their jobs, budget cuts on after-school programs, and rising school dropout rates. Worse, the Reagan administration cut budgets

for abortions, health clinics, sex education, and birth control programs. While rates of teen sex were just as high in Europe, rates of
teen pregnancy in England were half as high as they were in America
because, as the *Los Angeles Times* put it, "contraception is far more
common [there]," by which they mean it was easier for teenagers
to have access to free contraception thanks to the National Health
Service and health clinics. By 1989, one out of every ten American
girls was pregnant before her twentieth birthday.

So one could argue that teenagers in today's U.S. teen films
aren't more scared of sex than they were in the 1980s; they're just
being more responsible about it. This attitude shift is reflected in
their off-screen behavior: from 1991 to 2000 the number of teenage pregnancies fell by 50 percent across the United States, across
all demographics. But despite the strenuous efforts of the Christian
right and Republican Party, while American teenagers are having sex
slightly later than they were in 1988, they are not, in the vast main,
abstinent (all politicians would be very depressed if they knew how
little what they say affects teenagers' behavior). Instead, increased
use of contraception accounts for as much as 86 percent of the de-
cline in teenage pregnancies since 1990.

The rise in condom use also means that boys and men are taking more responsibility when having sex. So one could even look at
a film such as *Twilight* and see—beneath the scaremongering and
weirdness about sex—a sliver of modern relevance in that Edward,
in his own vampiric way, tries to be responsible with Bella and protect her from his death juice (or something).

This argument works less well, though, if one looks at the wider
culture alongside the facts as well as at the specifics of the films. For a
start, and most obviously, if teenagers are, as the figures strongly suggest, leading more responsible sex lives, then it makes no sense for
movies to be so hysterical about the subject, either suggesting that

all teens are having orgies or telling teenagers that sex will kill them. Fine, films shouldn't show teenagers having sex in every car on every street corner because, first, the gear stick digging into one's back is a major turnoff, but also because that's not how teenagers live today, and they never did. But teenagers also don't live lives in which if they have sex they are then emotionally damaged, publicly shamed, and turned into zombies.

"American movies have become much more conservative since they were in the 1980s, and this is partly because of the international market," says film producer Lynda Obst. Profits from China, for example, have grown by more than 400 percent in the past half decade. This then affects what studios feel they can and can't show on-screen, and one issue they are especially conscious of showing to the increasingly important foreign markets is teenagers having sex and abortions.

But the morality of American movies isn't just being determined by the morals of other countries: it also comes from within.

"Teen movies are much more conservative today than they were in the eighties because we've gone backwards domestically in terms of cultural attitudes, and studios have reacted to that," says Obst. "Pressure groups from the right have become much stronger over the past few decades, and this very much affects studios."

"We're like lobsters in a tank and don't notice how the temperature has been changing over the decades because we're in the pot. Hollywood has followed America in its move to the right and we're a much more conservative country now than we were then," says the editor of *Variety*, Steven Gaydos.

This growing conservatism has been very much reflected in America's attitudes toward teen sex: as part of the 1996 federal welfare reform legislation, Congress authorized $50 million annually to fund abstinence-only education. By 2008, the U.S. government had spent more than $1.5 billion on abstinence-only sex education, and federal guidance forbade any discussion of contraception except to emphasize its failure rates. Between 2006 and 2008 one in four teenagers in America received abstinence-only sex education with no instruction about birth control; in 1988 only 8 percent had done so. The Obama administration and Congress have since eliminated two abstinence-only sex education programs yet thirty-seven states still require sex education that includes abstinence. Twenty-six of those stress that abstinence is the best method, even though states that teach abstinence-only sex education, such as Mississippi, notoriously have the highest rate of teenage pregnancies. As of 2011, more than half of all women of reproductive age in the United States lived in a state hostile to abortion rights, an increase of 31 percent in just one decade.

The big teen films today are characterized by brutal and graphic violence in a way they never were in the eighties. In *Twilight*, the killings are depicted as romantic proof of Edward and Bella's love for one another as they (Edward, usually) knock off their enemies. In *The Hunger Games* teenagers kill each other to win a reality TV show. Sex, however, is anathema to these movies: in *Twilight* it is seen as dangerous, and in *The Hunger Games* it is an awkward inconvenience. Murder, though, is absolutely fine.

"One big problem is the [U.S.] motion picture ratings system: it is much harder these days on sex than violence and so if you don't want to get an R rating, which would kill the film, but to still attract the kids, you put in violence but leave out the sex. The ratings board is much harder on teen sex than violence and everyone knows it," said one producer who works in teen films.

It's true, the Motion Picture Association of America (MPAA) is easier on violence than it used to be for one big reason: computer-generated imagery (CGI). "We are seeing different kinds of violence with the rise of CGI and parents feel their children are able to filter what's real and what's not," says the MPAA's Joan Graves. As to whether it has become stricter about sex over the past thirty years, and especially teen sex, that, she says, is slightly trickier to say: "There has never been a round table discussion saying, 'Okay, we'll change this, we'll change that.' These changes happen over decades. But the ratings system is built to change. It's reflecting current standards rather than standards from twenty years ago. A movie that was made thirty years ago might well have a different rating today." In Britain, if a film has an 18 rating, no one under eighteen can see it, but in America, a film with an R rating can be seen by a child as long as they are accompanied by an adult. This then puts the onus on American parents to decide whether or not their child should see the film, and so the MPAA sees its role as equipping parents with the information to make that decision.

Thus, the U.S. ratings system is built to "reflect the standards of American parents," as Graves puts it, and if that sounds somewhat fluid, then it is. There is no strict rubric about what is and isn't allowed, only a sense of what "American parents" will tolerate. But Graves is very clear that the ratings board does not offer instructions to filmmakers about what they can and can't film—that's the studio's job. All it's there to do is "reflect [American] society," and in its angst about teen sex and relaxed attitude toward violence, in a country where three people are killed every hour by guns and abstinence is still part of many schools' curriculum, one can easily argue that it succeeds at that.

When there was talk at the beginning of the twenty-first century of remaking *Dirty Dancing*, Bergstein wondered how the studios would deal with the abortion plot in the film, especially as she owns the rights to the script. After all, when *Fame* was remade in 2009 the abortion plot was simply dropped, which also happened when the 1966 film *Alfie* was pointlessly remade starring Jude Law and Sienna Miller. In the end, it became a moot issue because—perhaps unsurprisingly—the remake never happened.

Instead, Bergstein turned the play into an international stage musical megahit and oomphed up the abortion plot, emphasizing the risks Baby's father, Dr. Houseman, took by helping Penny, endangering both his medical license and his freedom. People, Bergstein says, need to remember what it was like before, and what it could all too easily be like again:

> My feeling has always been that people who are anti-abortion are anti-sex and anti-pleasure for young women, and that's why I wanted to make a movie about both. That's why Baby and Johnny's first love scene comes after they've seen Penny nearly drowning in her own blood as a result of sex, and the song on the record player is [Solomon Burke's] "Cry to Me." It's not an idealized romantic scene, it's a scene about loneliness and terror and sex. But I wanted to say if you plunge into the physical world and if you do it with honor and without fear, you will attach yourself to a moral world.

More than that, *Dirty Dancing* taught my generation of women, and continues to teach generations of younger women, about their moral compass. We came for the sex, but we have stayed because it shows us something even more real and scary. It teaches us something about ourselves and the world. And, as Baby learns, only the best kind of sex can do that.

The Ten Best Power Ballads on an Eighties Movie Soundtrack

10 **"Up Where We Belong," by Joe Cocker and Jennifer Warnes, from *An Officer and a Gentleman***

Technically, a love song, yes. But a Cockerishly POWERFUL love song.

9 **"Glory of Love," by Peter Cetera, from *The Karate Kid II***

Say what you like about *The Karate Kid II* (it's terrible, for starters), but this song is grade-A singing-into-the-hairbrush material.

8 **"Shooting for the Moon," by Amy Holland, from *Teen Wolf***

He scored the winning point in the basketball game! And he wasn't even a werewolf! This song is a pure happy ending in sonic form. I enjoy this song so much I don't even notice that an extra in the background drops his trousers when it plays in the film.

7 **"Let the River Run," by Carly Simon, from *Working Girl***

Total singing-in-the-shower fodder, and that's the best kind of fodder.

"St. Elmo's Fire (Man in Motion)," by John Parr, from *St. Elmo's Fire*

John Parr tries as hard to get a St. Elmo's reference into his song as the characters do in the film, and makes about as little sense in his effort. God bless them all for trying.

 "*Flashdance*—What a Feeling," by Irene Cara, from *Flashdance*

The movie that made Hollywood decide to knock out films that look like movie videos, and this is the song that convinced them. The only song to weld and dance to.

 "Purple Rain," by Prince, from *Purple Rain*

I've seen this film hundreds of times, and I still have no idea what this song is about.

"We Don't Need Another Hero," by Tina Turner, from *Mad Max Beyond the Thunderdome*

TIIIIIINAAAAAAAAA!!!!

 "Holding Out for a Hero," by Bonnie Tyler, from *Footloose*

Nobody does power ballads like Bonnie does power ballads.

"Nothing's Gonna Stop Us Now," by Starship, from *Mannequin*

It is a scientific fact that if you don't enjoy this song, you have no soul. I'm sorry, but you can't argue with science.

The Princess Bride

It feels downright inconceivable* to devote only one chapter in a book about lessons gleaned from eighties movies to *The Princess Bride.* Why, just off the top of my head, while standing on my head, I can name five life lessons that this movie teaches you that you don't learn anywhere else:

1. "Never go against a Sicilian when DEATH is on the line!"
2. "Love is the greatest thing—except for a nice mutton, lettuce, and tomato sandwich when the mutton is nice and lean."
3. "Life is pain. Anyone who says differently is selling something."
4. Eventually, you learn not to mind the kissing parts.
5. And most important, "As you wish" = "I love you."

---

* I'm using Vizzini's definition of the word here, of course.

Such is the depth of wisdom in this film that in 2013, twenty-six years after its release, BuzzFeed devoted a list* to the lessons gleaned from it. A BuzzFeed list! Who needs the Oscars, *Princess Bride*, when you have that ultimate of modern-day accolades?

The Princess Bride is so adored that it's probably[†] now a clichéd response on Internet dating websites: walks on the beach, an open fire, sunsets, and *The Princess Bride*. And yet, despite this, love for *The Princess Bride* is not seen as desperately hackneyed or cheesily safe. *The Princess Bride* is what you'd need a prospective love interest to cite as their favorite movie for the relationship to progress,[‡] it's the one film that would make you rethink a lifelong friendship if you found out your best friend "just didn't get it"—not that they would ever say that, because I honestly don't know a single person of my generation who isn't obsessed with this film. And not just my generation: in *As You Wish*, a very enjoyable book about the making of *The Princess Bride*, Cary Elwes—who played Westley the farm boy, of course—recounts being told by both Pope John Paul II and Bill Clinton how much they loved the movie, proving that *The Princess Bride* appeals to saints and sinners alike.[§]

---

* Erin La Rosa, "17 Important Life Lessons from The Princess Bride," BuzzFeed, May 15, 2013. Seventeen! Pah! There are at least 1,374,978 lessons in that movie. Step it up with your listicles, BuzzFeed!

† I only managed to last a week on a dating website, so I'm afraid my research isn't as thorough as it could be. You see, because of *The Princess Bride*, I have high standards when it comes to love and I just didn't believe that any beautiful farm boys would be on match.com. How would he have Wi-Fi up in his mountainous hovel?

‡ The U.S. version of the TV show *The Office*, when it was still amazing, played on this idea in the second series when Pam chose *The Princess Bride* as one of her Desert Island movies choices, proving she is the right woman for Jim. Jim's current girlfriend Katy (played by Amy Adams), on the other hand, chooses *Legally Blonde*, which definitively establishes her inferiority to Pam.

§ If you love *The Princess Bride*, which I'm assuming you do if you're reading this chapter, and because you're presumably a sentient human being, you really should read *As*

Now, having said all that, I have a confession to make. I was not the big *Princess Bride* fan in my family when I was growing up. That title instead went to my sister, Nell. Our mother took us to see it at the movie theater when I must have been nine and Nell was seven, and even though the film was—incredibly—something of a commercial disappointment when it came out, the cinema was absolutely packed with kids like us. In my mind, everyone in the audience was utterly in thrall to this tale of Buttercup (Robin Wright), her true love Westley (Elwes), and their battles against Prince Humperdinck (Chris Sarandon), Vizzini (Wallace Shawn), and Count Rugen (Christopher Guest), and their eventual assistance from the brave swordsman Inigo (Mandy Patinkin), the giant Fezzik (the professional wrestler known as André the Giant), and Miracle Max (Billy Crystal).

Afterward, we stood in the cinema atrium as our mother bundled us back into our coats.

"Did you girls like it?" she asked.

Standing there in her corduroy dungarees and T-shirt, Nell looked in a state of semi-shock. "I LOVED IT. I WANT TO SEE IT AGAIN RIGHT NOW!" she practically shouted.

Now, *The Princess Bride* is wonderful, but in order to understand how unexpected this proclamation was, you have to know a little bit about my sister. Ever since she was old enough to throw a tantrum, my sister refused to wear dresses. She never played with dolls. She refused to let my mother brush her hair and had apparently no interest in her physical appearance. She did not like mushy stories—she didn't even like reading books. In other words, she was the complete opposite to me. How much of that was a deliberate reaction against

---

You Wish. Any book with an index that includes the entry "André the Giant: breaking wind, and, 123–126" should be on everyone's bookshelves by law.

me, a younger sibling defining herself in opposition to the older one, and how much of it was simply an innate part of Nell was already a moot point when we went to see *The Princess Bride*: Nell's parameters were so firmly set by then that her nickname in our family was "the tough customer." She would consent to drink only one kind of fruit juice (apple), and buy only one brand (Red Cheek), and only if it came out of a can (never a carton), so there was absolutely no negotiating with her about mushy princesses. Lord only knows how my mother got her to see the movie in the first place. She must have hidden the title from her.

And yet, like the grandson in the film, Kevin Arnold,* Nell found that, against all odds, she did enjoy the story, just as Kevin's grandfather, Columbo,† promises. I think Nell made my mother take her to see the film at the cinema at least three more times. As she wished.

When it came out on VHS, we bought it immediately and it was understood that the videocassette was officially Nell's, just as the videocassette for *Ferris Bueller's Day Off* was officially mine. When she found out that the film had originally been a book by William Goldman, who also wrote the screenplay, she asked my amazed mother to buy that, too. Nell read it over and over until the pages fell out, so she stuck them back in and then read the book again. *The Princess Bride* was the book that taught her to like books, as much as the movie taught her to relax some of her other rules. She developed a lifelong crush on Westley and, not long after, she started wearing dresses, too.

The reasons why Nell loved this film so much exemplify, I think,

---

* So called (by me) for the obvious reason that the grandson was played by Fred Savage, who went on to play Kevin Arnold in *The Wonder Years*. But you already got that, and I apologize for condescending to you by spelling it out.
† Because Peter Falk plays the grandfather and—What? You got it? Okay, cool. Just looking out for you, bro.

why it is universally adored in a way that, say, the vaguely similar and contemporary *The Never-Ending Story* is not. It's a fairy tale for those who love fairy tales, but it's also a self-aware spoof for those who don't; it's an adventure film for boys and—for once—girls, too, but without pandering to or excluding either; it's got a plot for kids, dialogue for adults, and jokes for everyone; it's a genre film and a satire of a genre film; it's a very funny movie in which everybody is playing it straight; it's smart and sweet and smart about its sweetness, but also sweet about its smarts. Unlike, say, *Shrek*, there are no jokes here for parents that go over the kids' heads: all generations enjoy it on exactly the same level. It's a movie that lets people who don't like certain things like those things, while at the same time not betraying the original fans. But most of all, *The Princess Bride* is about one thing in particular: "*The Princess Bride* is a story about love," says Cary Elwes. "So much happens in the movie—giants, fencing, kidnapping. But it's really a film about love."

This might seem like a statement of the obvious, but it isn't, actually. Yes, the film is ostensibly about the great true love between Buttercup and Westley, and their most perfect kiss that leaves all the other kisses in the world behind. Both Elwes and Wright were so astonishingly beautiful when they made the film that, watching them, it's hard to believe any love ever existed on this planet other than theirs. And they, rather pleasingly, were quite taken with one another. In his book, Elwes talks at length about how "smitten" he was with Wright, and she says precisely the same about him: "I was absolutely smitten with Cary. So obviously that helped with our on-screen chemistry. . . . It doesn't matter how many years go by, I will love Cary forever."

Disappointingly, however, Elwes insists that they remained just friends. "Everyone asks if there was more!" he says, sounding a little exasperated, apparently unable to see what everyone else can: namely, that it seems against the laws of nature for two such beautiful people not to have had sex at least once. The last scene that Elwes shot was of him and Wright kissing on horseback, creating "the most perfect kiss" of all time against a sunset. Surely that was romantic.

"Well, not really. Robin and I were friends by that point so we kept laughing, and [the director] Rob [Reiner] was going, 'Touch her face, touch her face!'" He laughs.

But Westley and Buttercup's love is only a part of the film, and only one of several love stories in the film. There is also, for a start, the great love between Inigo and Fezzik. The scene in which a drunken and broken Inigo looks up into Fezzik's face in the Thieves Forest and Fezzik says a simple, smiling hello is much more moving than the moment when Buttercup realizes the Dread Pirate Roberts is actually Westley (not least because she's just pushed him down a hill). Even if Inigo does become the Dread Pirate Roberts at the end of the film, as Westley suggests he should, it is as impossible to imagine him going off without Fezzik as it is to imagine Buttercup and Westley being severed.

This love between the two men is at the root of one of the film's subtlest lessons. Bad guys teach audiences how to think of opponents in life, and this is especially true of bad guys in books and films aimed at kids. Because stories for kids tend to be relatively simple, villains in these films are almost invariably evil, and that's all there is to be said about them. Cruella de Vil, Snow White's stepmother, the witch in *Rapunzel*: WHAT a bunch of moody bitches. This is also certainly true of movies for children in the 1980s, from the frankly terrifying Judge Doom (Christopher Lloyd) in *Who Framed Roger Rabbit* to the enjoyably evil Ursula in *The Little Mermaid*. It's a pleasingly basic approach, and one that validates most kids' (and adults') view of the world: "I am good and anyone who thwarts me is wicked and there is no point in trying to think about things from their point of view because they have no inner life of their own beyond pure evil and a desire to impede me." *The Princess Bride*, however, does something different.

It's easy to forget this once you've seen the movie and fallen in love with the characters but Inigo and Fezzik are, ostensibly, bad guys. When we first meet them in the movie, they knock our heroine, Buttercup, unconscious and kidnap her for Vizzini. We are also told they will kill her. Our princess! In the eyes of children, you can't get much more evil than that. They are hired guns in the revenge business, which is not a job for a good guy in any fairy tale. But Goldman flips it around. We quickly see Inigo and, in particular, Fezzik being extremely sweet with each other, doing their little rhymes together and trying to protect one another from Vizzini's ire. Their love for one another shows us there is more to these villains than villainy. Goldman then ups the ante even further by having Inigo describe to the Man in Black how he has devoted his life to avenging the death of his father, thus giving him the kind of emotional backstory kids can definitely understand, as well as adding another mission to the movie. Soon after beating (but not killing) Inigo, the Man in Black fights with Fezzik, who we already know has a similarly sad past ("unemployed—IN GREENLAND").

Plenty of villains were once good before crossing to the dark side: Darth Vader, many of Batman's nemeses, Voldemort. The point in those stories is that the difference between true evil and true greatness comes down to one wrong decision, one wrong turn, and there is no going back from that. But *The Princess Bride* does something more subtle: it suggests that good people sometimes end up doing bad things, but are still good, have stories of their own, and are capable of love. Inigo and Fezzik both killed people in the past for Vizzini, but they're all still good people. This is quite a message for kids (and adults) to take in: not everything is clear-cut when it comes to good and bad, even in fairy tales.

In the original novel, William Goldman goes into much greater detail about Fezzik and Inigo's friendship, and this is one of the reasons why I—in all honesty—prefer the book to the film.* But the film alludes to it enough in order for audiences to understand the real bond between the men, and partly this happens through the script and partly through the actors, especially one actor in particular. At one point, Arnold Schwarzenegger was considered for the role of Fezzik, but, thank heavens, he was already too expensive by the time the film finally started shooting. Where Schwarzenegger is all jarring rectangles and jutting jaw, André the Giant was all soft circles and goofy smiles. Where Schwarzenegger palpably punished himself to a superhuman extent to get the body he clearly wanted so badly, the man born André René Roussimoff suffered from gigantism due to acromegaly and had no choice about his size, just as Fezzik didn't, much to the latter's misery ("It's not my fault being the biggest and the strongest—I don't even exercise"). It would be a patronizing cliché to say André was born to play Fezzik, but he was certainly more right for the role than Schwarzenegger.

By the time he made *The Princess Bride*, André was seven feet, four inches and weighed more than 540 pounds. Easily the sweetest stories in Cary Elwes's book come from the cast and crew's memories of the wrestler, who died in 1993 at the age of forty-six, and this is not mere sentimentality. Quite a few of *The Princess Bride*'s cast have, sadly, since died, including Mel Smith, Peter Cook, and Peter Falk, but none of them prompts the same kind of fondness as that felt for

---

* Which is not to say I don't love the movie. I do, completely, love the movie. But I ADORE the book. Other reasons why I prefer the book are that Buttercup is allowed to be much funnier than she is in the film, and Goldman's authorial interjections in the text are worth the price of the book alone.

André. "It's safe to say that he was easily the most popular person on the movie," Elwes writes. "Everyone just loved him."

Partly this is due to the extraordinary nature of the man. Robin Wright recalls going out to a dinner with him where he ate "four or five entrees, three or four appetizers, a couple of baskets of bread, and then he's like, I'm ready for seconds. And then desserts. I think he went through a case of wine and he wasn't even tipsy."

But it was André's innately gentle nature that made him so beloved. His "compassion and protective nature," Elwes writes, helped Wallace Shawn overcome his almost paralyzing fear of heights when they were filming the climb up the Cliffs of Insanity. When Robin Wright felt chilly when filming outdoors, André would place one of his huge hands on top of Wright's head. "She said it was like having a giant hot water bottle up there. It certainly did the trick; he didn't even mess up her hair that much!" Elwes writes. When he died, William Goldman wrote his obituary in *New York* magazine. The last lines were as follows: "André once said to Billy Crystal, 'We do not live long, the big and the small.' Alas."

Next, on a smaller level, is the love between Miracle Max (Crystal) and his aged wife, Valerie (Carol Kane). Initially they seem simply like a squabbling old couple, playing purely for broad comedy (and their scene is the broadest comedic one in the film). But it soon becomes clear that Valerie is needling Max only because she wants him to get back his confidence in his work after Prince Humperdinck destroyed it by sacking them, and her little cheer when her husband agrees to make a miracle for Inigo is really very touching. By the end of their scene, they're working together, finishing one another's sentences, holding each other arm in arm, and whispering little asides to one another. As a portrait of elderly marriage goes, this one is a pretty lovely one.

Finally, there's the great love story that frames the whole movie:

the one between the grandson/Kevin Arnold (Fred Savage) and the grandfather/Columbo (Peter Falk). In the beginning of the movie, the grandson is irritated by his cheek-pinching grandfather and can hardly believe that he has to stop playing his adorably primitive-looking computer baseball game to listen to grandfather read a book.* As the film progresses, the relationship between the grandson and grandfather progresses almost like a traditional love story: the grandson slowly gets more interested, clutching his covers anxiously when Buttercup is almost eaten by the Shrieking Eels; then he gets angry, banging his bed with his fist when it seems like Westley has been killed; and finally, he comes around entirely and tells his grandfather to come back the next day to read the book again.

"As you wish." His grandfather smiles, and the film ends. "That wasn't actually in the script," Elwes says. "They came up with him saying that on, I think, the last day, and it really captures the love between the grandfather and grandson. You can also see the tenderness between Fred Savage and Peter Falk."

In Elwes's book, Savage recalls how comfortable Falk made him: "I don't even remember when we were shooting or when we weren't. He would sit in that chair, and I would be in the bed, and he would talk to me all day. . . . He just kind of became my grandfather."

This relationship feels especially significant because the reason this film exists is that of the bond between particular parents and their children. Rob Reiner first came across the book when it was given to him by his father, the comedian and actor Carl Reiner.

---

* This computer game is the one thing that dates the film. Other than those creaky graphics, the movie looks remarkably timeless—more so, really, than any other film from the eighties. This is partly because there aren't any eighties clothes in the film (other than the grandson's mother's weird mullet hairdo), and partly because instead of having a pop-and-synth soundtrack, Mark Knopfler wrote a simple instrumental piece.

Elwes, too, was given the novel when he was thirteen by his step-father, and his love for the book made him especially determined to get the role. And most of all, the reason the book was written in the first place was that of the love one father felt for his children. Back in 1970, William Goldman decided to write a story for his two daughters, then seven and four years old, to entertain them while he was away in Los Angeles working on a movie: "I said to them both, 'I'll write you a story, what do you want it to be about?' And one of them said 'princesses' and the other one said 'brides.' 'Then that will be the title,' I told them. And so it has remained."

Goldman has written a frankly ridiculous number of acclaimed novels (*Marathon Man*), screenplays (*Butch Cassidy and the Sundance Kid, All the President's Men, Misery*), and memoirs (*Adventures in the Screen Trade, Which Lie Did I Tell?*). But his favorite thing he ever wrote, he has said, is *The Princess Bride*. He lovingly turned it into a script in 1973, and then watched it languish for thirteen years, rejected by studio heads who all said the same thing: they loved it, but it was unfilmable. When it was finally picked up by Rob Reiner, Goldman was so anxious that Rob had to reshoot scenes because Goldman, standing behind the camera, was praying that the film would turn out okay and his prayers were picked up by the microphone.

"Please understand that this is a very personal project for me. Normally I don't care much for any of my work. But this one is different. It is my favorite thing I've ever written in my life. So if I appear a little nervous, that's the reason," Goldman told the cast.

The Princess Bride is funny, and exciting, and scary, and funny, and silly, and sweet, and funny (I might have mentioned that). But the reason it has endured is that it is such a warm film, one without cynicism or calculation, and a film as lovely as this one could only have been born out of love itself—all kinds of love.

And yet, this is also the reason the film was initially deemed something of a damp squib. While not a bomb, the movie was certainly not the commercial success it should have been—and would, eventually, become. But because the film isn't aimed at one particular demographic, exemplified by its multilayered depiction of love, the studio simply had no idea how to market it, or even of whom to aim it at. After all, it features a simply fairy-tale love, but also a deeper love about friendship, one about grandparents and grandchildren, and then a pair of squabbling geriatrics: who on earth is it aimed at? The correct answer, of course, is "everyone," but that is not an answer movie marketing departments understand. For all that I despair of the way movies are marketed and targeted today, it's not like they always got it right in the eighties, either. Despite the movie being one of the most exciting films ever made, the studio marketed it with one of the most boring posters of all time, featuring a silhouette of Kevin Arnold listening to Columbo read a book. Not even I especially want to see a movie featuring just that.

"Rob unfurled the poster on the way back from the Toronto Film Festival on the plane and we all gathered around and we thought, Gosh, there's not even a sign of Fezzik! How can anyone know what the movie's about without Fezzik?" recalls Cary Elwes, understandably still bemused. How could any marketing department see a film featuring a real live actual giant, and then leave the giant off the film poster, for heaven's sake?

The theatrical trailer was even worse and was quickly pulled from cinemas, and if you look it up on YouTube you'll see why.

"The movie opened the same weekend as *Fatal Attraction* and nobody went. The cast and crew were all pretty surprised and bummed but Goldman had warned us this might happen," says Elwes. "He said, 'Look, this is an oddball movie so it's going to be a tough sell. I won't lie to you, I've been through it, for more than a decade.'"

"We were in dangerous terrain—because when you mix genres in a movie, that's where you end up," Goldman writes in his delightful essay on *The Princess Bride*. It wasn't until the movie came out on VHS and audiences were able to discover the film for themselves, without the cack-handed meddlings of the studio, that it became the success it deserved to be.

The lesson that *The Princess Bride* taught the film industry is that it is possible to make a movie for kids and adults alike, and this is one it has remembered well.

Modernized fairy-tale films such as *Enchanted* and pretty much the whole output of Pixar all owe an enormous debt to *The Princess Bride*. *Shrek* in particular can be seen as the next generation's take on *The Princess Bride*, with its toying with tropes and tongue-in-cheek humor. But as much as I love *Shrek*, *The Princess Bride* has a simple sweetness that *Shrek* doesn't. *Shrek* is more knowing than *The Princess Bride*, with more winks over the heads of the kids to their parents. Part of the joy of *The Princess Bride* is that kids and adults enjoy it on the same level. It doesn't differentiate between what kids get and what adults enjoy. There is no irony to *The Princess Bride*, no nudging nods to contemporary adult references. For this reason, *The Princess Bride* is a much more clever film than *Shrek*, which is no slur on *Shrek*. After all, *The Princess Bride* is one of the cleverest and most original movies ever made, and this is exemplified in its depiction of love.

There are plenty of reasons why *The Princess Bride* could not be made today: "It would all be done by CGI, which would make the movie completely different," says Elwes. "Also, I seriously doubt that a studio would let a director cast two unknowns, as Robin and I were then, in the leads of such a big movie. They'd want a big box-office draw, like Tom Cruise, or whoever." But the most obvious reason is in its complex layering of different loves about different ages. Unlike movies today, which are nervily sliced up into their varying demographic quadrants, *The Princess Bride* has faith that children can cope with a love story between the elderly, just as adults are happy to watch a fairy tale that might lack in sex but more than makes up for it with a brilliant script.

Modern classic children's movies feature many kinds of love: the love between an elderly couple in *Up*; the love a boy feels for the plastic cowboy he is leaving behind in *Toy Story 3*; the love between a donkey and a dragon in *Shrek*. Ah, love in its infinite varieties! But I can't think of another children's movie in which there are so many different kinds of love featured, and all aimed fully at the children to understand. *The Princess Bride* teaches children that the love their grandparents feel for them, and what they feel for their grandparents, and the love friends have for one another, is true love, as important as Westley and Buttercup's true love. This is why Kevin Arnold—and Nell—learned not to mind the kissing parts, thanks to *The Princess Bride*.

Decades after Nell shouted about how much she loved *The Princess Bride* in the cinema, I got a job assignment from work. My editor asked me to interview someone who had just written a book, and I eagerly agreed. I don't usually bring family members on job assignments, but in this case I decided to make an exception. I called Nell and told her to meet me at an office block the next Monday. As it happened, she had just had her second baby but she instantly agreed. And so, on a cold December morning in northeast London, Nell, accompanied by her three-week-old daughter, Edith, met Westley. His hair was a little shorter, and his accent a touch more transatlantic after having spent three decades in the States, but he was definitely Westley.

"Look at this most beautiful girl!" cried Cary Elwes, reaching

toward Nell, but stopping a few inches short of her face and reaching down instead to the baby in her arms. "This is just the most
precious thing . . ." and his voice trailed away as he gazed at Edith,
utterly rapt.

Nell got her moment of great love with Westley. If it wasn't quite
as she'd imagined when she was seven, or seventeen, it was, ultimately, as she wished.

Top Ten Fashion Moments

10 **Kevin Kline's teeny-tiny running shorts, *The Big Chill* (see also: Tom Selleck in *Three Men and a Baby*)**

Coupled with some fine manly chest hair.

9 **Tom Hanks's white tux in *Big***

How all of us wish we could dress for an office party, if we're honest.

8 **Rob Lowe, *St. Elmo's Fire***

Sweaty Rob Lowe wears a yellow vest top with black bats patterned all over it, while playing the sax. Your life = complete.

7 **Michael J. Fox, *Back to the Future***

A T-shirt, a shirt, double denim, and the "life preserver." And to think, the characters in 1955 think people in the eighties dressed oddly.

6 **Nicolas Cage, *Valley Girl***

Frosted hair, a leather waistcoat, and a bare chest is a strong look, Nicolas.

Absolutely everything Michael Douglas wore in the decade

From his patterned blouson shirts undone to his mid-chest in *Romancing the Stone* and *The Jewel of the Nile*, to his braces in *Wall Street*, this man was eighties fashion in human form.

 The Heathers in *Heathers*

For services to shoulder-padded jackets and colored tights.

 Molly Ringwald and Jon Cryer, *Pretty in Pink*

God bless John Hughes and his belief that wearing weird clothes proves one is a sensitive soul. Extra points for Ringwald's hat, golden stars for Cryer's sunglasses.

 Melanie Griffith and Joan Cusack, *Working Girl*

Where to start? Melanie's mullet and white trainers? Melanie's extraordinary lingerie? Actually, let's just say Joan Cusack's wardrobe and leave it at that.

 Desperately Seeking Susan

The movie that proves everyone's life is improved by eighties fashion.

Top Five Comments About Fashion

5 "This jacket used to belong to Jimi Hendrix." "You bought a USED JACKET? What are we, poor?" (Rosanna Arquette and Mark Blum, *Desperately Seeking Susan*)

4 "Pink is my signature color." (Julia Roberts, *Steel Magnolias*)

3 "Does Barry Manilow know you raid his wardrobe?" (Judd Nelson, *The Breakfast Club*)

2 "This is a really volcanic ensemble you're wearing." (Jon Cryer, *Pretty in Pink*)

1 "Six thousand dollars?! It's nawt even leatha!" (Joan Cusack, *Working Girl*)

Pretty in Pink

Awkward Girls Should Never Have Makeovers

Until Molly Ringwald met John Hughes, she'd always felt wrong.

"I was growing up on the west coast and just so self-conscious about my looks," she recalls from her home in California, her two children shouting happily in the background. "Back then I was surrounded by images of Cheryl Tiegs and Farrah Fawcett, and that was the look then—that California blonde look, which was the opposite of what I was."

But Hughes—unusually, perhaps, for a thirty-something male director—recognized the appeal of the then fifteen-year-old Ringwald's looks from the start, and he saw something in her, something unconventional. As soon as he came across her head shot in his pack of photos while looking for young actresses for his next film, with her snub nose, slightly slack jaw, and bright red hair, he stuck it up on his billboard and, without even meeting her, wrote *Sixteen Candles* for her in two days.

Hughes could see the value of Ringwald's unfashionable looks for the same reason he was able to write films about teenagers that felt so true to young people at the time, and still do today: because, at heart, he was still the sensitive teenage outcast he loved to write about. "John was frozen in time emotionally in a way. He would not have been able to create the sense of truth in those characters had he not been so much like that himself," says director Howard Deutch, Hughes's frequent collaborator.

This meant he didn't see teen films as an easy means to get sexy girls in bikinis up on the screen, as screenwriters for the hugely successful *Porky's*—which came out in 1982, two years before Hughes's first teen film, *Sixteen Candles*—did. Rather, what he loved about teenagers was their complications as opposed to their cleavages.

"When I started to work with John, I realized my differences could work to my advantage because they made me stand out, but in a good way. So my skin got even paler and my hair got redder," Ringwald says. He wanted his teenage actors to stay totally true to their teenage selves, to the point that they were encouraged to pick out their own clothes for the films. One of the few times Hughes ever chided Ringwald was when she turned up on set wearing eye shadow: "He thought I was trying to be someone else." She smiles.

Hughes, more than any other filmmaker, made the 1980s the golden age of teen films because he realized that the trick to making good films about teenagers was to take them as seriously as they take themselves. "One of the great wonders about that age is your emotions are so open and raw. That's why I stuck around that genre for so long," he said in an interview. "At that age it feels as good to feel bad as it does to feel good." It's only as a teenager, Hughes believed, that you have this capacity for deep feeling, which explains why his own work was divided between the swoonily soulful teen films, including *Sixteen Candles*, *The Breakfast Club*, *Pretty in Pink*, *Ferris Bueller's Day Off*, and *Some Kind of Wonderful*, and the slapstick "dopey-ass comedy," as he put it, such as *National Lampoon's Vacation*, *The Great*

Outdoors, and, in the nineties, *Home Alone.** With the exception of *Weird Science*—which is a dopey-ass teen comedy and as a result is Hughes's least memorable teen film†—he kept these two sides to his filmmaking separate, even going so far as to fire Rick Moranis from *The Breakfast Club* as the janitor because he felt, rightly, that Moranis's humor was too broad for that film, and that's the only time I'll ever say a word against Moranis. Teen films were about deep emotions, and deep emotions were reserved for his teenage characters alone. "When you grow up," one of his characters in *The Breakfast Club* says, "your heart dies."

Even though Hughes wove plenty of autobiographical details into his films, he was a lot less interested in his own youth than he was in that of contemporary teenagers. Not many adults can say that. He would hang out with his teenage actors on the set, make them mixtapes, take them to concerts (Hughes genuinely loved music and, unlike a lot of eighties filmmakers, didn't just see it as merely a means to sell soundtracks), and he would infuriate his crew by cracking up along with the kids during embarrassing scenes. Hughes's teen films feel so heartfelt because they were written with such honest respect for his teenage actors, and the one with whom he felt the closest affinity was Ringwald: "We just instantly connected. He felt more like a friend than a director. We talked about everything," she says. So it is not surprising that the truest character Hughes ever wrote was one he created for her: Andie Walsh from *Pretty in Pink*.

By the time Hughes and Ringwald made *Pretty in Pink*, they

---

* This is not intended as an all-encompassing diss of Hughes's comedies. Personally, I would fight to the death for *Planes, Trains and Automobiles* and fight at least until grievous injury for *Uncle Buck*.

† For women, that is. Men, I have found, retain a strong fondness for this film about two boys who construct the perfect woman on their computers. Funny, that.

knew each other pretty well after having already worked on *Sixteen Candles* and *The Breakfast Club*. Ringwald's character, Sam, in the former is sparky, but the film is pretty unwatchable today due to being weirdly racist* and a bit rapey.† Hughes then cast Ringwald as popular and posh Claire in *The Breakfast Club*, because it amused him to cast her against type, and he gave the more interesting female character, Allison, to Ally Sheedy. It wasn't until *Pretty in Pink* that he created for Ringwald the role she deserved. "John always wrote best when he was writing for someone, and his real muse was Molly," says Howard Deutch, who directed *Pretty in Pink*. "A lot of who Molly was became the character he wrote for her in *Pretty in Pink*. So Molly inspired John to write that character and the writing of the character also impacted on Molly."

Like all Hughes's teen films, *Pretty in Pink* has a laughably simple premise: Andie, a high school girl from the wrong side of the tracks (literally, she lives next to the train tracks—no one could ever accuse Hughes of subtlety), wants to go to the prom with a wealthy boy called Blane, to the horror of her lifelong and fellow lower-middle-class friend, Duckie.

"When we were filming I remember thinking, This is about a girl going to a dance? Seriously? Who's going to want to see this? Really had my finger on the pulse there!" says a laughing Andrew McCarthy, who, thirty years on, has yet to escape the shadow of the film (although we fans of the 1989 comedy *Weekend at Bernie's* also associate him with near necrophilia; but that's a different story).

The Breakfast Club is more original as an eighties teen film in that it pretty much takes place in just one room (truly, this is one

---

* The Chinese exchange student character, Long Duk Dong, is a caricature so crude he makes the scenes featuring the Chinese villain in *The Hangover* look like an educational video from the UN.

† The awful Caroline and Geek ending, as ranted about in the Introduction.

eighties film that is begging to be turned into a play) and DOESN'T
EVEN HAVE A PROM, whereas *Pretty in Pink* ticks off all the classic clichés: pop song title, scenes in crowded school hallways, big
music number, climactic prom. But it is in many ways a more satisfying film, partly because it features some of the best acting ever
to appear in any of Hughes's films, especially from James Spader,
who nearly steals the whole movie, bringing his delicious Spaderish
creepiness unlike anything seen in any other teen film ever. Sometimes, when I'm feeling a little down on the world, I remember that
Spader was in a Hughes film and he says lines like "Any girl who did
that to me I would not be too JAZZED to hold on to," and my faith
in humanity is restored. Jon Cryer as Andie's heartsick and nerdy
friend Duckie is great, too, full of frustration and fury that the girl
he always revered turns out to lack the wisdom to fall for him, and
who among us has not felt so let down by a love interest? But what
really makes the film stand out is the character of Andie.

Before the eighties, young women didn't tend to do too well in
teen films. In the fifties they were generally ignored as movies focused
instead on the agonized plights of young men (*The Wild Ones*, *Rebel
Without a Cause*). In the sixties filmmakers realized that making movies about teenage protagonists made it even easier for them to shoot
endless scenes of young women in minimal amounts of clothing without having to bother too much about things such as plot or logic.
So young women were ostensibly given leading roles, but star billing
really went to their bikinis (the hugely popular Frankie Avalon and
Annette Funicello films). By the seventies, teen films were synonymous with horror movies (*Halloween*, *Carrie*) or movies sentimental-
izing teenagers from an earlier era (*American Graffiti*, *Grease*), and,
blood-soaked prom queens aside, they were utterly devoid of admirable female characters. But then Hughes arrived in the eighties, and
suddenly the girls started getting the good roles.

Hughes loved to write about awkward kids, but unlike too many male filmmakers, then and now, he didn't only write about awkward boys: he also grasped the extraordinary idea that teenage girls were humans—not sex objects or icy bitch temptresses—and his close friendship with Ringwald doubtless helped him with this. He said that some of Ringwald's roles in his films were "really a portrait of myself," and the fact that he gave the two best roles he wrote for her male names—Sam and Andie—further suggests his identification with them.

"When I first read John's scripts, I couldn't believe someone could write such amazing parts for young women. There had been movies with strong female protagonists before, but not ones with a strong female teenage protagonist," recalls Ringwald.

Hughes's teen films are peppered with awkward, truculent, even difficult young female characters: Jeanie, the patron saint of unhappy siblings everywhere, in *Ferris Bueller's Day Off*; Allison, making her dandruff blizzard out of her hair in *The Breakfast Club*; Watts, who proudly wears men's boxers instead of women's underwear in *Some Kind of Wonderful*; Iona, Andie's delightfully mouthy boss in *Pretty in Pink*, played by Annie Potts, aka Janine from *Ghostbusters*. In *The Breakfast Club*, Hughes showed he recognized one of the great plights of being a teenage girl when the two female characters discuss how to answer the question of whether or not you've "done it": "It's kind of a double-edged sword, isn't it?" Allison says to Claire. "If you say you haven't, you're a prude. And if you say you have, you're a slut. It's a trap. You want to but you can't, and when you do, you wish you didn't, right?" It's not only boys, Hughes knew, who struggle with sex. But of all Hughes's great female characters, there is none greater than Andie.

I first saw *Pretty in Pink* when I was nine, and while I, like every other heterosexual female, did promptly develop a lifelong crush on

McCarthy, it was Andie with whom I fell in love. She was the first girl I'd ever seen on-screen who felt recognizable to me. While I pretended sometimes I was Sloane from *Ferris Bueller*, all pretty and confident and with a boyfriend who picked me up from school in a car, I recognized that the teenager I would be was the awkward girl who drove herself to school. At the time, I lived in a Jewish enclave of Manhattan, meaning my life looked so different from the suburban white-bread ones depicted in John Hughes's films that I may as well have grown up in a different country. Yet even if the details of my life looked nothing like Hughes's movies, they nonetheless taught me something important: that I, a weird girl who lived too much inside her own head, whose looks somehow never seemed to coincide with the fashions of that day and wouldn't even kiss a boy until well into her third decade, deserved to be the star of my own movie.

This is not a message girls and young women can take for granted anymore. Until the *Twilight* series and *The Hunger Games* came along, studios had assumed for years that young women couldn't front franchises for teenagers. "Teenage girl [audiences] just weren't even in the equation until *Twilight* came around. When people talked about the teen market, they meant the male teen market," says film producer Lynda Obst. "This is because studios look at a movie's takings from the first weekend and teen boys tend to go out in packs on a first weekend, whereas girls didn't. Also, teen boys tended to match the international market, so studios would market to them, because the international market is so much more important these days. It wasn't until *Twilight* that it was the girls who came out in droves."

But Bella in *Twilight* and Katniss in *The Hunger Games* are, obviously, very different kinds of heroines from Andie. For a start, Bella is as passive and blank and tedious as the most retro of Disney heroines, always requiring the services of males to save her. She puts herself at risk for her creepy, cold, and dangerous boyfriend, and this is depicted as romantic. Whereas Andie refuses even to change her hat for Blane, Bella enthusiastically changes entire species in order to stay with her boyfriend, going from human to vampire, which is some makeover.

"Passive" is not a charge one would ever lay at the feet of Katniss Everdeen, one of the most admirable female characters to be seen in a teen film for some decades, albeit one who kills other teenagers. Many reviewers praised Katniss as a rare example of a strong female hero in modern movies, but strength doesn't always have to be demonstrated physically, despite what today's superhero-loving Hollywood might think. Katniss also lives in a completely different world from that of the audience. A film doesn't have to look familiar to inspire teenage audiences—after all, Hughes's high schools looked downright exotic to me—but at least there was a pretense of realism there. Audiences might sympathize with Katniss, and maybe even Bella, but they could empathize with Ringwald and her contemporaries.

But the real difference between Bella and Katniss and Andie is the kind of movies they are in. For a start, they are self-consciously dark films, reflecting a common belief among Hollywood filmmakers today that darkness equals depth and serves as a compensation for throwaway, forgettable scripts. It's easy to make a movie feel dramatic when the stakes are as high as the characters' lives, as they are in *Twilight* and *The Hunger Games*. Even a vaguely more realistic film like *The Fault in Our Stars*, which is like a twenty-first-century version of the Victorian novels that fetishized sufferers of consumption, plays on this, giving readers an almost perverse pleasure in reading about those more ill than themselves. It is trickier to give a movie emotional heft when it focuses on average people's average lives, and the fact is, most teen audiences will be average kids—they will not be superheroes or sufferers of terminal diseases. John Hughes told those kids that their stories were worth telling.

Hughes also understood that while American teenagers in the eighties didn't have the problems their parents had endured in their youth—Vietnam, namely—their daily anxieties felt no less pressing. This lesson was already forgotten by the nineties when the biggest teen films winkingly used plots from classical texts, such as Jane Austen's *Emma* (*Clueless*), *The Taming of the Shrew* (*10 Things I Hate About You*), and *Les Liaisons Dangereuses* (*Cruel Intentions*), simultaneously to mock the teen film genre and give it ironic credibility, as opposed to relying on the films to stand up for themselves (and thinking up their own plots, although, for the record, I do love *Clueless* and *10 Things I Hate About You*). These films didn't believe that the mundane details of the average teenager's life were interesting or important enough to make a film about, as eighties teen films definitely did, and Hughes especially did.

This reduced interest in female audiences has led to the rise of that dreaded stock (read: lazy) female film character whose presence has become such a given in certain types of films aimed at young people that she was eventually given a name. The Manic Pixie Dream Girl is a "bubbly, shallow cinematic creature that exists solely in the fevered imaginations of sensitive writer-directors to teach broodingly soulful young men to embrace life and its infinite mysteries and adventures," as journalist Nathan Rabin, who coined the term, put it. Many successful teen films very much feature the trope, such as 2009's *(500) Days of Summer* and 2012's *The Perks of Being a Wallflower*, in which, respectively, Zooey Deschanel and Emma Watson play attractively damaged pixies whose eyeliner and spontaneity rejuvenate their male leads while they themselves apparently have no inner lives (the vast majority of films featuring Manic Pixie Dream Girls, including these two, are written and directed by men). Most of all, they are not the star of their movie.

Stories serve as guides about how to live and what to expect from life, and if you're a girl who grows up believing that the most you can expect is to be a supporting character to a man, that's all you'll ever ask for. Rabin has since disowned the term, claiming, correctly, that misappropriation of the name has become as much of a cliché as the trope itself and the misappropriation tips into precisely the kind of sexism the term is supposed to satirize. But as Ben Beaumont-Thomas wrote in the *Guardian*: "Rabin is rightly uncomfortable in thinking about women in terms of stock subgroups, and yet this is exactly how a male-dominated film industry thinks about them—and after a trickle-down process, how ordinary men will end up thinking about them. By lampooning it in a tangy phrase like MPDG, a trope which has creeped along suddenly gets the light shined on it, and its ridiculousness becomes so well-articulated that it's difficult to get away with it again."

Andie is pretty much the opposite of a Manic Pixie Dream Girl. She exists totally in her own right. She is confident and insecure, wise and foolish, happy and furious, mature and childish, lustful and fearful, savvy but gauche. She is, in short, a teenager, and often unsure if she's worth what she wants. But as much as she doubts herself, she always stands up for herself: she screams in disarmingly unabashed rage at Blane when he lets her down, and she snaps back when Steff bullies her. I always liked that Hughes took the trouble to slip in the reason for Steff's hatred of Andie, and it has nothing to do with her being poor, or a nerd, or different—it's because she knocked him back. In other words, it's not about her, it's about him, and as messages to young female audiences go, telling them that misogyny often stems from male insecurity is a pretty good one. Most of all, Andie learns never to change herself for anyone.

When we first meet Andie in *Pretty in Pink*, there's a very big part of her that does want to be part of the popular and moneyed set, as much as she hates them. She drives down a street in the wealthy part of town and looks, longingly, at the big houses, much to Duckie's bemusement. There's no question that part of Blane's appeal to her is that he represents entry into that world, which is precisely why she's so conscious of him being from a different social class from her, despite her father reassuring her that it doesn't matter. It's only when she and Blane start dating that she realizes how much she values herself, and she refuses to change an iota for him.

All the men have to change in the movie: Blane, Andie's dad, Duckie, even Steff. The one person who doesn't change is Andie, and she still gets her dream boy—although that wasn't quite what Hughes intended, because in the original ending of the film Andie ends up with Duckie.

When he wrote the script, Hughes pictured Blane as fratty and obnoxious. Another Jake from *Sixteen Candles*, in other words, but with Ringwald getting together with the Geek in this film. Hughes and Deutch seriously considered the decidedly fratty-looking Charlie Sheen for the role of Blane and weird-but-undeniably-cute Robert Downey Jr. for Duckie, which would have worked, perfectly. But Hughes ultimately screwed his own film when he decided to cast the more sweetly soulful Andrew McCarthy, thereby making Blane seem more like a plausible boyfriend for Andie, despite his wealth.*

As any straight woman would have spotted from the start, McCarthy was so damn cute—his delicate looks so perfect for the beautiful but weak Blane—that there was no way female audiences were going to accept any ending other than one in which Andie gets together with him.

---

*The criminally underrated 1986 teen film *Lucas* later cast Sheen as the unexpectedly sensitive popular boy and, despite Sheen's underappreciated acting skills, and despite my deep love for this film, the truth is, he's not exactly plausible in the role. Every time he stands up for a nerd in the movie, I half expect Sheen to turn around and give him a wedgie.

But Hughes and Deutch, not being straight women, were "completely shocked" when test audiences affirmed this after seeing the film with the original ending: "The teenage girls were very clear about this: they wanted Andie to get what she wanted and to get with the cute boy, forget the frog, and I resented that," recalls Deutch. Speaking as a former teenage girl, teenage audiences would probably have found Downey Jr. to be a more acceptable consolation prize than Cryer, but that was no longer an option, and so, reluctantly, Hughes rewrote the ending, presumably throwing up on his own shoes as he sent his heroine off to live happily ever after with the town's "richie."

Hughes and Deutch absolutely hated this revised ending: "The movie became something else. Something that was not what the movie was supposed to be. It felt immoral," says Deutch. My biggest problem with the revised ending is that McCarthy had to wear a wig during the reshoot since he had since shaved off all his hair for a new movie and the obviously synthetic nature of this tonsorial monstrosity is a downright insult to his youthful, beautiful bouffant. But in all honesty, I don't mind that Andie ends up with Blane. After all, why shouldn't the awkward girl get the beautiful boy if that's who she lusts for? (And boy, does Andie lust for him—she practically eats him when they kiss.) Also, as Hughes shows through the storyline of Andie's heartbroken and abandoned father, women should not get together with nice men if they don't actually love them, or even feel attracted to them. That is a too little noted but important message, and too few movies appreciate that.*

But I think what I love most about this final scene, revised or otherwise, is what Andie's wearing, which is by anyone's measurement

---

* *Broadcast News* (1987) is also very smart about this, with Holly Hunter's character, Jane, falling for the shallow handsome newsreader (William Hurt) instead of the schlubby and nice producer (Albert Brooks), and that's just the way it is.

the ugliest prom dress of all time, and which she made for herself. "Oh my God, that dress!" groans Ringwald. "That is one thing in the film I won't take responsibility for. I remember thinking at the time that it was really funny because Andie wants to be a fashion designer, and she makes that dress. Pick a new career, Andie!" But in defense of this dress, it does encapsulate one of the truly great things about girls in eighties teen movies: they dress like shit.

When girls in eighties movies go on dates, they dress as demurely as the Amish: in *Valley Girl*, Julie's (Deborah Foreman) party outfit is a high-necked Victorian blouse and a pair of slacks; in *Lucas*, Maggie (Kerri Green) woos Cappie (Charlie Sheen) away from sexy cheerleading captain Alise (Ally McBeal's future nemesis Courtney Thorne-Smith) while wearing full-length skirts and shapeless jumpers; Chris (Elisabeth Shue) in *Adventures in Babysitting* attracts the attention of a college boy—a college boy!—while wearing her dead grandfather's coat; Boof (Susan Ursitti) in *Teen Wolf* dresses like a middle-aged suburban mother and she gets her dream boy/wolf; Watts (Mary Stuart Masterson) wears boys' clothes and still gets Eric Stoltz at the end of *Some Kind of Wonderful*; in *St. Elmo's Fire*—strictly speaking, a twenty-something movie as opposed to a teen movie, but a Brat Pack movie so, scientifically, it still counts—Leslie (Ally Sheedy) is every man's sexual fantasy despite dressing like a Quaker and sporting an amazing pudding-bowl haircut, while Wendy (Mare Winningham) pulls Rob freaking Lowe despite wearing her great-grandmother's wardrobe, right down to the underwear; Molly Ringwald's wardrobe in all her teen movies is a testament to the power of one's imagination if one apparently does not possess a full-length mirror.

These outfits are not actually a reflection of eighties fashion—in fact, it's usually the mean popular girls who wear the typically eighties clothes, from rah-rah skirts to cropped tops. Chris, let alone

Watts, would never wear a puffball skirt. Instead they reflect a female attitude that has been absent from teen films since the early nineties: dressing for oneself as opposed to dressing to look sexually available. Unlike teens in post-eighties movies, even good post-eighties teen movies, girls in eighties teen films don't dress to show off their "big boobs" (*Easy A*) or "to show a little skin—this reminds boys of being naked, and then they think of sex" (*Clueless*). They dress entirely for their own pleasure, even their own comfort.

By contrast, in 1999's *She's All That*, Laney (Rachael Leigh Cook) has to take off her glasses (obviously) and show off her breasts (OBVIOUSLY) in order to go from school joke to potential girlfriend for the popular boy, Zack (Freddie Prinze Jr.). Zack's sister even comes over before their date to pluck Laney's eyebrows, thereby ensuring that the date would be credible in the eyes of others, and the film blatantly approves of this, with the sister making "hilarious" comparisons between Laney and Bert from *Sesame Street*. Natural body hair on women: GROSSARAMA. And this brings us to a central teen movie issue: the makeover.

Eighties teen movies aren't averse to the occasional pointless makeover. One of the most misguided cinematic makeovers of all time takes place in *The Breakfast Club* when Allison (Sheedy) wins the glorious prize of Emilio Estevez's attention—but only after she swaps her fabulous eyeliner for pink blusher and a quite lame headband. And I like headbands. (This makeover is why Allison, in the pantheon of great Hughes female characters, is something of a disappointment. The worst thing about it is that it is only by changing that Allison catches a boy's attention, which is the diametric opposite message sent by *Pretty in Pink*. Sheedy herself was unsure about her makeover: "I didn't want it to be a makeover scene, as if somebody painted a face on Allison and suddenly she became acceptable. But I thought if she wore this heavy black eyeliner, then it would be like wiping off the mask to reveal the person underneath. I could have done without the bow in the hair, but it was a compromise.'") Looking further back, one of the most famous movie makeovers took place in a 1970s teen movie when Sandy in *Grease* swaps her lovely 1950s bobby-soxer clothes for the wardrobe of roller derby groupie and wins back her boyfriend in the process. (Fist pump! Go women!)

Some of the most popular makeovers in movies, from 1958's *Gigi* to 1990's *Pretty Woman*, have involved courtesans and prostitutes, emphasizing that cinematic makeovers are invariably about making the female characters look more sexually available. But it wasn't until the nineties that they became such a staple of teen movies that the stereotype was later satirized in 2001's *Not Another Teen Movie*, in which nerdy Janey (Chyler Leigh) is rendered slo-mo sexy simply by taking off her glasses and loosening her ponytail. In 1995's *Clueless*, Cher (Alicia Silverstone) makes Tai (Brittany Murphy) Beverly Hills–ready by reapplying her makeup and swapping her loose trousers for tiny miniskirts. In 1999's *Never Been Kissed*, Josie (the always lovely Drew Barrymore) is rescued from (undercover) high school hell thanks to some fashion and social help from her cooler brother Rob (David Arquette). Kat (Julia Stiles), the feminist protagonist in 1999's *10 Things I Hate About You*, endures a makeover from her little sister before the prom because everyone knows feminists are too ugly to be seen at social occasions unless heavily overhauled.

What a makeover means for women in a movie is "Conform and show off your boobs," and all the examples cited above say just that.

---

* "How could that have been allowed to happen?" wailed the badass actress Ellen Page in an interview with *New York* magazine when discussing *The Breakfast Club*. Films like that, Page tells the magazine, make tomboys like her "start judging ourselves, just because, you know, we'd rather climb trees than give blow jobs."

Change for men, in other words. By contrast, in the vast majority of eighties teen films, girls are celebrated for being their own gauche, unique selves, and this is a common theme in almost all eighties teen movies for all teenagers, from *Teen Wolf* to *Say Anything*. This celebration of the unique explains, I suspect, why so many kids in eighties teen films have such weird names (Boof and Styles in *Teen Wolf*), and especially in Hughes's teen films (Ferris, Bender, Sloane, Duckie, Blane, Watts).* With the exception of the makeover scene in *The Breakfast Club*, Hughes celebrates his leading ladies' quirks, and Andie's vintage clothes—which she wears because she can't afford new ones—are depicted as proof of her admirable creativity. If she does then wear the ugliest prom dress of all time, that's a price worth paying for individuality. *Pretty in Pink* is the anti-makeover movie.

Andie stays so true to her style, no matter how much she likes a boy, that Blane doesn't even realize she's dressed for their date when he picks her up from the record store and he suggests that she should go home and change (in true Andie style, she refuses). Laney Boggs in *She's All That*, by contrast, gets so overhauled before her date that her paramour doesn't even recognize her—and he likes her more for it. Nineties teen makeover scenes are all about stamping out a teenage girl's awkwardness and unique personality, whereas the girls in eighties teen movies celebrate those two qualities. Even Diane Court in *Say Anything*, the girl with "the body of a game show host," dresses undeniably, unapologetically, and gloriously badly, with her frumpy skirt suits that she wears on dates. And it was the very weirdness of these eighties girls, the Andies and

---

* Sweetly, in Hughes's world, it's the kids with relatively normal names who are mocked. Of Blane, Duckie rages, "Blane? His name is BLANE?! That's a major appliance, that's not a name!" In *The Breakfast Club*, Bender—BENDER—snorts, "Claire? CLAIRE?! That's a fat girl's name." As you can probably guess, this reversal of the usual attitudes to names served as great consolation to someone named Hadley.

the Dianes, that attracted the boys to them. They didn't even have to get out the tweezers.

Celestia Fox, a casting agent who discovered and worked with some of the most successful British and American teen actors in the eighties, says the reason teen films and teen characters are so much glossier today than they were thirty years ago can be summed up in one word: "*Clueless*. That changed everything. And, to a certain extent, *Beverly Hills 90210* did, too. These shows completely altered the look of American films and TV shows aimed at teenagers. In America, everything made after *Clueless* immediately became much more aspirational and glamorous, and it still is."

"*Clueless* was never meant to be a teen film exactly—it was a comedy of manners," says the film's director, Amy Heckerling, who also directed the 1980s teen film *Fast Times at Ridgemont High*. "I saw it as a satire, almost, whereas *Fast Times* was about how teenagers actually lived." But what was once satire soon set the standard, and not just in terms of how teenage actresses dressed.

Actresses in teen films and teen TV shows have also become progressively thinner over the past few decades, especially in the past decade. A comparison between the original cast of the TV show *Beverly Hills 90210* (1990–2000) and the cast of the revived series *90210* (2008–2013) is so jarring it's eye-watering: the actresses on the recent series look—and this is barely an exaggeration—half the size of those on the old show, and, shockingly, the original cast look almost chubby in comparison when they were seen at the time as very slim. Even the young actresses on the Disney Channel (aimed at nine- to fourteen-year-olds) are getting thinner, as a brief comparison between Hilary Duff (a star on the channel in 2000) and Bella Thorne (2010) proves. Not only are teenage girls seeing fewer representations of their lives on-screen; they're seeing fewer actresses who even vaguely resemble them.

Again, some of this can be traced back to *Clueless*, with its deliberate gloss and glamour. But the actresses in that film look almost chunky compared to the ones in films today. (The one *Clueless* actress who continued to work in popular movies after that film, the late Brittany Murphy, became, notoriously, much skinnier in her later films, thus fitting in with the new and increasingly limited aesthetic.) But really, this change has largely come from the fashion world. Films, especially films aimed at young women and teenage girls, have always taken their cues from fashion trends and there is no question that the fashion industry venerates a much skinnier look now than it did in the eighties, as the most skirting comparison between eighties supermodels and today's jarringly attenuated models proves. Fashion editors invariably say that models today look "much healthier" these days than they have of late, and this is true, but only if one thinks that looking better than the pale and miserable-looking Eastern European models popular at the beginning of this century is a triumph for health in itself as opposed to a decidedly minor and relative improvement.

"When I started in this business thirty years ago, teenage actresses were always about a size six, maybe a four; now they're always a size zero, or even a double zero," one fashion stylist who works for teen magazines told me. A costume designer who has worked on one of the biggest teen films of this century adds, "When I get clothes for these girls, I often have to shop in the children's section, even though they're sixteen. Teen actresses are not expected to look like teenagers anymore—they're expected to look like models, and this is because female celebrities have sort of taken the place of models. Just look at the covers of fashion magazines today and who do you see? Actresses and celebrities." When asked if Ringwald would get work today as the romantic lead in a teen film, the costume designer rolled her eyes.

Ringwald is one of the most successful teen actresses of all time, but her influence proved a lot shorter-lived than her fame. If *Pretty in Pink* were made today, the film would be told from Blane's point of view and Andie would be relegated to being a Manic Pixie Dream Girl, about twenty-five pounds lighter with heavy eyeliner and blow-dried hair. (See: *Along Came Polly*. Or, rather, don't.) Ringwald says:

> I feel like the films and TV shows today for teenagers are all about wanting to be famous and rich, and the girls are so skinny and sexualized in them, I just don't have the stomach for them. The kind of roles I played in teen films just don't seem to exist anymore. My elder daughter is almost ten and I wanted to show her something that would make her feel better so I was thinking and thinking and I thought, Oh my God! I made it! So we sat down together and watched *Pretty in Pink*. It was wonderful to watch it now but it also feels really sad that the only movie that hit the spot was made thirty years ago. But ever since my daughter watched *Pretty in Pink*, she doesn't want to watch those other shows anymore. She knows there's something else out there.

Plenty of awesome and weird heroines appeared in eighties teen films after *Pretty in Pink*. There's self-righteous and fearless watermelon carrier Baby in *Dirty Dancing*, which was released the following year; dorky and courageous Thor-obsessed Sara in *Adventures in Babysitting*; and most of all, Veronica in *Heathers*, the film that didn't just make female aggression scary, *Carrie*-style, but also triumphant, and really, really cool. By the end of the decade, audiences had become so used to teenage girls getting the good parts that Cameron Crowe was able to make one of the most sophisticated and feminist teen films of them all, *Say Anything*, in which the teenage boy, Lloyd (John Cusack), says specifically all he wants to do with his life is to support his brilliant girlfriend so she can shine. "This is a very differ-ent kind of knight and white horse. It's not, 'I'll take you away,' it's 'I'll enable you to be you.' If you're a terrific girl and you're brilliant, that's what you'd hope for," said *Say Anything*'s executive producer, James L. Brooks.

Thanks at least partly to Hughes, young actresses enjoyed lead roles in teen movies for a brief period in the nineties, such as Julia Stiles as the fuming feminist in *10 Things I Hate About You* and Alicia Silverstone in *Clueless*, as well as a brief flurry of independent films about tough girl heroines, such as 1996's *Girls Town*, 1998's *The Opposite of Sex*, and 2000's *Girlfight* and *Bring It On*. But the return of raunchy comedies and superhero films pushed them to the back again. There have been occasional teen films starring young women in the twenty-first century, such as, most obviously, 2004's *Mean Girls*, but these are the exceptions. From a Hollywood studio's point of view, it makes more sense to have a male lead, in the be-lief that they're more likely to attract a wider audience. (The closest raunchy nineties teen movies came to creating an Andie-like char-acter is Michelle in *American Pie* [played by Alyson Hannigan], the goofy flute player who is always utterly herself, even when consumed with lust. But she is played in the movie for laughs, and is really just a side character to the male lead.)

But Ringwald herself would never get to play another great Hughesian heroine because by the time *Pretty in Pink* came out, she and Hughes were barely talking. During the making of *Pretty in Pink*, Hughes told Deutch to ask Ringwald if she would appear in their next film, *Some Kind of Wonderful*, which Deutch also directed, as Watts, another awkward girl. But Ringwald felt it was time to grow up. She knew the film was just too similar to ones she'd done before, as *Some Kind of Wonderful* is really just a gender-reversed

Pretty in Pink, with the original ending reinstated. (Deutch insists that Hughes didn't write it as a reaction to having had to rewrite *Pretty in Pink* and somewhat improbably suggests that Hughes didn't see a connection between the two films.) So she turned it down, and Hughes stopped speaking to her and, after *Some Kind of Wonderful*, he never made another teen film. It turned out there was a downside to working with a director so in touch with his inner teenager: sometimes he really acted like a teenager.

"John could be very sullen—if his feelings were hurt, he'd shut down and not speak to you for days," says Matthew Broderick, the star of *Ferris Bueller's Day Off*.

Ringwald later wrote in the *New York Times*: "We were like the Darling children when they made the decision to leave Neverland. And John was Peter Pan, warning us that if we left we could never come back. And, true to his word, not only were we unable to return, but he went one step further. He did away with Neverland itself."

"There was a tremendous sense of loss for him when she moved on, as I think there was for her, too. They were very, very close and it was really sad to see that end," says Deutch.

Hughes died in 2009, at the ridiculously premature age of fifty-nine, of a heart attack: "When you grow up, your heart dies."

Reporting his death, newspaper coverage barely mentioned *Home Alone*, which was his most financially successful film by a hefty mile. Instead, the media focused on his teen films, especially those he made with Ringwald. In the *New York Times*, chief film critic A. O. Scott wrote: "Molly Ringwald was for Mr. Hughes what Jimmy Stewart was for Frank Capra: an emblem, a muse, a poster child and an alter-ego."

But Hughes and Ringwald never spoke again, and she instead

pursued an acting career without him. There was no final tearful makeup scene between her and her former mentor, no Hughesian climactic final scene. But that's the thing about awkward girls: they might get their happy endings, but they don't always follow the script.

Top Five British Bad Guys

 Charles Dance, *The Golden Child*

Charles Dance, phoning it in and all the funnier for it. I love that Kanye West cites him ("My sweet brother Numpsay!") in his song "Gone" on *Late Registration*.

 David Bowie, *Labyrinth*

One of the weirdest villains of the eighties and one of the weirdest songs, too. Nothing less is expected, David Bowie.

 Steven Berkoff, *Beverly Hills Cop*

It's the law for Berkoff to appear in any list of top villains: Shakespearean, James Bond, you name it. He clocked up a good few in the eighties, including in *Rambo First Blood Part II*. But obviously this one's my favorite.

2 **Terence Stamp,** *Superman 2*

"KNEEL BEFORE ZOD." For his facial hair alone, Stamp comes zooming in at number two.

Alan Rickman, *Die Hard*

No competition. Unbelievably, this was Rickman's first film role, and with his debut, he became the überBrit villain (albeit playing a German). Unbettered by anyone until Rickman played the Sheriff of Nottingham in 1991's *Robin Hood Prince of Thieves*.

When Harry Met Sally

Romcoms Don't Have to Make You Feel Like You're Having a Lobotomy

Come closer, children, come closer, and sit by your old granny's knee. I'm a-gonna tell you a tale from times of yore, of what life was like back in the olden days. Oh, it was all very different back then, I can tell you! Back then, we didn't have things like cell phones—good gracious, no! If you wanted to walk around with a phone that had a photo of you and your friends on the front, you'd have had to cut a handset off the wall and tape a Polaroid onto the back of it. What's that you ask? "What's a handset on a wall? What's a Polaroid?" Oh dear, I'm using old-world language. Let's try again. So as I was saying, back when your granny was a young child, we didn't have cell phones, we didn't have the Internet, and, perhaps most shockingly of all, romcoms weren't synonymous with mind-numbing retrograde crap that made you think all women were insane and all men horrible human beings. I know! It's like hearing about a time when people didn't have indoor plumbing, isn't it?

Those of us who were born before 1995 know that romcoms didn't used to be terrible, but we know this in the way that we know we used to love Michael Jackson and Bill Cosby in a manner wholly uncomplicated by their personal lives. We accept that time did exist, even if it does feel impossible today. The low status of the romcom today makes me very sad because it is so wrong. What's more fun to watch than romance and comedy, for heaven's sake? The answer is "ANYTHING" if by "romance and comedy" we now mean "misogynistic bullshit starring Katherine Heigl and Gerard Butler," as apparently we now do, judging by 2009's *The Ugly Truth*. And the result is, romcoms have been declared dead.

"RIP Romantic Comedies: Why Harry Couldn't Meet Sally in 2013," blared the *Hollywood Reporter*. "Why Are Romantic Comedies So Bad?" mused the *Atlantic*. "Death of the Romcom," read a graph on Box Office Mojo, showing how the romcom has tanked while movies about superheroes have soared.

Do we really want to live in a world in which Captain America is considered to be more universal than romance and comedy? Nobody, goes the theory, wants to see romcoms anymore, because they are terrible. The end. But the truth is, the only reason romcoms are terrible these days is that Hollywood stopped giving a shit about women. *Fin*.

Romcoms were once amazing. In fact, the romcom genre encompasses some of the finest—and most feminist—films ever made, from *The Philadelphia Story* in 1940 to *Annie Hall* thirty-seven years later. There were so many great romcoms in the 1980s that I feel like there should be a collective noun for them: a delight of romcoms, a swoon of romcoms. And they weren't just good—they were critically respected: romcoms such as *Moonstruck* and *Working Girl* won Golden Globes and Oscars. Sure, the Oscars are stupid and ultimately meaningless, but the only romcom of the past fifteen years that has been comparatively lauded was 2011's *Bridesmaids*, which—uniquely for today—was written by and starred women. Which brings me to the next point.

What marks eighties romcoms out is that so many of the best ones starred women. Whereas Woody Allen made himself the protagonist of his great seventies romcoms, such as the wonderful *Annie Hall* and the now pretty much unwatchable *Manhattan*, in the eighties he made his then-partner Mia Farrow the focus, and his movies became sweeter, more varied, and more interesting for it. She is very much the star in films such as *The Purple Rose of Cairo* and *Hannah and Her Sisters*, and therefore the subject of the film as opposed to just being the object within it, as Diane Keaton is in *Annie Hall*. Allen gave Farrow a voice in his eighties films, which is more than he's ever done for any actress since. Cher was forty-one when she starred in *Moonstruck* and Nicolas Cage, her romantic opposite, was twenty-three, and no one in the film ever comments on this (fairly obvious) disparity.* *Working Girl* transplanted the romcom to zeitgeisty eighties Wall Street, with a vague (very, very vague) feminist spin, and has three fabulous actresses at its core: Melanie Griffith, Sigourney Weaver, and Joan Cusack. Kathleen Turner proved that women can front romantic action films when she costarred with Michael Douglas in the sweetly screwball *Romancing the Stone* and *The Jewel of the Nile*.

"I was the first! The first female lead of an action movie. I knocked up a lot of firsts," hoots Turner. "But I don't remember that being discussed at the time—certainly no one expressed to me that they had any concerns. You know, I'm a strong woman and I was a terrific athlete so the only thing that they were worried about was they had to stop me from doing my stunts: 'No, Kathleen, you can't

---

* Possibly because everyone was too distracted by Cher and Cage's awesomely hammy acting and even more awesomely hammy lines, for example, "I ain't no monument to justice!" "A WOLF WITHOUT A FOOT!" Seriously, go watch this movie, it's just the business.

swing across the gorge on a vine, insurance doesn't cover that.' Ah, come on!"*

All these films attracted not just female audiences but (gasp! shock! amazement!) men, too. *The Princess Bride* proved that rom-coms didn't just have cross-gender appeal; they had a cross-generation one, as well, because only people without souls don't enjoy romance and comedy and men, women, and children alike all generally have souls.

The wonderful *Tootsie* showed that you could have a romcom that looked at love from both gender sides through one character. When aspiring actor Michael Dorsey (Dustin Hoffman) dresses up as a woman and redubs himself Dorothy Michaels, in order to get a role on a soap opera, this former selfish asshole finds himself helping to empower the women on the show against the sexist director (*9 to 5*'s Dabney Coleman, everyone's favorite sexist in the eighties). So far, so early eighties comedy. But Hoffman plays the part much more tenderly than audiences have come to expect from movies featuring actors cross-dressing. In an emotional interview with the American Film Institute in 2012, a tearful Hoffman described how shocked he was when he first saw himself made up as a woman because he wasn't beautiful. He then went home and cried and said to his wife that he had to make this movie. When she asked why, he replied: "Because I think I am an interesting woman when I look at myself on-screen. And I know that if I met myself at a party, I would never talk to that character. Because she doesn't fulfill physically the demands that we're brought up to think women have to have in order to ask them out. There's too many interesting women I have . . . not had the experience to know in this life because I have been brainwashed."

---

* Can we please have a moment of respectful silence for the hot tamale of awesomeness that is Kathleen Turner?

To the film's credit, it does show various men in the movie learning to appreciate Dorothy, despite her not being conventionally attractive, including her costar John (played by George Gaynes, better known to eighties movie fans as dippy Commandant Lassard from the *Police Academy* films), the father of a friend, and even, to a certain extent, Coleman. You can tell that Hoffman truly did respect both the character and the film because he managed to make a whole film about a man cross-dressing without once coming across as even slightly transphobic—a downright marvel, considering the film was made thirty-five years ago, and this is why it feels as timeless as the similarly transphobia-free *Some Like It Hot*. Nothing dates a film quicker than bigotry (that, and giving a cameo role to Paris Hilton). At most, the movie has a small plotline about his costar Julie thinking that Dorothy's a lesbian, but even this is done rather sweetly: when Michael-as-Dorothy tries to kiss her, Julie reels away in shock but, instead of being shocked or even horrified, she burbles apologetically, "I'm sure I've got the same impulses. Obviously I did. . . ."

But the movie flakes out when it ends with Michael getting together with Julie, played by the astonishingly beautiful Jessica Lange, whereas it would have been much more interesting if Michael himself had learned to see the appeal in women who don't necessarily look like goddesses—such as, for example, his best friend Sandy, who likes him, played by Teri Garr, but whom he dumps. Still, at least the point of the film is that women shouldn't date assholes, and if it takes Michael dressing as a woman to become the non-asshole that Julie deserves, fair play to them all. And at least Hoffman himself took something away from the movie (even if what I took away from it was that even five-foot-five-inch schmucks with big Jewish noses only want gorgeous blond shiksas). (Incidentally, I really do love this movie.)

Then, in the final year of that decade, the greatest of all eighties romcoms was released. It looked at love from the men's and women's points of view in a far more credible, funny, and moving way than *Tootsie*: *When Harry Met Sally* . . .

Along with *Ferris Bueller's Day Off* and *The Princess Bride*, *When Harry Met Sally* . . . is the most quotable film of the 1980s, the most quotable of all the decades. Nora Ephron wrote so many great lines in it that the self-restraint needed not to type them all out in one giant quote binge is actually giving me finger cramp.

"Thin. Pretty. Big tits. Your basic nightmare"—No! Stop it! "Someone is staring at you in personal growth"—Stop! You promised you wouldn't do this!

"You know, I'm so glad I never got involved with you. I just would have ended up being some woman you had to get up out of bed and leave at three in the morning and go clean your andirons, and you don't even have a fireplace—not that I would know this."

Ah well. It takes a stronger woman than me to resist the pithy power of the Ephron.

But as funny and wise as *When Harry Met Sally* . . . is—and it is so funny and wise, and we'll return to this—the funniest thing about it is that it was dismissed by the critics when it was released. The *New York Times* described it as "the sitcom version of a Woody Allen film" (critics can be real idiots) and it was nominated for only one Academy Award, Best Original Screenplay—and it lost that to *Dead Poets Society.** *Dead Poets Society*! Well, I did tell you the Oscars were stupid.

I get the surface comparisons with Allen—the white-on-black opening credits, the adoring shots of New York City, the privileged

---

* Other screenplays that lost that year to *Dead* freaking *Poets Society*: *Do the Right Thing*, *Crimes and Misdemeanors*, and *Sex, Lies, and Videotape*. The Oscars were completely hilarious that year.

uptown world, the hat-wearing women—but *When Harry Met Sally* . . . is nothing like a Woody Allen movie, even though plenty of critics still beg to differ on that point (writer Mark Harris memorably described it as "not *Annie Hall* but a movie about people who have seen *Annie Hall*").

Like the best of Ephron's writing—her journalism, *Heartburn*, her essays—*When Harry Met Sally* . . . has the precision of a personal story but is actually interested in drawing out universal truths. Allen, by contrast, is only ever interested in his stories and would never dream of suggesting that they somehow say something about anybody but him, and sometimes that's great and sometimes it's less so. When people talk today about the message of *When Harry Met Sally* . . . , they think of Harry's claim that "men and women can't be friends," and how the movie seems to confirm that. But Ephron said she didn't believe that at all. Instead, she wrote:

> What *When Harry Met Sally* . . . is really about is how different men and women are. The truth is that men don't want to be friends with women. Men know they don't understand women, and they don't much care. They want women as lovers, as wives, as mothers, but they're not really interested in them as friends. They have friends. Men are their friends. And they talk to their male friends about sport, and I have no idea what else. Women, on the other hand, are dying to be friends with men. Women know they don't understand men, and it bothers them: they think that if only they could be friends with them, they would understand them and, what's more (and this is their gravest mistake), it would help.

Gender generalizations are, as a generalization, abhorrent, but it takes a truly po-faced pedant not to delight in this one. Imagine a romcom today being built on this kind of subtle wisdom. And as abhorrent as gender generalizations are, I think only a man could ever claim that *When Harry Met Sally* . . . feels like an Allen movie. Sally and her female friends are so different from the kinds of women you find in Allen's movies they may as well be aliens, because the women in *When Harry Met Sally* . . . were written by someone who didn't just like women, but understood them.

Unusually for a romcom—or any movie, for that matter—*When Harry Met Sally* . . . is equally interested in the women in the film as it is in the men, and the reason for this is that Ephron was writing about real people. Harry was based on Rob Reiner, the film's director, and Sally was based on Ephron herself: "I realized that I had found a wonderful character in Rob Reiner. Rob is a very strange person. He is extremely funny, but he is also extremely depressed . . . but he wasn't at all depressed about being depressed; in fact, he loved his depression," Ephron wrote. "And because Harry was bleak and depressed, it followed absolutely that Sally would be cheerful and chirpy and relentlessly, pointlessly, unrealistically, idiotically optimistic. Which is, it turns out, very much like me."

Incidentally, the first great female character Allen ever wrote was also based on a real person—*Annie Hall*, which was a straight-up homage to his ex-girlfriend Diane Keaton (real name: Diane Hall). The next was Hannah in *Hannah and Her Sisters*, which was clearly and heavily based on Mia Farrow. Anyone who thinks that an author is cheating if they use real life in their fiction is a fool. Real life is often what gives fiction its truth, and good fiction in turn helps us understand real life. Ephron knew better than anyone that real life is the stuff great fiction is made of: "Everything is copy," was her mother's mantra and this attitude turned her into a legend when she turned her brutal divorce from Carl Bernstein into one of the funniest novels ever written, *Heartburn*. So it seems like the best way to honor her memory would be to write a little bit about the personal relationship I have to this movie.

I first saw *When Harry Met Sally . . .* when I was a teenager, almost a decade after it came out. I must have watched it in London, where we moved to from New York in 1989, in our living room on our dying VHS, and the character I related to immediately wasn't Sally, the female lead who wants to be a writer, but Harry, the miserable and proud-of-his-misery Jew. Harry was the first character I'd ever seen in a film who was Jewish the way I was Jewish: if someone was asked what religion they thought Harry and I are, they'd probably say "Jewish," but it wouldn't be the first personality attribute you'd list about either of us (that would be "self-absorbed"). This was Jewishness the way I knew Jewishness—being Jewish—and not the self-conscious outsider and faintly minstrel Jewyness that Woody Allen portrayed. Also, like Harry, I was miserable, in a way that only an extremely privileged, middle-class teenage girl from a very nice family can be miserable. And like Harry, I made the mistake of thinking that made me deep.

It wasn't—and it still isn't—easy being a female movie fan. Movies tend to be written and directed by men, which means that the female characters are generally insane or boring. I began to notice this only when I moved on from eighties teen films, where I had Molly Ringwald, Ally Sheedy, Winona Ryder, and Jennifer Jason Leigh for companionship, to nineties movies for grown-ups, where my options felt hugely reduced. So when I was a teenager and I wondered who would play me in the biopic of my life (I told you I was self-obsessed), I settled on Bill Murray. Only he had the qualities of humor, cynicism, and lovableness that I was sure would be appreciated in me one day. Until I saw *When Harry Met Sally . . .* , that is, and then I thought Billy Crystal might just make the cut. After all, he was Jewish. And miserable. And deep.

But as I grew older, I began to see a different strength in the movie, one I had entirely missed when I was younger because, like Harry, I was too self-obsessed: I began to see Sally. And this is when my life began to change thanks to *When Harry Met Sally*. (I'm going to skip the ellipses hereon: I get the point of them in the title but they're annoying to type and even more annoying to read, and I don't think Ephron would mind. She never even liked the title.)

So as I was saying, it's not always easy to be a female movie fan, especially a female fan of comedies. Men are generally the protagonists of comedies, because comedies tend to be written by men, so it's easy to grow up resenting your gender, a little. Why do you have to be a woman? Women are boring. Women are there just to laugh at the men's jokes, or be the disapproving shrew. Women don't get the good lines. Women are Margaret Dumont and men are the Marx Brothers, and I like Margaret Dumont (especially when she was wearing a swimming costume—her swimming costumes in the Marx Brothers films were amazing), but I prefer clowning to making moues of disapproval at Groucho. Worse, when you grow up watching men play leads in films, as I increasingly did, you get used to wanting everything to work out well for men, because you've been trained to be on their side. I spent years staying in relationships with men who were not worth my body, let alone my time, because I worried that if I broke up with them they'd be sad like Lloyd Dobler was in *Say Anything* (it turned out, they weren't, because Lloyd Dobler is fictional) (and also, 90 percent of the guys I went out with when I was young were idiots).

Until, that is, *When Harry Met Sally*. It's written by a very funny woman and therefore features many funny women. Sally is not just Harry's straight sidekick—the Sigourney Weaver to Dr. Venkman, or the Buttercup to his Westley. Sally doesn't even have to perform any of the three functions women are usually lumbered with in romcoms: pine desperately for the man, make the man grow up by being a nagging shrew, or be liberated from her frigid bitchiness by the power of his amazing penis. In fact, for the first half of the film it's Harry who's heartbroken after his ex-wife left him for Ira the accountant, making him the vulnerable, humiliated, needy one. Sally supports him—helping him lay carpet, singing songs from *Oklahoma!* with him—because she is seemingly over her ex-boyfriend Joe ("'I am over him,' Sally says, when she isn't over him at all; I have uttered that line far too many times in my life, and far too many times in my life I have believed it was true," Ephron wrote).

Here, I realized, was an adult female character who wanted love, but wasn't pathetic, and was loved, but also human. She wasn't just Harry's romantic quarry—she was her own person. I was thrilled when I read that Ephron based Sally on herself because that meant Sally must be Jewish. I'm not some cinematic Zionist who can enjoy her characters only if they're kosher, but this proved that the film doesn't follow that insufferable template of having a goyish woman fall for a Jewish man because of his allegedly adorable Jewish qualities, and the Jewish man falls for her in turn because she is not (mazel tov, sir!) a Jewish woman. Woody Allen populated the cliché and Judd Apatow has since flogged it to death (while Larry David has waved the flag for it on TV). In Sally, Ephron coined that rare-to-the-point-of-nonexistent film character: a desirable Jewish woman. A Jewish woman. Sally also pointed out to me that being miserable didn't mean I was deep. It meant that I was just ruining my own life.

Sally's relationship with her girlfriends, especially Marie (Carrie Fisher), is one of my favorite things about the movie. Her friends are portrayed as a source of support but also have lives of their own (an extreme rarity in a movie, in which friends usually exist merely to be friends with the protagonist). This makes their friendship feel utterly real. "You're right, you're right, I know you're right," Marie chants in self-recrimination whenever Sally tells her, for the ten thousandth time, that Marie's married lover will never leave his wife for her.

Like Sally and Marie, I lived in New York City in my early thirties and, like them, I dated some absolute shockers whom I should have been smart enough to avoid. It turned out, much to my surprise, that even those of us who grow up hoping to be as wise and cynical as Dr. Venkman make the same grim, boring, sad mistakes as so many other women, and for exactly the same reasons: we're hopeful, we're suckers, we're lonely. Ephron knew that, but didn't mock women for it, or depict them as pathetic for wanting companionship; rather, she regarded them with fond affection, and that made me do the same about myself, eventually. Bad romcoms stigmatize and deride feelings of heartbreak and loneliness, and make me feel like I'm being a shameful cliché for desiring love, like some subnormal character in a Kate Hudson or Katherine Heigl movie. Good romcoms, like *When Harry Met Sally*, reassure me that this is what it's like to be a human being. Every time my best friend Carol made these mistakes we'd call each other for reassurance, just as Sally and Marie do, and the other one would say, "You're right, you're right, I know you're right." And eventually, the point would sink in: don't beat yourself up about this, but get yourself together and move on.

Writing good romcoms is hard. You can't fake them because most people recognize when something is funny and most people have been in love, whereas no one is a superhero so you can do whatever you want there. I was amazed when I read in an essay that Ephron "struggled" with the screenplay for *When Harry Met Sally* and that "it was really hard" ("I was just doing it for the money," she cheerfully admits), because it reads as smoothly and effortlessly as a bunch of friends talking.

It makes me laugh when I hear male screenwriters today insist they don't write female characters because, well, how can they possibly understand women, what with them just being dumb lugs? In an interview with the *Guardian*, Evan Goldberg, writer of the bro-heavy comedies *Superbad* and *This Is the End*, offered what he thought was a reasonable explanation for why there are so few female roles in his movies: "I'm a guy! I'm not as good at writing about women. Kristen Wiig [who wrote *Bridesmaids*] is way better. I don't fully understand my wife's emotions—and I'm supposed to write an excellent female character and unravel the secret of women?"

And he learned this mentality from his mentor, Judd Apatow, who that same year said the following to the *New Yorker*: "The reality is, I'm a dude and I understand the dude thing, so I lean men just the way Spike Lee leans African-American." Imagine how different movies would be if more men realized that women are humans and not an entirely different species. Because insisting you can't write dialogue for the opposite gender is not being gender-sensitive, it's being lazy.

So what happened after Harry and Sally's ellipses? Well, there was an absolute glut of romcoms in the nineties, starting with the mighty behemoth of *Pretty Woman*, the timeless and romantic tale of what happens when a rich asshole picks up a hooker in Los Angeles for a blow job. Some nineties romcoms were a complete delight (*Four Weddings and a Funeral*, *Groundhog Day*, *The Wedding Singer*), but even Ephron's romcoms had diminishing returns, going from the magic of *When Harry Met Sally* to the sweetness of *Sleepless in Seattle* to the mehness of *You've Got Mail*. By the late nineties and early noughties, the trend had switched to raunch with male leads, kick-started by *There's Something About Mary*. Hollywood made more romcoms with male leads (*Along Came Polly*, *Garden State*), which were increasingly tired and formulaic and were written solely from a male perspective.

"Audiences aren't tired of romance, they're tiring of formulas," one director told the *Hollywood Reporter*, a claim that would make a lot more sense if Hollywood weren't subsisting on *The Avengers 7* and *Batman 22*. And without wishing to state the obvious, maybe if audiences really are tired of formulaic movies, Hollywood could make romcoms that are, you know, less formulaic. Just a thought, guys!

Even if no one had ever before made a romcom, audiences still wouldn't want to see awful junk like *He's Just Not That Into You*, *Love Actually*, or *Valentine's Day*, because they're terrible. And people definitely don't want to see them now because they know that romcoms can be good. If *When Harry Met Sally* were released today, people would definitely want to see it. But it probably wouldn't get released today because movies like that struggle to get made now.

"Women's films, like weepies and romcoms, don't get commissioned anymore because they don't work overseas. There's a different kind of funny today—less wit. Wit and nuance doesn't travel," says producer Lynda Obst, who worked in the romcom market for years before having to move on to sci-fi due to what she describes as "lack of windows for romcom." "Funny is an Asian man who's going to blow up your car. Comedies take place in the same style as action movies and they go from set piece to set piece—you don't see that in Cameron Crowe or Nora Ephron's films. You see writing and dialogue. Now it's about dialogue moving you to another set piece where something big will happen. Comedy writers are taught to write set pieces," she says.

"There is also a creeping sexualization of women in recent romcoms, particularly in those starring Jennifer Aniston," says film writer Melissa Silverstein, and she's right. It's amazing to see how "frumpy" (that is, normal) Sally looks, with her shaggy hair and baggy clothes, compared to the glossy female stars of today's romcoms.

Christopher Orr in the *Atlantic* argued that the reason romcoms struggle today is that, well, love is too easy now: "Among the most fundamental obligations of romantic comedy is that there must be an obstacle to nuptial bliss for the budding couple to overcome. And, put simply, such obstacles are getting harder and harder to come by. They used to lie thick on the ground: parental disapproval, difference in social class, a promise made to another. But society has spent decades busily uprooting any impediment to the marriage of true minds. Love is increasingly presumed—perhaps in Hollywood most of all—to transcend class, profession, faith, age, race, gender, and (on occasion) marital status."

Well, if Mr. Orr thinks love is easy these days, I'll have what he's having. Love is a freaking nightmare today, as it always was and always will be, and that's because human beings are ridiculous. There was no real impediment to Harry and Sally's love—they're the same age, often single at the same time, and they like each other—but it took them twelve years and three months to get together, because that's what people are like. Ephron knew that, and she was smart enough also to know that love wasn't about set pieces, or shticks, meet cutes, or clichéd impediments—it's about people. Jane Austen knew that, too, and even though so many of the relationships in her books seem to be rooted in issues about money (Darcy is richer than Elizabeth in *Pride and Prejudice*, Edward is richer than Elinor in *Sense and Sensibility*, and so on), the only real impediment to them is the characters themselves: Darcy is too proud, Elizabeth is too prejudiced; Edward is too loyal to his commitments, Elinor is too self-effacing; Anne Elliot in *Persuasion* was too easily persuaded by bad advice, and Captain Wentworth's pride was hurt; Emma in her eponymous novel is too immature to see what is in front of her face. This is why her novels have lasted, and it's why *When Harry Met Sally* has lasted: because stories that are about human emotions don't date. But it's hard to translate witty dialogue about complicated human emotions for overseas sales, I guess, and car explosions are a lot easier to write anyway.

Another factor is the lack of women working today behind the camera on movies. Women have been running studios in Hollywood since 1980, when Sherry Lansing became the president of 20th Century Fox, and Cheryl Boone Isaacs is currently president of the Academy of Motion Picture Arts and Sciences, the group behind the Oscars. But as the *New York Times* film critic Manohla Dargis notes: "trickle-down equality doesn't work in Hollywood, even when women are calling the shots and making the hires."

In 2013 women constituted just 10 percent of the writers working on the 250 top-grossing films. If the remaining 90 percent of working screenwriters are too lazy to write a movie from a woman's perspective, then the result is what we see now: an absolute dearth of movies written about women and for women. Amy Pascal, Sony's then cochairman, said, "You're talking about a dozen or so then female-driven comedies that got made over a dozen years, a period when hundreds of male-driven comedies got made. And every one of those female-driven comedies was written or directed or produced by a woman. It's a numbers game—it's about there being enough women writers and enough women with the power to get movies made."

Not that studios especially want these female-driven movies anyway: they want franchises, and romcoms and female comedies aren't seen as blockbuster material. "Studio executives think these movies' success is a one-off every time," Nancy Meyers, who wrote and directed *Something's Gotta Give* and *It's Complicated*, said. "They'll say, 'One of the big reasons that worked was because Jack was in it,' or 'We hadn't had a comedy for older women in forever.'" According to Melissa Silverstein, editor of *Women and Hollywood*, "Whenever a movie for women is successful, studios credit it to a million factors, and none of those factors is to do with women."

Romcoms aren't heart surgery, but they—at their best—explore and explain the human heart, and that's why great ones are so great and terrible ones are so very, very terrible. This is also why it feels like such a shame that studios simply think they're not worth their time anymore. To be fair, writers as wise and funny and fair as Ephron—and Austen, for that matter—don't come along every day. But things have reached a pretty pass when film trade publications admit that *When Harry Met Sally* wouldn't even get made anymore. There are many smart and funny women screenwriters around these days: Amy Schumer, Mindy Kaling, Lake Bell, Tina Fey, Jennifer Westfeldt, Katie Dippold, to name just half a dozen off the top of my head. The question is whether the men who still run movie studios have the courage to let them do their thing, without insisting on adding in what they imagine are male-audience-pleasing details (gross-out scenes, raunch, cutesifying the female lead, a schlubby male lead who is so clearly unworthy of the female counterpart).

Anyway, I grew up and the more I grew the more I became a mix of Harry (Jewish) and Sally (journalist, dependent on my friends, wanting love) and, like them, I eventually found the right person for me, although, also like them, I took my sweet time about it, and I sure didn't make it easy for myself along the way. Like Harry, I waited for someone who made me laugh, and like Sally, I waited for someone who wanted me to make them laugh. But the person in this movie whom I learned the most from was Ephron, because she taught me everything I know about, not just men and women, but love and marriage and friendship and funniness and good writing. And I know that's a lot to ask for from a movie but I don't think it's too much to ask for occasionally. I'm right, I'm right, you know I'm right.

Top Five Rick Moranis Moments

Ahhh, sweet Rick Moranis. He was the übernerd in the eighties and then, suddenly, he was nowhere. This bothered me for years, so finally I decided to ask the man himself: "Hey, Rick! What the hell happened?!"

And this is what he said: "I took a break because I was a single parent* and it got too hard, working and looking after my kids," he says. "The break got longer and longer and I realized I didn't miss what I had been doing, keeping in the mind that the last films I'd done weren't as gratifying as they weren't collaborative comedies.† Movies were changing, my kids were changing, so I decided just to stop doing it and one thing led to another. I didn't grow up wanting to be a performer or an actor. It was only after I had a pretty high degree of success and became a marketable commodity and was asked to act in other people's projects and to function as an actor and not comedian, and I didn't find it that enjoyable. So I just stopped."

Does he miss it?

"Oh goodness, no."

So very Moranis, don't you think? It makes me miss his sweet nerdy face even more. Still, at least we have his finest moments.

 Wayne Szalinski, *Honey, I Shrunk the Kids*

Moranis enters franchise hell. He clearly enjoyed the first one the best and he's (unsurprisingly) great as the batty scientist.

---

*Moranis's wife, Ann, died from cancer in 1991.
†Moranis's later films included *The Flintstones* and, er, *Honey, We Shrunk Ourselves*. So, you know, fair enough.

Nathan, *Parenthood*

A rare non-nerdy role for Moranis, and he's adorable in it. Bonus points for singing a Carpenters song, too.

 Dark Helmet, *Spaceballs*

Rick Moranis as Darth Vader, aka Dark Helmet! For God's sake, what more do you want, people?

 Seymour, *Little Shop of Horrors*

Okay, so he's not Pavarotti but the man can honestly sing.

 Louis Tully, *Ghostbusters*

He is hilarious as the accountant throwing the worst party ever ("Everybody, this is Ted and Annette Fleming. Ted has a small carpet cleaning company in receivership, but Annette is drawing a salary from a deferred bonus from two years ago . . ."), and adorable as the demonic Key Master. Moranis at his most Moranisish.

Ghostbusters

(with a Segue into *Top Gun*): How to Be a Man

I've read a lot of film books and they've taught me a few things about how film books should be written if they are to be taken seriously, and these are lessons that I feel are as useful in life:

1. Drop in random French phrases wherever possible so it looks like you're quoting from the French film magazine *Cahiers du Cinéma*, because even if you don't know what the hell you're talking about, nobody will be able to tell;

2. When in doubt, start waffling on about Godard;

3. Never describe a film as your "favorite film." This looks unprofessional and childish. Instead, claim—in ringing tones *comme les écrivains de Cahiers du Cinéma*—that it is the Greatest Film.

Zut alors! Malheureusement, not all the French in the world could convince anyone that I am more interested in Godard than *The Goonies*, so that's a nonstarter. But I shall make use of one of these handy life lessons and state that the best, most brilliant, most extraordinary, the most deftly created piece of auteur film work of all time is *Ghostbusters*.

For pretty much most of my life, I'd assumed that this was a fact accepted by everybody: *Ghostbusters* is the greatest movie ever made. Sure, people tend to say random words like "*Citizen Kane!*" and "*Vertigo!*" when asked by *Cahiers du Cinéma* for their favorite film. But I thought they did this just as, when asked who they'd like to have at their dream dinner party, they say, "Mother Teresa and Nelson Mandela!" as opposed to who everybody would actually like, which is, obviously, Madonna and Bill Murray.

Now, one could take my massive assumption that my tastes reflect those of everyone else on the planet two ways:

1. I have an ego the size of Asia coupled with a narcissist's complex and incipient sociopathic tendencies;

2. *Ghostbusters* is so good that even if it's not everyone's FAVORITE movie, it is probably in their top ten and so whenever I mention my love of *Ghostbusters* people say, "Oh yeah, everyone loves *Ghostbusters*."

For the purposes of this chapter, we will go with option 2.

I never thought of my *Ghostbusters* obsession—and it is, I fully admit, an obsession—as remarkable. If anything, I saw it as a perfectly natural response to a great work of art. Devoting an entire shelf to books and articles by or about the people involved, however tangentially, in the making of this movie? Commendable intellectual curiosity. Spending two hundred dollars on a book about *Ghostbusters* that came out the year the film was released, just because it finally explains why the character of Winston is squeezed out of the movie? Hey, that's an investment piece! Refusing to go on a second date with someone because they failed to recognize a completely random (and not, to be honest, wildly relevant) *Ghostbusters* quote over dinner?* Well, why waste time with losers? It wasn't until I found myself awake at 2 a.m. at the age of thirty-three on a Tuesday scrolling through eBay in search of a rumored copy of Bill Murray's original *Ghostbusters* script, which obviously was not going to be on eBay, that I felt it might be time to look at what, precisely, was going on here and why, after all this time, *Ghostbusters* still feels so special, maybe even more special, to me.

There is sentimentality, for sure, not exactly for my childhood but for the city of my childhood. *Ghostbusters* is as much a love letter to New York as anything by Woody Allen, and a less self-conscious one at that, showing New Yorkers reacting with relative normality to an invasion of the undead.† Many of the jokes in *Ghostbusters* stem from the idea that, ghosts aside, Manhattan itself is an out-of-control Wild West place, a Gotham city where a man could collapse against the windows of the Tavern on the Green, the ritzy restaurant that used to be in Central Park, and the diners would simply ignore him. Trash is piled on the sidewalks and Checker cabs whizz around corners: this re-creation of New York, 1984—the New York of my childhood—is still how I think of the city, even though it has, for better or worse, changed a lot since then.

Even the hilarious anachronisms give me a sentimental frisson: Louis being mocked for his love of vitamins and mineral water; Ray and Peter snarfing down cigarettes while toting nuclear reactors on their backs; Larry King in a cloud of cigarette smoke while chatting drily on the radio; the bad guy being the man from the

---

* Failures to recognize quotes from *When Harry Met Sally* and *Indiana Jones* were also date deal breakers. It really is astounding I was single until the age of thirty-five.
† The very English comic horror film *Shaun of the Dead* (2004), which depicts a north London overtaken by zombies, owes a pretty hefty debt to *Ghostbusters*.

Environmental Protection Agency. These all look particularly out of date in the Manhattan of today, and I can't help but feel the city is a little poorer for it. But my absolute favorite New Yorky moment in the film is at the end, when a doorman brings Ecto1 round after the *Ghostbusters* have saved the world—or at least Central Park West—from destruction. Despite having battled a giant marshmallow man, Dan Aykroyd still has a couple of dollar bills in the pocket of his ghost uniform with which to tip the doorman. You cannot get more New York than that.

But there is something else in *Ghostbusters* that makes me sentimental, something else that I love in it that doesn't exist anymore. That is, its depiction of how a man should be.

Just in terms of sheer variety, one could do a lot worse than turn to eighties movies for lessons in how to be a man. When most people think of masculinity in eighties movies, they probably think of that strange genre that sprouted and bulged up in that decade like Popeye's biceps after eating spinach, consisting of men who look like condoms stuffed with walnuts[*] speaking their lines in confused accents and emphasizing random syllables, strongly suggesting they'd learned the words phonetically: Schwarzenegger, Lundgren, Stallone,[†] and, toward the end of the decade, Van Damme. Chuck Norris, too, can be included here, despite his lack of walnutness, but he earns membership in this group with his similar lack of obvious acting talent and strong fondness for right-wing messages in his films.[‡]

---

[*] Copyright: the great Clive James.

[†] Technically, if not obviously, a native English speaker.

[‡] During the 2012 U.S. election, Chuck Norris and his wife, Gena, made a video in which they issued a "dire warning" to America, suggesting that were Barack Obama to win the presidency, we would be sentencing "our children" to "a thousand years

But there is more to eighties men than that. For a start, there are the men who raise babies and children (*Mr. Mom, Three Men and a Baby, Uncle Buck*), which some feminist critics argued at the time was a backlash against feminism because the films seemed to mock the idea of feminized men.

In fact, in retrospect, these films look more like movies awkwardly coming to grips with feminism (*Tootsie*, too, can be included here, with a man pretending to be a woman, and occasionally looking after a child, and becoming a better person for it). *Mr. Mom* (1983), in which Michael Keaton loses his job and looks after the kids while his wife works, is clearly none too sure what to make of this "feminist" thing: the movie's message is that the swapping of traditional gender roles will probably destroy the marriage and almost certainly the house (somewhat dismayingly, the film was written by John Hughes).

But by 1987, *Three Men and a Baby* was getting much more of a handle on things. The men (Tom Selleck, Steve Guttenberg, and Ted Danson) are unexpectedly lumbered with a baby girl and, by the end of the film, very much want her to stay with them in their bachelor shag pad, even after the baby's dippy English (foreigners—tchuh!) mother turns back up. It turns out that, unlike *Mr. Mom*, they are capable of looking after a baby without causing havoc to domestic appliances (men—amirite??). The men in *Three Men and a Baby* are notably much less obnoxious than *les mecs* in the original French version, *Trois Hommes et un Couffin*, who have a pact never to let a woman stay more than one night in their flat and have a tendency to call the baby "a swine" when it has an accident on the sofa. *Ahh, les Français—ils sont tres masculins, ooh la la!**

---

of darkness." Action stars never fade away—they just become more themselves. See also: Steven Seagal.

* See? Random French words. They always work.

Which is not to say that the American version is without its anxieties. *Three Men and a Baby* goes to such lengths in order to reassure audiences of the übermasculinity of the three guys, despite their TERRIFYINGLY FEMINIZED baby-raising skills, that they become hilariously camp. Peak camp is reached, for me, when Selleck goes out jogging wearing little more than a tiny pair of shorts and an enormous mustache, and he picks up a sports magazine full of photos of muscled-up half-naked men. Now, if that isn't the definition of throbbing heterosexual masculinity, I don't know what is.

Yes, the eighties were a different time and American movies in that era seemed to think that *homosexual* was merely Latin for "psycho killer or flouncy interior decorator." But nonetheless, whenever I watch this movie (which is more often than I'm going to commit to print) I think it's a shame the director (who was the late Leonard Nimoy, very pleasingly) didn't just go with the obvious option here and make the guys gay, living in a happy yuppie *ménage à trois*. After all, this would explain why three apparently very solvent guys in high-flying careers* in their thirties would choose to share an apartment in midtown Manhattan as opposed to getting their own *American Psycho*–style bachelor pads. And for heaven's sake, have you looked at that Broadway-themed mural Steve Guttenberg paints of the three of them in the atrium of their apartment? No amount of references from Selleck to his love of sport can obscure the fact he and his two friends are living in the campiest New York apartment north of Fourteenth Street. These guys—the actor! the architect! the cartoonist!—are basically the eighties yuppie version of the Village People.

And let's talk about that homoeroticism! Accidental

---

* More high-flying, incidentally, than the characters in the French version. Typical Americans! So career obsessed! So competitive! Bof.

homoeroticism is yet another one of the great joys of eighties movies, and it was the last decade that would be blessed with the pleasure
because from the nineties onward, gay culture and references would
be too mainstream and recognizable to slip past studios unnoticed.

The plethora of eighties buddy movies easily and frequently tip
into accidental homoeroticism, with the female characters being explicitly excluded from pretty much the whole film and all sorts of
intense emotion between the two male leads. *Lethal Weapon* is one
example and an even more obvious one is *Stakeout*, in which Emilio
Estevez and Richard Dreyfuss spend an entire movie living together
in faux domesticity and, in the case of Estevez, voyeuristically spying
on his male partner's sexual encounters.

The Lost Boys is the most blatantly homoerotic mainstream movie
ever made for teenage boys. In this film, young Michael (charisma
vortex Jason Patric) is initiated into the manly life of a new town
by going into a cave with Kiefer Sutherland and his male buddies
(none of whom seems the least bit interested in the fact that a half-
naked Jami Gertz is wandering around drunkenly in front of them)
and drinking their body fluids. Sure, why not, right? Vampires are
inherently homoerotic and the director Joel Schumacher (who later
homoeroticized *Batman*—not difficult, admittedly—by sticking
nipples on the batsuit) revels in the connection in this movie in a
way *Twilight* later determinedly, somewhat dismayingly avoids. Michael does at some point have what looks like deeply unsatisfying sex
with Jami Gertz, but the person he gazes at with the most intensity
is young Jack Bauer. And I haven't even mentioned that Michael's
little brother Sam (Corey Haim), who dresses like he's trying out for
Wham!, has a poster on the door of his closet of Rob Lowe lifting up
his shirt. Because sure, why not, right?

The Lost Boys is not the only eighties movie to suggest that the
way a man becomes a man is by rejecting the world of women and

gazing lustfully at other men. Now, there are lots of things I've never understood about *Top Gun*—namely, who on earth Maverick is fighting at the end of the movie. But I do pride myself on recognizing homoeroticism when it's waggled right in my face. *Top Gun* is officially the most homoerotic thing that has ever existed, and I say that as someone who spent eight years covering men's fashion shows in Milan.

Most of überproducers Jerry Bruckheimer and Don Simpson's films—including *Flashdance, Top Gun, Beverly Hills Cop*, and, in the nineties, *Days of Thunder* and *Bad Boys*—are, at the very least, camp because they are, as the late producer Julia Phillips put it, "a series of soundtracks in search of a movie." More simply, they are extended music videos—in fact, some of the scenes are nothing but music videos, with montages set to a power ballad—and, to my mind, that is not a criticism. I love eighties music videos, I adore montages, and anyone who doesn't thrill to a power ballad is lying to themselves. These movies are fun (well, except for *Days of Thunder*) because they are about pure sensation. But they also easily become camp because camp is about exaggeration and surface aesthetics, which is a perfect description of Simpson and Bruckheimer's films.

Simpson himself was known for the kind of exaggerated macho posturing similar to that of his films: the drinking, the hedonism, the voracious use of call girls. And so, as is always the way with self-consciously macho men, there was something extraordinarily camp about him. This is especially true of macho men in the eighties, when straight men dressed like George Michael, blow-dried their hair, and took an open interest in bodybuilding. Simpson himself was the Liberace of eighties heterosexual Hollywood: he was obsessed with plastic surgery and body image, he spent ridiculous amounts on clothes and cars, and he cultivated a self-image that included fabricating stories about his own childhood. His films almost invariably feature an especially close and yet emphatically platonic male friendship—in *Top Gun*, most famously, there's the tortured triangle of Maverick's (Tom Cruise, obviously) intensely loving relationship with Goose (Anthony Edwards) and his lustful one with Iceman (Val Kilmer). Even Maverick's alleged girlfriend, Charlie (Kelly McGillis), has a male name.* All of this, unsurprisingly, reflected Simpson's life off-screen. His relationship with Bruckheimer was extremely close and while neither man was or is gay, there was

---

* In the best moment in the otherwise deservedly forgotten 1990s film *Sleep with Me*, Quentin Tarantino expands on Pauline Kael's description of *Top Gun* as "a homoerotic commercial" at pleasing length: "*Top Gun* is a story about a man's struggle with his own homosexuality. It is! That is what *Top Gun* is about, man. You've got Maverick, all right? He's on the edge, man. He's right on the fucking line, all right? And you've got Iceman, and all his crew. They're gay, they represent the gay man, all right? And they're saying, go, go the gay way, go the gay way. He could go both ways. Kelly McGillis, she's heterosexuality. She's saying: no, no, no, no, no, no, go the normal way, play by the rules, go the normal way. They're saying no, go the gay way, be the gay way, go for the gay way, all right? That is what's going on throughout that whole movie. . . . He goes to her house, all right? It looks like they're going to have sex, you know, they're just kind of sitting back, he's takin' a shower and everything. They don't have sex. He gets on the motorcycle, drives away. She's like, 'What the fuck, what the fuck is going on here?' Next scene, next scene you see her, she's in the elevator, she is dressed like a guy. She's got the cap on, she's got the aviator glasses, she's wearing the same jacket that the Iceman wears. She is, okay, this is how I gotta get this guy, this guy's going towards the gay way, I gotta bring him back, I gotta bring him back from the gay way, so I'll do that through subterfuge, I'm gonna dress like a man. All right? That is how she approaches it. But the REAL ending of the movie is when they fight the MiGs at the end, all right? Because he has passed over into the gay way. They are this gay fighting fucking force, all right? And they're beating the Russians, the gays are beating the Russians. And it's over, and they fucking land, and Iceman's been trying to get Maverick the entire time, and finally, he's got him, all right? And what is the last fucking line that they have together? They're all hugging and kissing and happy with each other, and Ice comes up to Maverick, and he says, 'Man, you can ride my tail, anytime!' And what does Maverick say? 'You can ride mine!' Swordfight! Swordfight! Fuckin' A, man!" In fact, Tarantino unnecessarily overegged the homoerotic pudding here. The truth is, what Iceman actually says to Maverick at the end is "You can be my wingman anytime." But I think we can all agree that his point still stands.

something bizarrely camp about them as a duo. During the making of *Top Gun*, they bought matching black Ferraris and matching black Mustang convertibles, they designed their houses to match, and, as if to ensure they definitely looked like evil camp villains, they hired identical twin secretaries. They reveled in supermacho displays, ones that frequently seemed to disguise their own insecurities or outright lacks: every Friday night during the making of *Top Gun*, the cast and crew would throw a huge pool party to which Simpson would bring dozens of young women he picked up on the beach. One particular Friday, the cast and pilots working on *Top Gun* decided to throw Bruckheimer and Simpson into the pool. Bruckheimer relented— but only after he prissily took off his expensive cowboy boots. Simpson clung desperately to metal railings but he could not fight off the pilots and they threw him into the pool. Simpson promptly "sank to the bottom, having been too embarrassed to tell anyone he could not swim."

Bruckheimer loyally remained colleagues with the increasingly out-of-control Simpson, until even he could no longer tolerate his friend's excesses. And then, like that other image of camp American heterosexuality, Elvis Presley, Simpson eventually died, bloated and battered and far too young, on his own toilet.

In fact, if anyone wanted to learn how to be the ultimate eighties movie man, the obvious place to start would be, not *Ghostbusters*, but *Top Gun*. Besides homoeroticism, this movie features the two other major takes on masculinity in movies from that decade: a fist-pumping love for the American military, and the celebration of the maverick.

The eighties was the decade when American politicians, led primarily by President Reagan, began to rewrite the story of the Vietnam War, pitching it not as a tragic and wasteful period in America's history, but rather as "a noble cause," to use Reagan's favored phrase.

Reagan followed up this revisionism by launching a series of military ventures in Central America and Libya, acting as palate cleansers to wash away the old taste of Vietnam loss and replace it with, instead, newfound American militarism.

Hollywood happily reflected this switch, with movies such as *Red Dawn* and *Top Gun*. Even films like *Rambo: First Blood Part II* and *Predator*, which are ostensibly about the failure of the American military top brass in Vietnam, celebrate the strength of individual soldiers over dubious natives. These films looked like pure propaganda, which is precisely what they were: many were made with assistance from the military in exchange for script approval, as the Pentagon saw these movies as an excellent means of recruitment. Which, again, they were: according to David Sirota, recruitment went up 400 percent when *Top Gun* was released, thanks in part, as the *Los Angeles Times* reported at the time, to the navy's clever wheeze of "setting up manned tables outside movie houses during *Top Gun* premieres to answer questions from would-be flyboys emerging with a newfound need for speed from an F14 warplane." Of course, most of these young people didn't realize that they were watching what were little more than ads for the military, nor did their parents, whose taxes were partially subsidizing the tanks and guns featured in these movies to tempt their children to enlist.

Hollywood had collaborated with the military plenty of times before the 1980s, going all the way back to 1927 with the film *Wings*, the very first winner of a Best Picture Oscar, which the military helped to produce. But given *Top Gun's* enormous success, the number of collaborations between Hollywood studios and the military increased exponentially in the eighties, with studio bosses convinced that churning out pro-war propaganda in exchange for access to military equipment was a guaranteed winner of a formula, and the military was now fully persuaded that recruitment through movies was the way forward. And so, alongside anguished films about Vietnam such as *Platoon*, *Full Metal Jacket*, and *Good Morning, Vietnam* came what *Movieline* describes as "hyper-macho, bazooka-toting fantasy fare," like *Top Gun*.

This is one movie lesson from the eighties that is still very much alive today. Michael Bay's deadening *Transformers* franchise, the laughable 2012 flop *Battleship*, which starred Rihanna as a weapons specialist, and the 2012 film *Act of Valor* (which *Movieline* describes as a "Navy SEAL porn flick") were all underwritten by the Pentagon, and all dutifully present a defiantly macho, determinedly pro-military message. Nor is it just bad films that get made this way: 2013's *Captain Phillips*, starring Tom Hanks as a captain taken hostage by Somali pirates, was also made with the military's cooperation and it, too, presents an utterly sterling view of the Americans in uniform. "When you know that you're going to need the military's assistance, and you know they are going to be looking at your script, you write it to make them happy right from the beginning," writes David Robb.

But of course, *Top Gun* isn't just about falling in line with the military. Hell no! It's about (somewhat contradictorily) rebelling against it, too! Because that's what real men are like, you see. A real man isn't a pencil pusher—he's the lone wolf, the renegade, the MAVERICK. Women have sex with the mavericks, but men ARE the mavericks, and they ride their motorcycles against a sunset into the danger zone. High-five, low-five! Yeah! And just in case that isn't entirely clear in the script, Cruise's character's name is, of course, Maverick (real men also don't bother with fey subtlety).

The idea of the male rebel outsider was hardly coined in the eighties, but the idea of the rebel outsider fighting against the inept or even evil American government was one that not only gained enormous traction in the eighties, but was encouraged by, of all things, the American government—or, to be more precise, President Ronald Reagan. "I've always felt that the nine most terrifying words in the English language are, 'I'm from the government and I'm here to help,'" Reagan said in 1986. Reagan had cannily picked up on this national mood that had been burgeoning in the seventies in the wake of the disaster of the Vietnam War and the humiliation of the Watergate scandal. Antigovernment moral mavericks started to emerge in films of that time, including Han Solo (another character who, like Maverick, was blessed with nominative determinism), the sexy outsider who made money working against the Empire, and, of course, Clint Eastwood's Dirty Harry. Tellingly, Reagan—a B-list actor through and through—was especially fond of using references from the films of both those characters, referring to the Soviet Union as "the Evil Empire," much to George Lucas's horror, and notoriously telling tax increasers in 1986 to "go ahead—make my day," echoing Harry Callahan's statement in *Sudden Impact*. Movie nerds like myself around the world sympathize with this tactic of Reagan's: if you can't get cast in the movie, quote the movie.

Thus, the mentality of the eighties in America began to take shape: government collectivism is bad, the male renegade outsider is good, even if both are ultimately working toward the same goal, that is, to protect America. It was this idea that was instantly reflected in TV shows (*The A-Team*, *Knight Rider*, *The Dukes of Hazzard*, *Moonlighting*) and movies. Wild buccaneer-for-profit Jack Colton (Michael Douglas) in *Romancing the Stone* and *The Jewel of the Nile* is a straight rip-off of Han Solo. So is Indiana Jones, for that matter, the renegade archaeologist, trying to save cultural and religious artifacts from collectors and Nazis. As if Spielberg wanted to make this point extra clear, he then cast the same actor who played Han to play Indy. *Lethal Weapon*, *Die Hard*, and *Beverly Hills Cop* also play on this idea of the rule-breaking maverick, with, respectively, crazy ol'

Riggs (Mel Gibson), sweaty ol' John McClane (Bruce Willis), and wisecrackin' Axel Foley (Eddie Murphy) determinedly giving ulcers to their fat superiors with their maverick—and ultimately COR-RECT—ways.

E.T. is probably the most obvious and—for those who saw it as kids—most formative example of a movie that pitches the U.S. government as actually nefarious. In the film, faceless government agents tear through Elliott's home like zombies rampaging through the family's sleepy suburbia, in a classic horror movie trope. The government then doesn't just kidnap sweet and innocent *E.T.* (and, ostensibly, Elliott)—it nearly kills them both, and they are saved only by Elliott's pure childlike nature, not the clumsy, oafish ways of the evil government. *Splash* and *Project X* completely ripped off . . . I mean paid heavy homage to *E.T.* with their distinctly similar plots featuring, respectively, in place of an alien, a mermaid and monkeys that had to be kept safe from meddling government agents.

But it's in *Top Gun* where this trope that the rule-breaking maverick is awesome is at its most ridiculous because it is so heavily and paradoxically tied to the theory that the American military is awesome. And this means the movie's ending is utterly insane.

The filmmakers were so averse to making Maverick's maverickness seem in any way misguided that they refused to give the movie the story arc it so obviously needed: for him to be the reason his partner Goose dies. But despite Maverick's guilt after the crash, Goose's death has nothing to do with him—it was due to faulty equipment. Maverick's brash arrogance and reckless selfishness turn out to have been the correct instincts all along, so there is really no message. Music videos feature more interesting emotional journeys than *Top Gun*. The only lesson Maverick (and audiences) learn from this incident is that Maverick should not have let the death of his best friend cause him to lose his confidence, because that is when he is at his least manly, repulsive both to his girlfriend (Charlie) and his boyfriend (Ice). It is only when he gets his confidence back that he becomes a triumphant "flyboy" again and Ice invites him to ride his tail, again.

This, the movie suggests, is how the military will survive, just as the police are dependent on rule-breakers like Riggs in *Lethal Weapon*, McClane in *Die Hard*, and Axel Foley in *Beverly Hills Cop*. These movies aren't arguing for the dismantling of institutions, just for the triumph of the unleashed individual within, and that's because these movies were made in the eighties: the era of selfish individualism, yes, not full-on revolution.˙

Being a man the *Top Gun* way is still very much a popular message in today's American movies and, for that matter, politics. The Tea Party is explicitly based on the premise that federal collectivism is deeply suspect and individualism is the way of the future. If the U.S. government nearly killed *E.T.*, no wonder millions of Americans don't trust it to look after the national health-care system. Has President Obama forgotten how *E.T.* turned a crusty shade of white when the government got its hands on him? White, for gawd's sake! It's not natural for an alien!

To be a true man in these films is ultimately about breaking the rules in order to restore the conventional hierarchy: the bad guys in jail, the police chiefs in charge, the flying instructors still instructing flying. Maverick behavior in pursuit of civic responsibility, in other words. Another movie demonstrated this better than any, and it did so without recourse to homoeroticism, the military, or howling lone wolves. Its version of masculinity might have something to do with

---

˙ The result of this veneration of mavericks in eighties movies is that the villains of these films are often completely in the right: Iceman is completely right that Maverick is dangerous, just as the Environmental Protection Agency is right that the Ghostbusters look like unlicensed clowns and Mr. Rooney is right that Ferris should be in school.

looking after kids, but that wasn't its main point. And yet, unlike the *Top Gun* way, it's one that's hardly endorsed at all by today's movies, or, indeed, any American pop culture at all, even though it is far, far preferable. And that is, the *Ghostbusters* way.

Ever since I saw this movie at the age of six, sharing my fold-down seat in the cinema with my mother's big purse for added weight so the seat wouldn't snap back up and swallow me up like the killer plant in *Little Shop of Horrors*, the Ghostbusters have represented to me an ideal of masculinity. This is not just because I fancy all of them, which I definitely do—the Ghostbusters are all total hotties, although this fact is rarely noted, for some mystifying reason. Young Aykroyd, for a start, is very much in my top five, maybe even my top three, and the only thing hotter than him greeting the crowds at the end of *Ghostbusters* with a cigarette in his mouth on Central Park West is him looking all sweet and poor and forlorn in *Trading Places* (mmm, sweet poor forlorn Aykroyd . . .). ANYWAY, I digress.

It might seem odd, this idea that a bunch of dudes running around Manhattan wearing cartoon insignia on their uniforms and car represent masculine goodness, and some people would disagree with me.[*] In fact, some dark souls have accused *Ghostbusters* of sexism, and to be fair to these people and their souls it's not wildly difficult to see why: the ghosts are all female (minus Slimer, of course) and are trying either to kill the Ghostbusters (Zuul, Gozer) or give them oral sex;[†] Venkman sexually harasses or patronizes any woman

---

[*] Crazy people.

[†] The scene in which Ray (Aykroyd) dreams a ghost is going down on him in the film is, by some measure, the weirdest and worst moment in the film. It makes absolutely no sense, mainly because it was part of another scene that was cut. That it was written at all, and stayed in the film, serves as a handy little reminder that Aykroyd is, as we shall discuss, kind of an odd fellow.

in his path. Read this way, the film sounds like a terrible precursor to a terrible Adam Sandler film—and it could have been, had it starred and been written by anyone else. (Just imagine if it were a Gene Wilder and Richard Pryor film. Or, you know, don't.) While defending the movie from such accusations, writer and *Ghostbusters* mega-fan Adam Bertocci writes that the confusions come from the fact that the film is actually about "ancient power struggles in which the boundary was between two worlds, masculine and feminine, and all that they represented: Apollo versus Dionysus, yang versus yin, sun versus moon, fire versus water, ego versus id, reason versus emotion, science versus magic." This is sweet, but it does also emphasize the alleged gender distinctions in the film. Journalist Noah Berlatsky puts it a little less forgivingly, describing *Ghostbusters* as "totally sexist" because it "denigrated and (literally) demonized women" and "bodily fluids are viewed as ectoplasmic ick."

Now, leaving aside the fact that it isn't, last time I checked, only women who produce bodily fluids, I can (just about) see Berlatsky's point—but he's wrong. Damn wrong! To accuse *Ghostbusters* of sexism is to apply a very basic algorithm to determine its sexual politics. This means, then, that the subtle and very sweet ways *Ghostbusters* subverts the sexist tropes of male-led comedies, made both in the eighties and still very much made now, are overlooked. There is a reason, in my personal and objective experience, why women love this film as much as men, and it isn't that they've been possessed by Zuul and turned into dogs.

First, there's the depiction of male friendship. The three primary Ghostbusters—Peter Venkman (Bill Murray), Ray Stantz (Dan Aykroyd), and Egon Spengler (Harold Ramis)—are all friends. Good friends. They like each other, they're amused by each other, and they stick together when they're fired at the beginning of the film from their university jobs. There's nothing eroticized about their friendship, no overcompensation of machoness, no competitive banter. No cruelty, in other words (although Peter is a little cavalier about making Ray mortgage his parents' house to fund the business). Nor is there any suggestion that male friendship is so special it must be protected from all outsiders who threaten it—namely, women.

In *Ghostbusters* and *Ghostbusters II*, Ray and Egon are nice to Dana: they welcome her into their group and they try to protect her from Peter's excesses. Compare this to the treatment meted out to the female love interests in modern-day equivalent movies such as *The 40-Year-Old Virgin*, *Anchorman*, and *Knocked Up*, or less broad bromance films such as *Sideways*, in which the male friends are all, without fail, horrible to the women (read: INVADERS). While Venkman might tease some of the women in his orbit (mocking Janine for her "bug eyes," lusting after Dana), he always immediately apologizes, and neither the film nor his buddies praise him for his foolishness. This strikes me as a lot more significant than the gender of ghosts.

The Ghostbusters also never fall out with one another. This, too, is appealing and makes them rarities in the world of male friendship in movies. In today's more recent male-led comedies, such as *I Love You, Man* and *Anchorman*, the male friends always fall out at some point, followed by an emotional reunion. That's because, in those films, the friendship between the male leads has become so celebrated that it is a (barely) platonic romance and therefore the trajectory of the friendship is like that of a clichéd film love story: boy meets boy, boy loses boy, boy gets boy back. The Ghostbusters never fall out with one another, because they are friends—just friends—and they are grown-ups. I'll return to this point later.

Just as the overly close friendships in *Top Gun* were a reflection of the one between the filmmakers off-camera, so the relationships in *Ghostbusters* were an expression of those behind the movie. The original idea for the film was born out of one particular friendship: the one between Aykroyd and his best friend and former *Saturday Night Live* castmate, John Belushi. By the time Aykroyd sat down to write what would be the first draft of the movie, the bearishly sweet but wildly self-destructive Belushi had been flailing around in film flops and drug addiction since the pair's last film, 1980's *The Blues Brothers*, and Aykroyd pictured his ghost film as the dual project his best friend needed: "Abbott and Costello, Dean Martin and Jerry Lewis—everyone did a ghost picture," Aykroyd said. And yet, despite those comic precedents, Aykroyd did not envisage the film as a comedy.

Instead, he saw it as a semiserious look at the paranormal and parapsychology, an idea that makes a tiny bit more sense when one takes into account that Aykroyd is a spiritualist and grew up reading journals from the American Society of Psychical Research. In fact, some of his ancestors were mystics and his father wrote what *Vanity Fair* describes with an apparently straight face as "a well-regarded history of ghosts."* For Aykroyd, this was a deeply personal project on several levels: on the one hand, he was exploring what he calls "the family business"; on the other, he was trying to rescue his best friend. But on a warm and bright March afternoon in 1982, just as Aykroyd was at home in New York writing a line for his friend, the phone rang. It was Belushi's manager, Bernie Brillstein, calling from Los Angeles: Belushi had died in the Chateau Marmont hotel after overdosing on cocaine and heroin. He was thirty-three years old.

Aykroyd was devastated. Photos from Belushi's funeral on

---

* Incidentally, Aykroyd also has webbed feet and is married to the Dream Girl from *Wayne's World* (Donna Dixon). Although he's generally only spotted flogging vodka these days, there is no denying that Aykroyd is a pretty extraordinary dude.

Martha's Vineyard show a shocked-looking Aykroyd leading the procession on a motorcycle—and a young Bill Murray, who revered Belushi, grimacing while placing a flower on the dead comedian's coffin. Aykroyd soon after decided that his *Saturday Night Live* cast-mate Murray should play the part he had written for Belushi, and it was the part that ultimately truly made Murray's name, just as Aykroyd once hoped it would make Belushi's. But he would still keep his late friend in the film in his own way: Slimer is a direct homage to Belushi, who, like the green blob, would steal food off room service trays in hotel hallways and generally cause chaos. More obliquely, the movie would be made by Black Rhino Productions, which is Aykroyd's production company—named in honor of a dream he had after Belushi died, in which his friend's face was on a charging rhino.

It's easy to overstate the influence of Belushi on eighties American comedy, just out of sentimentality and sadness for his premature death. But it's equally easy to underplay it because he died so young and so long ago. The impact of it heavily affected the movie that would soon become the most successful comedy of all time, giving it a sweetness that other comedies from that same era, starring the same actors and made by the same director, do not have. "Belushi's death was the soul of the film for Danny, and it played into my own sensibilities of friendship and humanity," says the film's director, Ivan Reitman. "I went in knowing that what was important was that the audience had to care about these guys, they had to want to be friends with them and to care about their friendship."

Aykroyd's original script, which he showed to Reitman, was set in the future, on various planets and over several dimensions. "My first draft," Aykroyd later said, "was written in a way that your basic acceleration physicist might have enjoyed more than the mass audience."

"Danny's first draft," Reitman recalls, "was basically unfilm-able." But Reitman loved the script's basic premise: a bunch of guys acting like firefighters but catching ghosts. So he took Aykroyd out to lunch and suggested some changes, such as setting it in present-day New York ("It became my New York movie," Reitman says with a smile). The always amenable Aykroyd agreed to all the changes. Murray had already told Aykroyd that he liked the script and made characteristically vague noises about maybe committing to it. Reit-man then suggested hiring Harold Ramis, with whom he'd made the 1981 army comedy *Stripes*, which also starred Murray. After getting Columbia to commit to a $25 million budget—which was seen then as an obscene amount of money to invest in a comedy—Ramis, Aykroyd, and Reitman decamped to Martha's Vineyard to rewrite Aykroyd's script. All these men were already old friends and would soon become even better ones. "Those weeks on Martha's Vineyard," Reitman recalls, "were two of the most fun weeks of my life."

First, they created the different character traits for the three Ghostbusters who before had, in Aykroyd's original script, been pretty much interchangeable: "Put [the characters of Peter Venk-man, Raymond Stantz, and Egon Spengler] together, and you have the Scarecrow, the Lion, and the Tin Man," Aykroyd said.

"For actors, especially in group comedy, those kinds of arche-types always seem to work," said Ramis.

They also used character traits from each other, with Venkman taking on Murray's already well-honed sarcastic outsider tone and Stantz becoming the paranormal nerd, just as Aykroyd was and is. It is impossible not to take delight in watching an actor play a role that he was seemingly born to play, whether it's Clark Gable as Rhett Butler or Humphrey Bogart as Rick. With *Ghostbusters*, you get that three times over: Murray as the wiseass, Ramis as the egghead, and Aykroyd as the lunkish geek. From then on, any time any of them branched out of these types—Murray as the depressed father in *Rushmore*, Aykroyd as the southern good ol' boy in *Driving Miss Daisy*, Ramis as the stoner dad in *Knocked Up*—it felt to me both daring and unsettling, as though I'd caught my father cross-dressing.

Next, they jettisoned all the interplanetary time travel from Aykroyd's script, wisely cutting out all the spiritual woo-woo stuff but keeping in all the geeky science: the proton packs, the containment units, the streams that must never be crossed. Geeky science was already becoming one of the defining characteristics of eighties movies, particularly in male-led comedies, and would feature in films from *Weird Science* to *Short Circuit* (aka *E.T.* as a robot) to *Batteries Not Included* to Bill and Ted's time-traveling phone booth in *Bill and Ted's Excellent Adventure* to the greatest eighties film science experiment of them all, the DeLorean with the flux capacitor. This is my kind of sci-fi, and my kind of masculinity: gleefully, nonsensically, sweetly nerdy.

Notably, this kind of sci-fi and accompanying special effects—the nerdy nonsense kind—has endured a lot better than the more grandiose visions of, say, *Star Wars*, with all those tediously phallic light-sabers. At times the film makes fun of its tackiness, such as Egon using a colander to read Louis's (Rick Moranis) mind. But with the exception of the demon dog that crashes Louis's party, which was done using stop-motion puppets, the special effects in *Ghostbusters* still look just as good today as they did in the eighties, just as they do in *Back to the Future*, *Bill and Ted's Excellent Adventure*, and the grievously underrated *Young Sherlock Holmes*. And this is at least partly why these movies have lasted so well and why they still attract audiences who weren't even born when DeLoreans were being manufactured.

Murray, meanwhile, was in India filming another movie. The day he arrived back in New York, Reitman and Ramis met him at

LaGuardia Airport and took him out to a restaurant in Queens to show him the script. But Murray trusted his friends so much he barely looked at it, said "about two words about the script," Ramis later recalled, and flew back out again. "It was trust. *Ghostbusters* was the first film he committed to without fighting like crazy," Ramis said.

But of course, *Ghostbusters* does not only star the Ghostbusters themselves. Other actors and actresses had to work within this already existing strong friendship. When Aykroyd wrote the script, he envisaged a role for John Candy, and Reitman approached him to play Louis. When Candy suggested playing the role with a heavy accent and two dogs, Reitman decided he was going too broad, even for *Ghostbusters*. So instead, he cast the Canadian comedian Rick Moranis, then little known to American audiences.

"My career was completely luck," says Moranis. "Different things would come up and I would pick what I felt was the most fun and who would be the most interesting to work with. I wasn't being offered a lot of the Schwarzenegger parts: you have a round Jewish face and you don't wear contacts and you're five foot five, you're going to get certain parts. People always thought of me as the nerdy guy, even in non-nerdy parts."

Because the part of Louis had been written for Candy, Moranis set about shaping it more to his image: he suggested that Louis be an accountant and be more nerdy and less lecherous over women, as they'd written originally. "Ivan let me work with my character, which was wonderful. They were all extremely friendly and supportive guys and really encouraged my input, even though they'd all known each other for years and I was really the outsider," says Moranis.

Sigourney Weaver also ended up shaping her role to the benefit of the film. She came in to audition for the part of Dana, "which I know sounds ridiculous—we made Sigourney audition, when she'd already done *Alien* and *The Year of Living Dangerously*," says Reitman with a laugh. "But she'd never done comedy. Little did I know that comedy was her true love."

Weaver proved her comedic skills by opening her audition with the suggestion that Dana become a dog in the movie, and she promptly climbed up on Reitman's coffee table, got down on all fours, and howled.

"And I was just fascinated—it was so goofy!" says Reitman, sounding very much like he's still recovering from the encounter more than thirty years later. "And I thought, you know, that's a good idea, we should look at it."

Weaver also suggested that Dana be a musician instead of a model, as was originally written in the script, and she made similar suggestions throughout the shoot in order to make her character more than a cipher. In the scene when Venkman first goes to Dana's flat to check out her haunted refrigerator, Dana was written as very passive in the script: she doesn't get it when Venkman is making salacious come-ons to her, and she seems scared of him, threatening to scream at one point. In the film, Weaver rolls her eyes at Venkman and clearly just finds him ridiculous and, in doing so, makes the scene a lot less creepy than it could have been—after all, Venkman is basically sexually harassing Dana in her own apartment. But because Dana stands up to him, and Murray himself looks and acts like such a tongue-tied nebbish next to Weaver's patrician, cool glamour, the power tips more in her favor. The scene becomes sweet instead of stupid, therefore proving the rarely acknowledged fact that when female characters are allowed to be stronger than a wet rag, it does everyone in the movie a favor.

"Sigourney insisted, without being obnoxious in any way, on making her character real," said Ramis. "Often in comedies, you see characters doing all these outlandish things while the people around them are acting like stooges, as though nothing out of the ordinary is happening. And so when Sigourney was able to stand there like a real person and say to Bill [in that scene], 'You are so odd,' it was totally genuine—and she came up with that line herself. I loved it, because it let the audience off the hook and allowed them to say, 'Yeah, he IS odd.'"

Ramis also admitted, "We [Ramis and Aykroyd] had never written women very well," which is a disappointing cop-out from him. *Ghostbusters* does, sadly, fail the Bechdel Test and is a classic example of Katha Pollitt's Smurfette Principle. But at least they had the sense and ego strength to take Weaver's suggestions and allow the main female character more agency than they'd written, which is a helluva lot more than the filmmakers behind today's male-led comedies do.* Dana is more interesting than a generic love interest, largely due to Weaver, and the fact that Reitman cast the lead actress from *Alien* strongly proves he wanted an actress whom the audience would recognize as powerful. The film even tweaks and literalizes what is now an infamous trope in comic books and comic book movies, *women in refrigerators*, referring to the tendency for female characters to be killed or injured as a plot device. (The name derives from a storyline in *The Green Lantern* comic books in which a female character is killed and stuffed into a fridge, for no reason.) In *Ghostbusters*, Dana becomes imbued with the powers of her actual refrigerator, and lives to tell the tale (and snog Murray on Fifth Avenue).

Another factor here is Murray, who has been, from the beginning

---

* When actress Katherine Heigl later—and rightly (if somewhat belatedly)—complained about the female characters in *Knocked Up*, her male costar Seth Rogen sneered on Howard Stern's radio show in July 2009, "It's not like we're the only people she said some batshit crazy things about. That's kind of her bag now." The depiction of female characters in Apatow and Rogen's films has remained unchanged ever since.

of his career in *Meatballs* (1979), the master of taking awful characters and tweaking them just enough so that their creepiness is un-
dercut and they become palatable. Even in the opening scene of
Ghostbusters, when we meet him at the university and he is trying
to seduce the pretty female student, with his mugging and hesitan-
cies he comes across as more laughable than a predatory creep. The
fact that he is literally electrocuting a male student in order to get
his quarry emphasizes that the film wants us to see this guy as, not
cool, but a jerk. Later, Venkman refuses to sleep with Dana when
she's possessed and begging him to do so, proving there are, in fact,
moral depths to this formerly lecherous university professor, and this
is reiterated by his look of heartbreak when he thinks Dana is dead.
Ghostbusters is a male-led comedy, for sure. But by no means does it
respect only men.

In fact, the cast member who found it hardest to penetrate
Aykroyd-Ramis-Reitman-Murray's wall of white male friendship
was not a white woman, but a black man: Ernie Hudson, who plays
Winston Zeddemore, the fourth Ghostbuster, and this led to the
biggest flaw in *Ghostbusters*, and in its depiction of masculinity. Back
in the eighties, Hudson was a jobbing actor and a single dad, working hard to support his two sons. "As soon as I read the script I
thought, Wow, this is really cool, this could change everything for
us," he remembers.

In the version Hudson read, Winston becomes part of the Ghostbuster team from almost the beginning of the film, but in the version
that they ended up shooting he doesn't appear until nearly the end,
meaning most of his lines had been cut out. For years *Ghostbusters*
fans speculated that Winston's part was cut because Eddie Murphy
turned down the role to make *Beverly Hills Cop* and they didn't want
to give so many lines to a relative unknown like Hudson. Others
suggested that racism played a part, with white Hollywood once

again stiffing the black guy. Reitman has denied the Murphy rumor ("Murphy was never a consideration"), but Aykroyd has said that he originally wrote the film with Murphy in mind as a Ghostbuster. Reitman also hastily dismisses accusations that Hudson's crunched-down role feels uncomfortably like the Token Black Guy: "It was always written for these three guys, we grew up together, so this was the comedy troupe, so to speak. I cast Ernie because he was really different in his energy from the other guys."

Hudson was devastated by the script change but tried to stay pragmatic about it: "I think the studio thought they could sell the guys as they were from *Saturday Night Live*, and they wanted to include Winston marginally. I don't know. I blame the studio because in my mind it's easier for me to say 'some exec' rather than the guy sitting next to me. I don't think it came from the guys [Aykroyd, Ramis, and Reitman], the guys are great, but what do I know?" He tried, he says, "not to go to the racial side of it," because he didn't want to send a defeatist message to his sons.

The studio was almost certainly less excited about the bankability of Hudson compared to Aykroyd and Murray. But the truth is, it was Ramis and Aykroyd who cut down Winston's part, for the precise reasons that Hudson feared—race and star power, but not quite as he imagined. According to Ramis:

> As writers, we'd never done a black character. The Writer's Guild sends out letters about this regularly—"Let's see more women and minorities." So when we wrote Winston, I think we had our own little reverse backlash going. We bent over backwards to make Winston's character good—and in doing so, we made him so good that he was the best character in the movie. We looked at it and said, "Jesus! He's got all the good lines." At the same time, everybody was saying Bill's character was a little

weak. So, little by little, we started shifting Winston's attitude to Bill's character—which made perfect sense—and we also ended up delaying Winston's introduction until much later in the film.

This explains why there are two skeptical outsiders among the Ghostbusters—Venkman and Winston—which always felt like overkill to me. It's only because Murray plays the part "so odd," as Dana says, that he doesn't feel like an everyman, as Winston does, and the overlap isn't more obvious than it already is.

Once they started shooting, Reitman says, they realized Hudson was so funny they decided to re-expand his part, but only up to a point. Winston does still get some good lines ("I've seen shit that'll turn you white!" "I love this town!"), but his role is unquestionably squeezed. And Hudson's disappointments continued after the movie: he was turned down to voice his own character in the cartoon of *Ghostbusters* (they gave it to Arsenio Hall instead), and his part was, once again, nearly pushed out of the (pretty meh) sequel to the film. "That was difficult for me because that I really didn't understand. But once you get angry, it's all over. So I stayed positive and kept working. And I can also say that the original *Ghostbusters* is a perfect movie as it is," says Hudson.

And it is, and not just in the way it depicts (white) masculinity in opposition to everything else, from the government to women to black men. What makes it feel especially perfect today, particularly in regard to the subject of masculinity, is the fact that the guys in it are grown-ups.

It's extraordinary watching eighties comedies now, especially ones starring men and featuring male friendships, such as *Ghostbusters*, *Trading Places*, *When Harry Met Sally*, *Three Men and a Baby*, even *Three Amigos!*, for heaven's sake, because as silly as the men are in those movies—and they are often very silly—they still behave like adults. Not stunted adolescents, not misogynistic overgrown babies, but adults. They like women, they usually have jobs, they don't wish they were nineteen, they don't sit around smoking bongs all day, and they're not jerks. This distinguishes eighties comedies strongly from today's male-led comedies. Yes, contemporary male-led movies all show that this is because the guys are immature and need to grow up, but what they also show is that guys are a lot more fun whereas women are tedious shrews whose only function in life is to drag the poor menfolk away from their PlayStations and into the sad, drab world of maturity. These movies accept that men have to grow up, but they don't like it.

"I don't know anyone who wants to grow up," says Judd Apatow, who, along with Adam Sandler* and filmmaker Adam McKay (*Anchorman*, *Step Brothers*), has been at the forefront of popularizing the trope of the overgrown man-boy. "For me it's natural to tell stories about people who are resisting the maturation process—there's nothing that's fun about having responsibilities and dealing with real world problems. I'm always fascinated by the moment people are expected to define themselves as an adult. I also like stories about feeling time pressure. Everyone feels they need to get things done by certain stages—getting married, having kids. We all hear this ticking clock all the time and it drives us crazy so I write about that a lot."

Even though Apatow cites eighties movies as his most formative source of inspiration, especially *Ghostbusters*, *Fast Times at Ridgemont High*, *Say Anything*, and the John Hughes films, he concedes that there are no films from that era that feature men resisting growing up. In fact, it's often the reverse. In *St. Elmo's Fire*, for example, which

---

* In fact, Sandler and Apatow shared an apartment when they were both starting out. Ladies, we can only look back and regret that we never got to hang out in Sandler and Apatow's woman-repelling bachelor pad.

focuses on the usual Apatow demographic—twenty-somethings wondering what to do with their lives—the male characters are desperate to grow up, pleading with the various women to marry them (Judd Nelson, Jon Cutler), live with them (Andrew McCarthy), or at least have a relationship with them (Emilio Estevez). It's the women (respectively, Ally Sheedy, Mare Winningham, Ally Sheedy again, and Andie MacDowell) who push them away. "Didn't you think women were dying to get married?" asks a bemused Nelson, after being rejected again. It's the male character in the film who refuses to grow up, Billy (Rob Lowe), who tries to stay a student forever, who is mocked most by his friends and the film.

There is one eighties movie that seems to exemplify Apatow's theory—*Diner*, Barry Levinson's 1982 film set in 1959 about a bunch of young men hanging out during the run-up to a friend's marriage. "One of the things I love about *Diner* is that it shows the moment they have to grow up and get married. I don't know why, but it is a moment I keep going back to in my movies because so much happens in that transition," Apatow says. But in that film, Levinson takes care to emphasize the cruelty of the young men's immaturity, showing how much they hurt their wives when they scream at them for not putting their records back correctly. This, the movie suggests, is a form of spousal abuse. When Pete is caught lying to his wife so he can play sports games, in Apatow's *Knocked Up*, he's just having, the movie says, immature, male-bonding fun. The men are not fun in *Diner* when they behave like jerks, and there's no intimation that they'd be happier if they stayed that way forever—they're just mean.

The guys in *Ghostbusters*, by comparison, behave like recognizable adults, and seem far more grown-up than men in most pop culture today. And when the Ghostbusters seem like relative paragons of maturity, then something weird is going on.

"Yes, exactly!" cries Reitman excitedly, as though he has been waiting to make this point for years.

> As silly and as raw as those eighties films are, they're not coarse. I think now, with the last few generations, these things have evolved. Kids stay in school as long as they can these days, and especially with the masculine gender, there seems to be a desire to put off settling down for as long as possible. So many of the ideas that go into these movies are about that—the childishness of young adult males. I think it's funny enough for a while but I've seen it already and it's time for something else. It's one of the reasons I think those films don't tend to hold up in multiple viewings in much the way that I keep hearing about those [eighties movies] that people tend to view over and over again.

Yes, kids do tend to stay in school longer and, yes, there is a melding between the generations that has never heretofore existed, with grandparents poking their grandkids on Facebook and mothers and daughters shopping together in Topshop. Never has it been easier to stay part of the youth culture for longer. But as much as I'd like to blame Facebook for absolutely all evils in the modern world, the truth is that young men today are no more like Adam Sandler in *Billy Madison* than they ever were (thank God). The telling thing here is that it's men who are depicted as stunted adolescents, not women.* And this is because the trope of the overgrown man-boy is simply the laziest and lowest answer to a question that has been building up

---

* *Bridesmaids*, *Train Wreck*, and the HBO show *Girls*, all produced by Apatow, depict young women struggling to grow up. But these remain anomalies and the amount of attention these projects received, when they were merely showing women do what men had been doing on-screen for decades, underlined the different expectations placed on male and female fictional characters.

in pop culture for decades: how to incorporate male-based storylines into a society that is increasingly enlightened by feminism.

Despite still getting the vast majority of starring roles and storylines, men do not get a great deal in pop culture today. A particularly popular trope for fathers on TV shows today, from *The Simpsons* to *Modern Family* to *Peppa Pig*, is to depict them as incompetent manboys, haplessly trying to keep up with their far more mature wives. Compare, say, useless Phil Dunphy in *Modern Family*, always getting things wrong, always buying the wrong kind of car, always mocked by his kids, with Cliff Huxtable in *The Cosby Show*, the patrician doctor whose kids respected him despite his wildly questionable taste in knitwear. In American movie comedies today, men are not sweetly silly, as they were in the eighties, keen but not desperate for female attention—they are overgrown teenagers who regard women as bitches to humiliate or mother figures to worship. Women, bromance movies suggest, are a necessity in life, but it's only by hanging out with one's male friends, swapping porn films with them, taking mushrooms in Vegas with them, and making homophobic gags while playing computer games with them that a man is truly at ease with himself.

Why this has happened can be gleaned, not from films, but TV. The most celebrated recent TV blockbusters all depict the erosion of patriarchy: "Tony [Soprano], Walter [White] and Don [Draper] are the last of the patriarchs," writes the *New York Times*' film critic A. O. Scott. "[But] it seems that, in doing away with patriarchal authority, we have also, perhaps unwittingly, killed off all the grown ups. . . . In my main line of work as a film critic, I have watched over the past 15 years as the studios committed their vast financial and imaginative resources to the cultivation of franchises that advance an essentially juvenile vision of the world. Comic-book movies, family-friendly animated adventures, tales of adolescent heroism and comedies of arrested development do not only make up the commercial center of 21st century Hollywood. They are its artistic heart." This genre of film, Scott continues, is "a cesspool of nervous homophobia and lazy racial stereotyping. Its postures of revolt tend to exemplify the reactionary habit of pretending that those with the most social power are really the most beleaguered and oppressed." The man-boy, in other words, is a petulant temper tantrum about the demise of simple patriarchal structures, a giant shrug of confusion about how men should be if they can no longer act like Don Draper without being arrested. It is a form of rebellion when the only thing to rebel against is women and themselves, and it is a giant step backward from the comparatively enlightened likes of *Three Men and a Baby*.

One could easily argue that it was the eighties that started this trend of infantilization and especially infantilized men, which makes sense as this was the decade of the so-called backlash against feminism. After all, it was the eighties that saw a huge rise in youth culture, with MTV and teen movies dominating the pop culture, as well as the growth of high-concept movies, which are the definition of an infantilized art form. In his both fascinating and charmingly pretentious essay on 1989's *Indiana Jones and the Last Crusade*, Peter Biskind argues that George Lucas and, in particular, Steven Spielberg popularized in the seventies and especially the eighties "the echt lesson of the sixties: don't trust adults, particularly those in authority." *Star Wars*, most obviously, is a film about kids versus parents (that is, the Empire), with the kids being very much on the side of the good. Lucas then described *Close Encounters of the Third Kind* as a movie "for the kids in all of us," and movies like *Star Wars* and *Indiana Jones* encourage a childlike unquestioning sense of awe in audiences of all ages ("I want a movie to overwhelm me," Spielberg once said), bludgeoning them with spectacle and old-fashioned derring-do, replacing the more complex and anguished post-Vietnam films of the 1970s with something far more simple, with clear-cut good guys and bad guys.

Spielberg has been fond of the wisdom-of-children-versus-the-obtuseness-of-adults trope in his films for decades, and this is perhaps most obvious in the films he made in the eighties. In *E.T.*, Elliott is shown to be the one who should control the situation, not his mother and certainly not the U.S. government. In *Indiana Jones and the Last Crusade*, Indy is emphatically in the child's role, locked in an Oedipal battle with his father (Sean Connery), whom he resents but also wants desperately to please, like the neediest of adolescent boys.

The eighties saw a weird flurry of actual man-boys in a slew of utterly disposable films about fathers, grandfathers, and sons swapping bodies: *Vice Versa* (Judge Reinhold and Fred Savage), *18 Again!* (George Burns and Charlie Schlatter), *Like Father, Like Son* (Dudley Moore and Kirk Cameron), and *Dream a Little Dream* (Jason Robards and Corey Feldman—not, I suspect, a film Robards looked back on with much pride). Yet all these movies show that being an adult is preferable: you get to have sex, drive cars, not go to school, and not listen to your parents. Being a kid, in these films, sucks.

The wonderful if deeply, deeply weird 1988 film *Big* comes closer to the current mentality that idealizes man-boys. When thirteen-year-old Josh Baskin asks the arcade game Zoltar the Magnificent to make him big, he becomes Tom Hanks, replete with Tom Hanks's chest hair and Tom Hanks's penis, which is more than I ever got from an arcade game. As an adult but with a child's mentality, he charms women and work colleagues at his new job at a toy manufacturer, the insinuation being that his delightful innocence is just what the world of adulthood needs. This theory works well enough in the arena of Josh's job—who better to come up with ideas for toys for kids than a kid?—but gets decidedly icky when it comes to Josh's love life. The intimation here is that what a jaded thirty-something career woman needs in her life is a man who is—and acts like—a prepubescent virgin. If I ever went back to a man's apartment with him and he suggested we sleep on different levels of a bunk bed, as happens to Susan (Elizabeth Perkins) when she goes to Josh's loft for the first time, I wouldn't think, Wow, what a sweet guy! I'm so girlishly excited about his innocent way of seeing the world! Instead, I would pick up the phone and say, "Hello? Operator? Put me through to the Weirdos on the Loose Unit." This, however, is not Susan's reaction and she eventually sleeps with and moves in with the dude Carrie Bradshaw would refer to as Bunk Bed Guy, which is weird in itself, but even weirder for the audience who knows that Josh—I repeat—is thirteen years old.

"It's emphasized in the screenplay that it was a secret he was a little boy," says Tom Hanks, a little defensively when I asked him about this. "And when we shot the scene when they're about to be intimate for the first time and there's that bit when he turns the light back on because I thought, Well, there's no way a thirteen-year-old boy wouldn't want to see this."

Sure, the sex scene is believable but that doesn't mean it's not weird, right? He's THIRTEEN. "Yeah," he agrees. "It was weird."

But at least in the case of *Big* and all the body swap films, the reason the man is acting like a boy is that he is, actually, a boy. In none of these films, no matter how much they celebrate George Lucas's "the child within us all," is there any suggestion that men should resist growing up, or that this is even their natural inclination. The reason the Ghostbusters represent an idealized sort of masculinity to me is that they're neither patrician nor man-boys—they're just funny, friendly guys whose funniness doesn't depend on misogyny or insecurity. Is that really too much to ask for these days?* They were enough like my father when I was a kid to feel reassured by them (Harold Ramis), they were enough like me so that I wanted them to be my friends and giggle with them (Bill Murray), and they were handsome enough so that I wanted to do things to them I was only starting to understand (Aykroyd, obviously†). And those things still hold true, on-screen and, it turns out, off.

In early 2014 I was sent by the *Guardian*, where I work when I'm not watching eighties movies, to Los Angeles to cover the Oscars and the *Vanity Fair* party, the famous post-ceremony event. It so happened that Bill Murray had presented an award and had made an impromptu tribute to Harold Ramis, who'd died that year. When I saw him at the party, I didn't even stop to think or take the time to feel shy. I just instinctively ran up to him in an unashamedly starstruck way.

"Mr. Murray, *Ghostbusters* is my favorite movie in the world. What is the secret of *Ghostbusters'* everlasting appeal?" I burbled breathlessly, simultaneously terrified and elated in that way you are when you meet your heroes.

He looked down at me (Murray is surprisingly tall), his hair now gray, but still as skewwhiff as Peter Venkman's after a ghost shoot-out. For a mortifying second, I thought he'd tell me to get lost.

"Friendship," he replied without a pause. And then he gave me a noogie.

---

* Yes.

† I'm sensing that I'm not really convincing you of my whole "Aykroyd = total hottie" argument.

Top Five Montages

(Yes, I left out the *Rocky* training montage. Too easy.)

 The volleyball game, "Playing with the Boys" by Kenny Loggins, *Top Gun*

Topless sweaty men playing sport and a song called "Playing with the Boys" by Kenny Loggins—seriously, what else can you possibly want from an eighties montage?

 The Ghostbusters get successful, *"Ghostbusters"* by Ray Parker Jr., *Ghostbusters*

Classic montage with newspaper front pages spinning across the screen, and a VERY cute photo of Aykroyd on the cover of *Time* magazine.* The cameos from real eighties DJs, such as Casey Kasem and Larry King, make me go a little weepy.

 Alex practices dancing, "Maniac" by Michael Sembello, *Flashdance*

She welds—and then she dances! And when she dances there are a thousand close-ups on her arse. This is pure Bruckheimer and Simpson as they were hitting their stride.

---

* Yes, I am still going on about how cute young Aykroyd was.

2 Baby learns to dance, "Hungry Eyes" by Eric Carmen, *Dirty Dancing*

So sexy, so adorable. I just love the bit when her sneakers suddenly morph into dancing shoes. I could watch this montage a million times, and I probably have.

1 The trip to the Chicago Institute of Art, "Please, Please, Please" by the Dream Academy, *Ferris Bueller's Day Off*

John Hughes's self-described "self-indulgent" scene, and all the more moving for it. This is the scene that confirms *Ferris Bueller* to be the most poetic of all teen films ever, and it is quite possibly my favorite movie moment of all time.

Ferris Bueller's Day Off

The Impact of Social Class

The eighties, goes the general thinking, was the decade of venality. No one in America—heck, in the WORLD—had been interested in making money before the 1980s came along and corrupted us all. It was, apparently, the era in which everyone walked around in gold lamé and regarded Ivana Trump as the last word in understated chic. Seriously, you couldn't take the dog for a walk in the eighties without tripping over a giant Versace gold logo. And a pair of giant shoulder pads. And a massive pile of cocaine. And cocaine plays absolute HAVOC with one's Armani stilettos.

Maybe it was—far be it from me to cast aspersions on lazy descriptions of an era—but a little-remarked-upon truth is that this is not, in fact, the mentality depicted in many mainstream eighties movies. Many Hollywood movies argued for, if not actual class warfare, then certainly a suspicion of wealth. Repeatedly, wealthy people are depicted as disgusting, shallow, and even murderous, while working-class people are noble and good-intentioned, such as in not exactly niche films like *Wall Street*,* *Beverly Hills Cop*, *Ruthless People*, *Raising Arizona*, and *Overboard*. Contrast this with today's films like *Iron Man*, in which the billionaire is the superhero (and is inspired by actual billionaire Elon Musk), and the deeply, deeply weird *The Dark Knight Rises*, in which the villain advocates the redistribution of wealth—HE MUST BE DESTROYED. But the eighties films that were the most interested in issues of class were, of all things, the teen films.

The motivating force of almost every single classic eighties teen film was not, in fact, selling soundtracks, watching an eighteen-year-old Tom Cruise try to get laid, or seeing what ridiculous hairdo Nicolas Cage would sport this time round. It was social class. There's *The Karate Kid*, in which the son of a single mother unsuccessfully tries to hide his poverty from the cool kids at school who make fun of his mother's car; *Dirty Dancing*, in which a middle-class girl dates a working-class boy, much to her liberal father's horror; *Can't Buy Me Love*, in which a school nerd gains popularity by paying for it; *Valley Girl*, in which an upper-middle-class girl dates a working-class boy; *Say Anything*, in which a privileged girl dates a lower-middle-class army brat and her father turns out to be a financial criminal; *The Flamingo Kid*, in which a working-class kid is dazzled by a wealthy country club and starts to break away from his blue-collar father; and all John Hughes's teen films.

Of course, issues of class can be found in the undercurrents of pretty much any American movie, from *The Philadelphia Story* to

---

* *Wall Street* is pretty much the film equivalent of "Born in the USA" in the way it was misunderstood and reappropriated by precisely the people it was satirizing: just as Gordon Gekko's mantra "Greed is good" was adopted by Wall Street bankers, so Springsteen's protest against the Vietnam War was clunkily adopted by Ronald Reagan's 1984 campaign for the presidency.

The Godfather. The difference with eighties teen films is that they were completely overt in their treatment of it: class is the major motivator of plot, even if it's easy to miss next to the pop songs and Eric Stoltz's smile. All these films stress emphatically that the money your family has determines everything, from who your friends are, to who you date, your social standing in school, your parents' happiness and aspirations, and your future. They, to varying degrees, rage against the failure of the American Dream. They stress that true class mobility is pretty much impossible, and certainly interclass friendships and romances are unlikely, for the simple reason that rich people are assholes and lower-middle-class and working-class people are good. Which was unfortunate because according to the vast majority of eighties teen movies, the only way a teenager could truly move up out of their socioeconomic group was if they dated someone wealthier than them, Cinderella-style.

The one exception to this rule is *Back to the Future*, which definitely does not rage against the American system; instead, it concludes that, yes, money does buy happiness and that's just great. When Marty returns from 1955 to 1985, he realizes that he has inadvertently changed history so that now his parents, formerly poor and therefore miserable and barely on speaking terms, are now rich and therefore happy and cheerfully smack each other's backsides: "I remember how upset Crispin [Glover, who played George McFly] and Eric [Stoltz, who was originally cast as Marty] were about the ending of *Back to the Future*: now that they have money they're happy," recalls Lea Thompson, who played Lorraine Baines McFly. "They thought it was really outrageous. It went right over my head, of course. Maybe because I was poor and when I got wealthy I was happy!" This is indeed a subject that still riles Glover enormously. For decades he has spoken out against what he describes as "corporate movies"—that is, studio movies—that peddle "propaganda" and he is currently writing a book on the subject addressing, he says, "the *Back to the Future* issue in great detail."

"The main idea was that the family was in love and I felt that if there was any indication that money equals happiness, that was a bad message to put out," he says, the exasperation still palpable in his voice thirty years on. "I was not given the screenplay before we shot the film because Universal and Spielberg were at the time making it apparent that they needed to keep their movie under wraps. Which I understand but as an actor you have to investigate the psychology of the character, and you can't do that until you've read it. Now I would be very insistent [about reading a script before committing to a film], but I was twenty years old at the time and it was a Universal movie; of course I was glad to be in it. So I wasn't given the opportunity to read it before I was hired and so it was fair for me to be asking these questions but they did not think it was fair. When you raise questions people say 'You're crazy, you're weird,' because you're questioning the authority that people have been brought up to think is the only correct way to think, when there are many correct ways to think."

Ultimately, Glover says, he was so disgusted with the message of *Back to the Future* he refused to be in the sequel.*†

"The point [of making the McFly family wealthy] was that self-confidence and the ability to stand up for yourself are qualities that lead to success," says Bob Gale, cowriter of *Back to the Future*. "So

---

* He has also said in the past that another factor in his refusal to be in the sequel involved a pay dispute. With delightful and characteristic Gloverishness, he does not seem to see any contradiction between his moral stance against the film's celebration of wealth and his demand for more pay.

† This refusal then led to Zemeckis's re-creating Glover's face in the sequel through the use of film and prosthetics on another actor. Glover in turn sued the filmmakers and the case was settled out of court. As you can imagine, Glover has quite a lot of feelings on this subject, too, which, sadly, we have neither the time nor space to get into here.

we showed George and Lorraine had an improved standard of living, we showed them loving toward each other, and we showed that George was a successful author. It was the way to show the audience that George had indeed become a better man. And, of course, in the beginning, we depicted George as a loser, Lorraine as a drunk, with a terrible car and a house full of mismatched and worn-out furnishings."

Back to the Future is such a charming film that it's easy to be swept along by it and not notice this equation of lower-middle-class status with being a "loser." But it does echo precisely the same message that other eighties teen films sent: the class you are born into dictates every aspect of your life.

"Class has always been the central story in America, not race—class," says Eleanor Bergstein, the writer and producer of *Dirty Dancing*. "And when you're a teenager you really start to notice this." And there was no teen filmmaker who felt this as deeply as Hughes.

David Thomson complains in his majestic *Biographical Dictionary of Film* that in Hughes's teen films "the fidelity of observation, the wit and the tenderness for kids never quite transcend the general air of problem solving and putting on a piously cheerful face. No one has yet dared in America to portray the boredom or hopelessness of many teenage lives—think of Mike Leigh's pictures to see what could be done." The first thing to say is that to complain that John Hughes isn't enough like Mike Leigh is like getting annoyed that a chocolate cookie is not trying hard enough if it's not a roast chicken. But it isn't fair to dismiss Hughes's movies as devoid of "hopelessness" since his repeated depiction of class issues in his films definitely shows the "hopelessness" in these American teenagers' lives. *Pretty in Pink* (lower-middle-class girl falls for wealthy boy) and *Some Kind of Wonderful* (lower-middle-class boy falls for lower-middle-class girl who has gained acceptance among the rich kids through her looks) are the most obvious examples of Hughes's teen films that were obsessed with class injustice and how difficult it is for kids from different classes to connect (Hughes, despite his inherently romantic nature, apparently thought they couldn't, really). But it's there in all his teen films, including *Sixteen Candles* (Jake's house is notably bigger and flashier than Samantha's) and *The Breakfast Club* (Bender's somewhat implausible-sounding home life* is compared to pampered Claire's world, in which she can give out diamond earrings on a whim). But the film that really emphasizes how unfair he thought the system is is *Ferris Bueller's Day Off.*

There are many reasons to love *Ferris Bueller's Day Off,* and I've gone through all of them. As I said in the introduction, this was the first what I called REAL MOVIE (that is, neither animated nor a musical) I was allowed to see and it instantly became my first love and Ferris my first crush. It represented everything to me, everything I wasn't and didn't have and wanted: teenagehood, freedom, coolness, sexiness. Every day after school, for a whole year, I would come home, go straight to the TV room, carefully close the door to keep out my dorky parents and Jeanie-ish younger sister, and watch *Ferris Bueller's Day Off.* Every. Single. Day. I carefully transcribed the script into my diary, which I still have, and at some point I decided my sister was sufficiently acceptable to allow her to reenact scenes from the movie with me, using my transcribed script. That summer, I taught my sister about making out, using the scene in which Ferris makes out with Sloane in the museum as a guide, and the two of us would duly writhe around on the living room, making out with our imaginary boyfriends (Ferris for me, Marty McFly for her), while our parents, watching from the doorway, wondered what new

---

*Although to be fair to Hughes, the implausibility may be more of a reflection on Judd Nelson's attempts at Method acting than Hughes's writing.

game their innocent little nine- and seven-year-old daughters had invented. This is perhaps the only time in my sister's and my lives that our parents underestimated us.

As a kid, I loved the film and Ferris because I thought Ferris was so cool—he was cute, he was funny, and, most thrillingly of all, he could drive a car. I fantasized about him driving me to school, holding my hand all the way. (Yes, that was my sexual fantasy. Like I said, I had a pretty sheltered childhood.)

When I finally, and contrary to all my expectations, became a teenager and realized driving a car wasn't quite as rare a skill as I'd believed as a nine-year-old, I decided that the real reason to love this film was that it was so weird. Like all of Hughes's teen films, it has a simple premise (boy skips school and brings his best friend, Cameron, and girlfriend, Sloane, along for the ride) and takes place over a tiny period of time (like *The Breakfast Club*, *Ferris Bueller's Day Off* doesn't even cover twenty-four hours). But it is a much stranger beast than anything else Hughes ever wrote. While all Hughes's other teen films deal with the emotional minutiae of being a teenager, *Ferris Bueller's Day Off* doesn't make even the slightest pretense to realism. The characters are all surreal exaggerations of recognizable characters—the teenager, Ferris, is just that little bit too cocky, the principal, Ed Rooney (Jeffrey Jones), is definitely too demented—and the situations it depicts are, quite clearly, impossible.

"John always meant for the movie to be a fable," says Matthew Broderick. "In the original, longer version of the film there were some somber Hughesian musings about how when you're an adult nothing matters anymore. But when he was editing he decided to make it clear that it was a comedy fantasy and so cut all that out. From the start, he knew it wasn't going to be a messagey movie, like *The Breakfast Club*. He wanted it to be about having a good time."

For years I had a theory—and I was very proud of this theory—that *Ferris Bueller's Day Off* isn't about Ferris at all: it's about his miserable best friend, Cameron, and the whole movie is actually seen through Cameron's eyes.* This is why we see Ferris as this golden boy, the one who can do no wrong, the one for whom everything always goes right and the one whom everyone loves: because that's how Cameron sees him. Everyone had a friend in high school—and some still later in life—who, to their mind, exists within some kind of gilded halo, who is always funnier, smarter, cooler, and more popular than they could ever be, and that is who Ferris is for Cameron. While Ferris happily makes out with his girlfriend by the stained-glass windows in the Art Institute of Chicago (in what is the greatest montage scene of the eighties and my favorite cinematic moment of all time), Cameron has a mini nervous breakdown while staring at Georges Seurat's *Un dimanche après-midi à l'Île de la Grande Jatte*, as he realizes that he, like the child in the painting, is nothing more than a series of meaningless dots. Nothing comes easy for Cameron, who thinks too much about everything, but everything comes easy to Ferris, who thinks deeply about nothing. The clinching piece of evidence to my theory is that it's Cameron who goes through an emotional change during the movie. He learns that, in order for him to achieve happiness at last in his life, he's going to have to stand up to his father, for once. Ferris, by contrast, is as blithe and content at the end of the film as he is at the beginning.

I liked this theory a lot, mainly because I came up with it, but also because it explained all the things in the movie that I treasured. I loved the movie's dreamy surrealism, with Ferris frequently breaking

---

*There is a popular Internet conspiracy theory that says Ferris is actually a figment of Cameron's imagination, and there is merit in that. But personally, I don't want to live in a world where Ferris doesn't exist, albeit only on-screen.

the fourth wall (Hughes loved to have his teen characters break the fourth wall but nowhere did he do it better, or as much, as in *Ferris Bueller's Day Off*) and the strange characters with their strange peccadilloes: Grace, the school secretary, pulling pens out of her enormous hair; Charlie Sheen as the druggy punk dispensing life advice in the police station; the teachers whose classes are so boring they feel like a lobotomy.* They are all exaggerations, and that feels right if the movie is seen through a teenager's eyes because teenagers do exaggerate everything as they feel everything so intensely. And most of all, I loved Cameron, Ferris's miserable best friend, who increasingly felt like the heart of the film to me. Ferris, I realized, might be kind of a jerk: he borrows his best friend's dad's vintage car, much to his friend's horror (license plate: "NRVOUS"), just because he wants to borrow it. He manipulates his parents' blind love for him, he torments his younger sister, and he lies to pretty much every single person in the movie.

"It was definitely a concern when we were making the movie—is Ferris actually just an asshole?" Broderick says with a laugh. "But I

---

*The economics teacher who roll-calls "Bueller . . . Bueller . . ." was played by Hughes's friend and noted economist Ben Stein, who has said that acting in *Ferris Bueller's Day Off* was the happiest day of his life: "[My obituary will] have a picture of me and above it will say 'Bueller . . . Bueller.' The fact that I went to Yale Law School, was a columnist for the *Wall Street Journal* and the *New York Times*, wrote thirty books, that will all be washed away and it'll just be, 'Bueller . . . Bueller.' And that will be just fine" (from Susanna Gora, *You Couldn't Ignore Me If You Tried*). Stein omits from his list of achievements that he was also a speechwriter for Nixon, a game show host, an advertising spokesperson (which led to him being sacked by the *New York Times*), and author of a famously laughable defense of Dominique Strauss-Kahn, the former head of the International Monetary Fund who in 2011 was accused of raping a hotel maid. Stein pooh-poohed the allegation with the ironclad argument that "people who commit crimes are criminals," and not rich, important men like Strauss-Kahn. Maybe those achievements didn't feel as noteworthy to Stein as his attendance at Yale Law School? But no matter. In this book at least, a good *Ferris Bueller's Day Off* appearance can momentarily wash away all sins.

saw him as the maître d' of the movie, and it's right that he shouldn't have emotional development. He's hosting the film."

In Ferris's defense, he is definitely not "just an asshole." Okay, sure, he drives his best friend to near suicide and his sister to the brink of self-destruction, but he is also the ultimate bringer of joy, making everyone happier and better for being part of his world (with the exception of Mr. Rooney, that is, and there really is no helping that man—he won't even accept a consolation Gummy Bear!). But it is true that Ferris never experiences the sort of emotional journey one might expect of a film hero, and especially of a Hughesian hero.

All these issues further convinced me of the rectitude of my theory: of course the film must be Cameron's fantasy because only a teenager like Cameron (or a kid like me) would think that Ferris was cool. All adults think he is a jerk. Of course the movie was seen through Cameron's eyes. But as an adult, I've realized none of this is right either. What makes *Ferris Bueller's Day Off* feel so special and warm isn't that it's about Cameron or the relationships behind the camera: it's that it's about John Hughes and, in particular, a subject especially close to his heart—social class.

Hughes wrote all his teen scripts quickly and with seeming Ferris-like ease, and this, his masterpiece, was no exception. He wrote it, incredibly, in just two nights: "You know how Salieri looked at *Amadeus* with rage when he'd pulled it out of thin air?" his collaborator Howard Deutch said, remembering Hughes working on *Ferris*, and using another eighties classic film as an analogy. "That was me looking at John writing a script. I'd be like, 'How?! How?!'"

The reason Hughes was able to write his teen scripts so quickly was that he wrote so much of himself in them, both emotionally and in the details. It's easy to mock the homogeneity of the world presented in these films, a world in which everyone's white, suburban, and straight. But Hughes never meant his films to be seen as universal—they were utterly personal portraits of his own child-hood, growing up as a teenager in the suburbs of Illinois (almost no one made movies set in Chicago until Hughes came along). But like Ephron, while the stories were personal, the emotions in the film are universal, and with their simplistic narratives and familiar tropes, their clean divisions between good and bad, Hughes's teen films have become to the latter half of the twentieth century what Western films were to the first: they are as central to the way Americans raised on them see their own lives, and the way non-Americans raised on them see America. There is a part of me that still feels, and probably always will feel, that I didn't go to a REAL high school be-cause mine—private, all girls, urban—looked nothing like the pub-lic, coed suburban schools I grew up watching. At my school in New York, we didn't even have a high school—we had an "upper school." So whenever people ask me about my "high school" experiences, for a few initial seconds I envisage myself at Shermer High School, Hill Valley High School, or even Westerberg High School. And then I remember the boring truth.

To cite all the references Hughes put into his films that came straight from his own life would take up a whole book, but a few select ones from *Ferris Bueller's Day Off* alone include Ferris's home address (his house number is 2800, Hughes grew up in 2800 Shan-non Road); the "Shermer High" school scenes were shot in Hughes's old high school, Glenbrook North High School; Hughes and his high school best friend used to talk their way into fancy restaurants, as Ferris does when he takes his friends to Chez Quis (a punning reference, as writer Susannah Gora points out, to the American pizza chain Shakey's). But probably the most autobiographical moment in the film comes when Ferris takes Cameron and Sloane to the Art Institute of Chicago. When Hughes was in high school the museum was, he said, "a place of refuge for me" (in *Some Kind of Wonderful,* the male protagonist, Keith, describes the museum as "my sanctuary") and "this was a chance for me to go back into this building and show the paintings that were my favorites." But whereas Hughes would go to the museum alone as a teenager, here he has the teenage male lead of the film bring his girlfriend and best friend (and Hughes himself now brings his entire audience with him).

Ferris Bueller's Day Off isn't Cameron's fantasy about Ferris—it's a former teenage outsider's self-fantasy about what their teenage life should have been like, and this is why it appeals so much to Hughes's audience, which is largely made up of current and former teenage outsiders. *Ferris Bueller's Day Off* presents a nerd's idealized view of teenage life: sanitized, safe, and sweet, in which you are universally adored for being your own weird self and can do whatever you damn well want. This is a vision that would appeal enormously to a former teenage outcast (Hughes) and a future one (me as a child).

"I sort of saw Cameron and Ferris as the two sides to John Hughes, because he could be moody and quiet, John. But he had another side to him that didn't give a damn about anything and could be really funny," says Broderick.

Hughes wrote *Ferris Bueller's Day Off* after *Pretty in Pink* and during his reworking of *Some Kind of Wonderful*, and both of those films feature archetypal Hughesian outcasts: Duckie (Jon Cryer) and Keith (Eric Stoltz). Ferris, by rights, should fit into this group, seeing as he is odd, has no interest in doing what people in authority tell him to do, and likes New Romantic English singers. Like Duckie, he favors animal print (Duckie: shoes; Ferris: waistcoat), he talks to himself, and he dances to old-school singers.* And also like Duckie,

---

*Ferris and Duckie's dance styles are pretty similar, too, which is not that surprising as the man who choreographed Ferris's parade dance, the great Kenny Ortega, also choreographed Duckie's dance to "Try a Little Tenderness" in *Pretty in Pink*. He later he would be insufferably annoying if he weren't so sweet. (That Jon Cryer looked almost identical to Broderick as a teenager further encourages identification between their characters.) But there are two key differences between Ferris and Duckie and Keith: Ferris is rich and popular and Duckie and Keith are poor and outcasts and, in an eighties teen movie, these issues are inextricably connected.

Hughes grew up in a lower-middle-class family in an upper-middle-class neighborhood, an artistic outsider in a typical suburban high school, and he never forgot how it felt to be "on the lower end of a rich community," as he told the *New York Times*. The divisions he draws between the wealthy and poor kids are done with a hand so heavy they could only belong to a man who once felt himself to be the victim of class snobbery. To be rich, in Hughes's films, means that you are a jerk but granted instant popularity, while the noble working-class kids muddle through in the shadows.

So when Hughes decided to write a film about—for the one and only time in his career—a popular but likable kid, he simply took the nerd from his previous film, Duckie, and made him rich. This, in Hughes's world, was how a kid, even one as odd as Duckie/Ferris, was guaranteed popularity. The Buellers definitely have money, enough to give their son a computer and their daughter a car. Where Duckie apparently sleeps on a mattress in a bare room in *Pretty in Pink*, his alter ego Ferris sleeps in a room surrounded by computers and a giant stereo system. Where Duckie pines hopelessly after his female best friend and fantasizes in vain about marrying her, Ferris dates the prettiest girl in school and she is desperate to marry him. And where Duckie seems to have no parental figures at all in his life, Ferris's parents think he's wonderful, even when the school principal

---

went on to choreograph *Dirty Dancing* and, somewhat less excitingly in this book's opinion, *High School Musical*.

tells them he really isn't. *Ferris Bueller's Day Off* is like Duckie's fantasy, which it is, to an extent, because it's Hughes's fantasy. But because this is a Hughes film, there is, inevitably, a dig about wealth in it and this is done through Cameron.

Cameron is, clearly, much richer than Ferris. Whereas Ferris's house is a typical but very plush upper-middle-class suburban house, Cameron lives in what looks like a multimillion-dollar bunker for a Bond villain. His father's collection of vintage cars alone probably costs twice as much as the Bueller homestead. And Cameron is emphatically miserable. Hughes suggested that Cameron's parents simply don't love him (the reason there is a close-up on Mary Cassatt's painting *Mother and Child* in the museum montage is that, Hughes said, "I thought it was very relevant to Cameron, the tenderness between a mother and a child which he didn't have"), and Cameron knows that his father loves his Ferrari more than he loves his family. Even in a film that ostensibly lightens up on wealthy kids, Hughes couldn't help but make the point, again, that being a rich teenager—despite how it might look from the outside—actually sucks. Even if you yourself are not a jerk, like Steff in *Pretty in Pink* or Hardy in *Some Kind of Wonderful*, chances are your parents will be.

"Class consciousness was very important to John, and you can see it as he wrote about it so much," says Broderick. "He didn't talk about things like that so much but as time has passed I've realized that although he was very conservative politically, I think, he had a real problem with wealth when it was too concentrated. He always writes about it, even in something like *Planes, Trains and Automobiles*. There's very often somebody with money and somebody without. With Ferris, he tried to keep it on a fable level but those elements are definitely still in there."

This issue of class consciousness became, thanks largely to Hughes, such a staple of eighties teen movies it is as much of a cliché as the climactic prom. But it is the one ingredient to the genre that has never been picked up by its many copyists. Plenty of films have come out in the past decade that pay explicit homage to eighties teen films, and especially Hughes's teen films, from *Easy A* to *21 Jump Street*, which the film's star and producer, Jonah Hill, described as "a mix of *Bad Boys* and a John Hughes film." But none of these films ever deals with the class issues that Hughes depicted. Partly this is because the people who make these homages are remembering the films from when they saw them as kids and, by and very large, kids didn't notice all these arguments about social mobility, focusing instead on the power ballads and fights in the school canteen. But it is also because Hollywood—and by extension America—doesn't talk about class issues the way it used to.

"There is an avoidance of talk about class identification now. You'll hear talk of gender identification, sexuality identification, race identification, but never class," says Eileen Jones, a lecturer in film and media at the University of California, Berkeley, and a writer for the socialist-leaning magazine *Jacobin*. "Class identification, in America at least, is going through what feminism went through in the eighties: it is completely passé."

What is even more passé is to say that social mobility is impossible. This goes specifically against the American dream and therefore verges dangerously into the kind of talk that will get a filmmaker denounced by Fox News. Mainstream Hollywood movies that have depicted social mobility in the past twenty years, such as *Erin Brockovich* or even *Pretty Woman*, have all suggested that it is possible to lift oneself out of one's class (even if one has to become a prostitute and—even worse—spend a week with Richard Gere in Beverly Hills to do so). Teen movies of the 1980s argue precisely the opposite. "Eighties films were willing to deal with being poor and people's lives being screwed over by economic structures. You hardly see that at all in movies today," says James Russell, principal lecturer in film at De Montfort University in London.

The reason American teen movies specifically stopped featuring class issues after the eighties can be traced, again, back to one specific film: *Clueless*. *Clueless* was so big it inevitably changed everything about how teen films were framed, including the trend in teen pop culture of showing, not how middle-class American teenagers actually live, but how they didn't even know they would like to live. Already by the mid-1990s teen films such as *10 Things I Hate About You* and *American Pie* were depicting a world in which all teenagers came from the same upper-middle social class, in which everyone lived in big houses and drove big cars. Sure, there were still cliques and outcasts in the schools, but these had nothing to do with social class. Instead, the idea of a poor or even lower-middle-class kid appearing in a teen film today feels as outdated as a movie about workers' unions.

But instead of looking at why American teen movies in particular don't deal with class anymore, the question could be instead why so many of them did in the eighties.

"Never underestimate Hollywood's eagerness to copy something successful," laughs *Dirty Dancing*'s Eleanor Bergstein. "The reason so many teen movies talked about class is because those movies were successful, so then more movies would come along just like them."

Another factor is the demographic of the people who made the films. Hughes was from a lower-middle-class family, Bergstein grew up in a similar economic situation, and *Dirty Dancing* was born out of memories of her childhood, "and these were subjects that we talked about," she says. It is impossible to find precise statistics about the demographics of who works in Hollywood now but one thing is widely agreed on: "Hollywood has never been culturally diverse, but it's getting narrower, and it's definitely narrower than it was thirty years ago," says Russell. "It's much more male and more white and largely college-educated and middle-class. It doesn't draw from a particularly broad background, at least at the top end. It's hard to imagine Sam Peckinpah getting in today."

But probably the most crucial factor of all is the fact that movies today are more dependent than ever on the international market.

"You can't sell a movie to Japan or China that is about specific American cultural issues. So while American movies are still set in America, they are much vaguer and certainly not about American social issues," says Russell. "Also, it tended to be mid-budget films that dealt with social issues in the eighties, and Hollywood doesn't make films with those budgets anymore. It makes big blockbusters or low-budget independents." Hollywood in the 1980s produced hundreds of films about American social issues. Four alone were produced about the 1980s farm crisis: *Field of Dreams*, *Places in the Heart*, *Country*, and *The River*. These days, social engagement is left to the niche independents while the big-budget movies that are aimed at the masses take care to talk about nothing specific at all.

Ferris Bueller's Day Off isn't just a fantasy about wealth, it's about growing up. The best of Hughes's teen films—*The Breakfast Club*, *Pretty in Pink*, and *Ferris Bueller's Day Off*—are ultimately about the dread of growing up, of moving away, of losing that sparkle you have as a teenager and becoming as dead inside as all the adults seem to be around you. As the man wrote, in what is possibly his most famous line of all, when you grow up your heart dies. Everyone who watches those films as a teenager grows up with that dread and, eventually, regret about it. And this is something Hughes struggled with as much as any of his fans. It is ironic that Hughes, who made such a sparkling film fantasizing about what it would be like to be rich and popular, struggled when he attained that status for himself.

By the time he started shooting *Ferris Bueller's Day Off*, Hughes was already, as Broderick puts it, "the godlike Spielberg figure of teen movies." By the time it came out, and became his biggest success, he was one of the most sought-after directors and writers in Hollywood. Everyone wanted to meet and work with the former kid who used to lurk around museums on his own. "And John, I think, really didn't like it," says Howard Deutch. "He always felt like an outsider, and that's how he was able to write those characters. When he became successful out in L.A. and everybody wanted him, from Spielberg to Katzenberg, and all the power elite all wanted to do business with him, he found himself as a member of the insiders boy club. I think he felt like it was actually an obstacle to writing these characters that he believed in because he no longer felt like himself."

So Hughes and his family moved back to Chicago, Hughes's hometown, where he always felt happiest, and he continued to write. But the films he wrote "never had the emotional impact I recognized as John's real skill," says Molly Ringwald. Instead, particularly from 1990 onward, he wrote his "dopey-ass comedies": *Beethoven, 101 Dalmatians,* and, of course, *Home Alone.* He no longer wrote about soulful teenage outcasts, maybe because he knew he no longer was one.

He also cut himself off from almost all the friends he'd made on those teen films, leaving them behind when he left the genre. "I went to John's funeral and I realized when I was there that I hadn't actually seen him in over a decade," recalls Broderick. "It was sad because it had been such a happy set when we were making the film, and even afterwards John would invite Jennifer [Grey] and me to his house and we'd hang out in the pool with his family." He smiles at the memory, and then sighs: "But then he just disappeared."

Ferris had his one perfect day. It's what comes after that can be a drag.

I found that out for myself, too. I would never have believed it when I was nine, but I did eventually grow up and when I was about thirty-one, I moved back to New York after having spent twenty years in London. I don't know, maybe I was trying to recapture my youth, like Hughes did with his films. But that only really works in the movies and, the truth was, I felt as lonely and confused as Cameron Frye did when he was eighteen. I tried dating for a while, but it turned out that dating as a thirty-something woman in New York was about as tedious and riddled with clichés as trying to get a date to the prom when you're the school nerd in an eighties teen film. So eventually, I gave up the men and got a dog. As it happened, one of my neighbors had as little of a life as I did and our evening dog walks often synched. At first we just smiled at each other while our dogs sniffed one another's butts. But eventually, as we picked up dog poop together on Seventh Avenue for the tenth night in a row, it got too awkward not to introduce ourselves—after all, our dogs already knew one another's anal glands. So I went first.

"So, um, I'm Hadley," I stammered.

"I'm Matthew," he mumbled back. But I knew that already, of course. Because it was Matthew Broderick.

I didn't make out with him on my parents' living room rug. I didn't even hold his hand. But none of that mattered—as I headed out again every evening, knowing I'd be picking up dog poop with Matthew Broderick, it felt like I finally got my Hughesian happy ending.

The Top Ten Best Love Songs on an Eighties Movie Soundtrack

 "Almost Paradise," by Mike Reno and Ann Wilson, from *Footloose*

The song from when the kids are waiting for the prom to start. A classic eighties duet.

 "It Might Be You," by Stephen Bishop, from *Tootsie*

One giant cheese mountain of a song, and that is no bad thing.

 "Let's Hear It for the Boy," by Deniece Williams, from *Footloose*

Everything about this song, including the spelling of the singer's name, is adorable.

This song should be better known. The movie, on the other hand, should not.

 "(I've Had) the Time of My Life," by Bill Medley and Jennifer Warnes, from *Dirty Dancing*

It is a testament to the quality of love songs from eighties films that this classic is not at number one.

"Hungry Eyes," by Eric Carmen, from *Dirty Dancing*

Quality keyboard intro, bonus points for use in the second-best montage of the decade.

 "Take My Breath Away," by Berlin, from *Top Gun*

This song is so good it makes having sex with Tom Cruise seem almost sexy.

 "I Melt with You," by Modern English, from *Valley Girl*

 "Waiting for a Star to Fall," by Boy Meets Girl, from *Mannequin*

Terrible film, amazing song from the best one-hit-wonder band of all time.

2 **"In Your Eyes," by Peter Gabriel, from *Say Anything***

The most beautiful song in the world, and that is a scientific fact.

1 **"She's Like the Wind," by Patrick Swayze, from *Dirty Dancing***

Patrick Swayze sang AND wrote this little piece of genius. Obviously it's number one.

Steel Magnolias

Women Are Interesting

Of all the many extraordinary qualities that eighties Hollywood movies possess—the glorious hairstyles, their respect for power ballads, the endearing amount of confidence they had in the acting abilities of Steve Guttenberg—their depiction of women is not generally cited as being among their strengths. Eighties movies, the theory has long gone, were absolutely awful when it came to women, and no one argued this more vociferously at the time than feminist critics. "The backlash [against feminism] shaped much of Hollywood's portrayal of women in the eighties," Susan Faludi writes in the 1990s *Backlash*, in her famous chapter looking specifically at mainstream eighties movies and how they expressed the social backlash against second-wave feminism. "Hollywood restated and reinforced the backlash thesis: women were unhappy because they were too free; their liberation had denied them marriage and motherhood . . . [whereas] in the 1970s, the film industry would have a brief infatuation with the feminist cause."

Faludi is right about one thing: between the seventies and the eighties movies did change their attitude toward feminism. In the seventies there was a slew of overtly feminist films about independent women, such as *Private Benjamin, My Brilliant Career, Norma Rae*, and *Alice Doesn't Live Here Anymore*. Marriage was shown to be a prison for women in films such as, most famously, *The Stepford Wives*. Of course, not all movies were so charmed with feminism: in 1979's bafflingly much-lauded *Kramer vs. Kramer*, feminism is portrayed as something kooky and selfish. It is explicitly blamed for the breakdown of Ted (Dustin Hoffman) and Joanna's (Meryl Streep) marriage* and, the movie insinuates, will probably result in the couple's doe-eyed son spending the rest of his life hating women BECAUSE FEMINISM RUINS EVERYTHING. But it is fair to say that movies weren't as explicitly interested in feminism in the eighties as they were in the seventies—with the noted and glorious exception of 1980's *9 to 5*. In this still very funny film, Dolly Parton, Jane Fonda, and the glorious Lily Tomlin fight their sexist pig of a boss (Dabney Coleman) for equal pay, flexible working hours, and an in-office nursery. (Come back, Dolly, Jane, and Lily! We working women of the twenty-first century still need you!)

The popular argument that the eighties were terrible for women in movies is primarily based on one ridiculously OTT and all-dominating piece of evidence: *Fatal Attraction*. Directed by British former adman Adrian Lyne, *Fatal Attraction* was so clearly designed to needle liberal women that it might well have been written by Fox News. The film's message is that women who work and aren't married by the decrepit age of thirty-six are pathetic, crazed with baby hunger, and deserve to be shot by good and humble housewives

---

* Faludi doesn't mention *Kramer vs. Kramer* in her discussion of 1970s films as a feminist utopia, but I of all people can hardly criticize her for providing a selective view of a decade's movies.

(I am not exaggerating—this is literally the message of the movie). Along with S&M romcom *9½ Weeks*, which was also directed by Lyne, *Fatal Attraction* tends to skew all discussions about women in eighties movies, and that's a shame.

Sure, Lyne and his fantasies about how all women are masochistic bunny boilers are pretty attention-grabbing, but to let them grab all the attention is essentially doing Lyne's work for him.* Because, contrary to what Lyne seemed to think, there is a lot more to eighties women than stalkers and masochists. There were so many interesting female film characters in the eighties, and so many great movies about women. Not all of them were explicitly feminist, but the fact that these films were made at all, with largely female casts, featuring female stories, feels so feminist compared with today's movies they make Andrea Dworkin look a bit watered down. So much so, in fact, that feminist critics—ones who grew up reading Faludi—now look back to the eighties as the last high point for women in movies: "The status of women in movies has gotten worse since the 1980s," wrote journalist Amanda Hess, in a 2014 discussion of *Backlash* and eighties films.

"Just look at 1983, for example. I don't know what was going on but you had *Yentl*, *Terms of Endearment*, and *Silkwood*—all big films for women. Then there were movies like *Frances*, *Places in the Heart*, *Gorillas in the Mist*. . . . But now, well, we know what's happened now," says film writer Melissa Silverstein.

---

* For a start, there were other movies around that were far smarter about male infidelity than *Fatal Attraction*, such as, for example, *Moonstruck*. In this movie, Olympia Dukakis has to contend with her aged husband's compulsive womanizing. But because this movie was sensible and not stupid like *Fatal Attraction*—or, more recently, the appalling *The Other Woman* (2014)—*Moonstruck* shows that marriage is about more than just point-scoring, infidelity is about more than just sex, and the betrayed wife is a smart woman in her own right. So don't watch *Fatal Attraction*—watch *Moonstruck*.

This is all true, and it is dismayingly impossible to imagine these films being made now. But let's not underestimate perhaps an even more mainstream depiction of women in eighties movies, and one that is equally difficult to envisage existing today: the classic women's movies.

Most people know about the Bechdel Test, which was coined by the cartoonist Alison Bechdel to ascertain how well represented women are in a film by posing the following rubric:

1. It has to have at least two women in it . . .
2. Who talk to each other . . .
3. About something besides a man.

Well, I'd like to coin the Magnolia Test, named for a movie that is particularly close to my heart, which judges whether or not a movie is a proper women's movie:

1. The cast is largely, maybe even solely female . . .
2. The female characters talk to each other about a million things other than men and genuinely like each other . . .
3. And the relationship between the women is far more important than any they have with a man . . .
4. Bonus points if any of the following are in the film: Shirley MacLaine, Dolly Parton, Bette Midler, Olympia Dukakis. Triple for Sally Field.

In an ideal world, these films would just be known as "movies," as opposed to "women's movies." But as the ongoing success of Michael Bay proves, we do not live in an ideal world. And so, for too long, when it comes to leading roles in movies, women have been seen as the exception rather than the norm. Movies that focus on

women's stories are—now more than ever—dismissed as "niche,"
even though women make up more than half the human race and
(arguably more to the point) cinema audiences. So the gendering
is, gratingly, necessary, just as, apparently, Michael Bay is to Hollywood's current financial success.

Some people snark about women's movies and dismiss them as
"domestic," as though that were a negative thing. Home is a place
most of us know and to write off "domestic" as an embarrassment
is to dismiss the lives that millions and millions of women lead as
worthless. I've also heard complaints that whereas men get action
movies and westerns, women "only" get domestic dramas and big ol'
weepies. Well, if I want to see movies set in jungles or outer space,
I will, and thanks to eighties movies I can see those movies starring
kick-ass women in the form of, respectively, *Romancing the Stone*
and *Aliens*.

What I love about classic women's movies is that they tell women
that their daily lives are interesting. Westerns and action movies and
other genres considered to be the area of menfolk do not, because
they do not depict lives led by most men, although heaven knows
there are plenty of other movies out there that depict nothing but
the daily lives of men. Women's movies show women living normal daily lives—raising their children, dealing with breast cancer,
laughing with their friends, contending with unfaithful husbands,
fighting sexist bosses: in other words, things that women around the
world deal with every day.

These movies also respect the value of women's emotional lives
and show women talking to each other about things other than
men. Men see this about themselves in pretty much any other
movie. Women? Not so much. In women's movies, women exist in
their own right, not as appendages, not as lonely spinsters, or idealized quarries, or someone's wife or someone's mother, but as funny,

sad, angry, kind, supportive, independent human beings—and how many movies can claim that? So yeah, sure, men have their westerns and their stoicism and tumbleweed. But women get to bond over cheesecake with Dolly Parton. If men make sneering comments about women's films, it's because they're jealous, and I really can't blame them.

9 to 5 amply passes the Magnolia Test, as do those ne plus ultra eighties women's movies, *Terms of Endearment* and *Beaches*, two of the most classic women's weepies of all time. These movies starred women, were made for women, told distinctly women's stories involving breast cancer, straying husbands, and motherhood, and the few men on-screen are repeatedly shown to be a disappointment, whereas the women are there for one another until death. *Beaches* comes with the obvious added bonus of being the last film to provide truly great hairbrush-microphone-in-front-of-the-mirror singing, thanks to Bette Midler's irresistible soundtrack, a quality frustratingly lacking from movies today, and it serves as some distraction from Barbara Hershey's lips seemingly inflating and deflating during the film. *Terms of Endearment* is probably not a film you've seen recently, but you should—it is as delightful as you'd expect a movie to be featuring Shirley MacLaine as a crotchety busybody and Jack Nicholson as her astronaut (!) lover. But the real heart of the film is the relationship between MacLaine and her charmingly daffy daughter (Debra Winger), who, while married to one useless man (Jeff Daniels) and being wooed by another (John Lithgow), develops breast cancer. These two films are both sad but, like the best weepies, they are also very funny, and this brings me to a quick defense of women's weepies.

American feminist film critic Mollie Haskell, writing a decade before the eighties, was very dismissive of women's movies and, in particular, women's weepies in her classic text *From Reverence to*

*Rape: The Treatment of Women in the Movies:** "The woman's film,"
she writes, "fills a masturbatory need, it is soft-core emotional porn
for the frustrated housewife. The weepies are founded on a mock-
Aristotelian and politically conservative aesthetic whereby women
spectators are moved, not by pity and fear but by self-pity and tears
to accept, rather than reject, their lot. That there should be a need
and an audience for such an opiate suggests an unholy amount of
real misery."

Well, first, unlike Haskell, I don't see too much wrong with
providing fodder for masturbation, especially if that other person is
frustrated. Seems like simple generosity to me. Second, the idea that
crying at sad movies is a form of transference is, to be frank, grade-A
baloney. A movie that makes you both laugh and cry is as satisfying
as a pop song that is both moving and ecstatic.† It's about the pleasure of experiencing the full gamut of emotions from a single piece
of art, that feeling of standing up at the end, exhausted by the emotional pummeling but still giggling at some of the jokes. After all
(cue stirring instrumental eighties women's movie theme song), isn't
that what life itself is like? I can understand why some critics—and
especially feminist critics—object to the trope of a woman dying in
the women's movie (belated spoiler: someone dies in both *Terms of
Endearment* and *Beaches*). But that is, in fact, only a tiny part of both
of those films: they are really about female friendship and mothers
and daughters. It's just that the deaths ramp up the tears and the
tears are part of the way female audiences (by which, once again, I
obviously mean "me") bond with the movies and bond with each
other while watching the movie. A movie that makes you cry is a

---

* One day I shall write a book about the mighty titles of feminist texts and studies.
They are all reliably awesome.
† See: the oeuvre of the Cure and New Order—in the eighties, obviously.

movie you have to love, and crying while watching a movie with a female friend is as intimate as getting drunk with them.

But the really telling detail is that these movies make (the largely female) audiences cry over the death of a woman. So often, women who die in movies (and books) are either idealized or completely anonymous, and it's impossible to cry over such characters today (I have never, for example, cried over the death of tedious Miss Melanie in *Gone with the Wind*). But with the women in *Terms of Endearment* and *Beaches*, we got to know them pretty well—their sexual desires, their flaws, their jealousies. That female audiences still cry at the end of these films is a testament to how hard the films work to make these female characters feel real.

This is why, of all the great eighties women's movies, my favorite one is *Steel Magnolias*. I watch this film at least twice a year (and always if I happen to come across it on TV). It still makes me laugh out loud ("I'm not crazy, M'Lynn—I've just been in a very bad MOOD for forty years," Shirley MacLaine's character, Ouiser, says to Sally Field's M'Lynn at one point, and that quote in particular has proven astonishingly useful in real life) and, yes, I still cry, every time, at the end. "Laughter through tears is my favorite emotion," says Dolly Parton's character, Truvy, in the film, which could be the motto of the film, and it's apparently everyone else's, too. Twenty-five years on, this film is still adored, so much so that it was remade (badly, sadly*) in 2012 with an all-black cast.

"People still talk to me about *Steel Magnolias* today—today!" says one of the film's stars, Olympia Dukakis. "At benefits I ask women to put their hands up if they've seen the film five times, ten times, fifteen times. The other day I got up to twenty-seven times. These women had seen the movie twenty-seven times! What a draw

---

* Says Hadley, madly.

that film has. It tells women that female friendship is profound, and women watch it together and cry together, still."

But even more important than weeping and hooting is the way it teaches audiences to expect more from movies when it comes to the representation of women.

For a start, this movie stars six female characters and there is not a single bitch fight. Not once do they even fight over a man. Imagine that! What next, a movie suggesting women can work together without throwing tampons at one another? A movie suggesting women like and respect each other—get outta town! Each of the six female characters gets her own story, some more lightly sketched out than others: Truvy (Parton) has to deal with a deadbeat husband and son; Annelle (Daryl Hannah) is coming out of a bad marriage and making a new life for herself; Clairee (Olympia Dukakis) has just entered widowhood; Ouiser (MacLaine) is starting a new relationship; M'Lynn (Field) is facing the loss of her daughter; and Shelby (Julia Roberts) is giving everything she has to have a much-longed-for baby. These are all classic women's stories, acted by six actresses who, between them, had an average age of fifty when the film came out.

It is impossible to imagine a studio film being made today featuring such everyday, even "domestic" stories about women so unforgivably north of thirty-five. The only vaguely equivalent film that has been released in the past decade is *The Help*, in which the five leading actresses (Emma Stone, Octavia Spencer, Viola Davis, Jessica Chastain, Bryce Dallas Howard) had an average age of 34.8 between them when the film came out and instead of just focusing on real women's lives, it took as its plot one of Hollywood's most beloved storylines: white people solve racism. In fact, Hollywood hasn't made a classic women's movie since the nineties with *Fried Green Tomatoes* and *A League of Their Own*.

But if the telltale sign of a classic women's movie is that it illuminates the reality of women's lives, then it's no surprise that *Steel Magnolias* is so good, because the reason it was written was to illuminate one particular woman's life. When pediatric nurse Susan Robinson, a sweet-faced brunette from Louisiana, died suddenly in 1985 from complications stemming from diabetes at the age of thirty-three, leaving behind a two-year-old son, her brother, Bob Harling, was distraught. But when his sister's widower, Pat, remarried a mere five months after Susan's death, he knew he had to do something. "It was very, very hard. I mean, it was just five months which was a little, you know," says Harling, from his house in Natchitoches, Louisiana, his and Susan's hometown. "Susan had gone through all this out of devotion to her son and when I heard him call another woman 'mama,' I thought, No way, he needs to know the story of his mother and his grandmother."

Harling had worked as an actor and had never written "a thing" before. But he became, he says, "obsessed" with telling Susan's story. So, with the encouragement of some friends who were writers, he wrote it as a play about six women set in a beauty parlor, renaming his sister "Shelby." "I wrote it very quickly because I wanted to capture how the women spoke. But I had no idea that anyone would do anything with it, I just wanted to make a document that celebrated Susan," he says in his gentle Louisiana accent.

The first thing that someone did with it was to turn it into an off-Broadway play, and it opened to huge critical praise. To Harling's amazement, Hollywood studios then approached him, asking him to adapt it as a screenplay. This being the eighties, the fact that the play had an all-female cast did not dissuade producers from thinking this play could make a hit film, and there was a bidding war. "I think it spoiled me for the rest of my career, actually, because we had so many suitors for the film," Harling says.

But one producer, Ray Stark, knew that for the movie to work, it had to feel real, and the best way to start that was to film it in the town where the story actually happened. And so, when Stark suggested making the movie in Natchitoches, among the places that Susan had known and the people who had known her, Harling signed with him.

Harling and his parents, Robert and Margaret, then had the extraordinary experience of watching their lives and the lives of their friends being played out in their hometown by some of the best-known actors of their day: "I had what was called 'casting consultation,' and they were very generous about that and let me hang around for all that." He smiles. "But when they come to you and say, Sally [Field] wants to play your mother and Shirley [MacLaine] wants to play Ouiser, and Olympia [Dukakis]—she just won the Oscar two or three weeks ago [Best Supporting Actress, in *Moonstruck*]—she'll be Clairee, well, you're not going to say no."

Being a southern family, they were, understandably, especially excited at the prospect of Dolly Parton playing the beauty parlor owner, Truvy: "Dolly was a little more glamorous than the original woman Truvy was based on, but that's just to be expected," says Harling, with southern sangfroid.

Meg Ryan was originally cast to play Shelby, but she dropped out when she got the lead in *When Harry Met Sally*. The near-unknown Julia Roberts was cast in her stead "and as soon as I saw that smile I said, 'There's Susan,'" Harling recalls.

Roberts visited the Harlings frequently, looking through their family albums and hearing stories about Susan from people who knew her in the town. Field, on the other hand, kept more to herself, wanting to create her own character, "and my mother, being a southern belle, would never want to impose. Also, if you're a woman from a small southern town and Sally Field is playing you in a movie, you go, Okay, you go, girl, whatever you do is fine by me."

Although some things in the film were changed for dramatic effect—whereas Shelby collapses at home with her baby son, Susan in fact fell into a coma in the hospital—the movie was remarkably true to the women and their stories, Harling says. His mother did in fact donate her kidney to her daughter, his sister did risk everything to have a baby, and the women the characters were based on talked just as they do in the film, in "bumper sticker slogans," as Harling puts it: "Your husband is a boil on the butt of humanity"; "If you can't say anything nice, come sit by me."

"What I wanted to show was the strength of these women, and the strength they gave each other," says Harling, who then went on to write *Soapdish*, also starring Sally Field, in the nineties. "I enjoy writing women's emotional journeys, but it's hard today to get movies made that aren't based on comic books. Character-driven films are the domain of the independents which a studio is never going to attack because they're all corporations. It's getting harder and harder to [get films made] with human roles, and a part of that is that it's much harder to get films made with women's roles."

"I don't think that *Steel Magnolias* would be considered 'industry friendly' today," says Dukakis with more than a touch of wryness.

Where once studios made women's movies, now they make "the negative sisterhood movie," to use Wesley Morris's memorable phrase. This is what the women's movie has become today and it is a bafflingly popular genre, one that suggests the women hate each other and should be duly punished for their stupidity by having to spend their lives fighting over men and being humiliated on-screen as much as possible. You know these movies: they're 2009's *Bride Wars*, 2014's *The Other Woman*, the toxic glut of overly monikered films like *What to Expect When You're Expecting*, *He's Just Not That Into You*, *I Don't Know How She Does It*, pretty much anything starring Kate Hudson.

One could argue that this genre was kick-started in the eighties. *Working Girl*, as discussed in the chapter on *Baby Boom*, is a perfect example of the genre, in which Melanie Griffith and Sigourney Weaver engage in a wearily predictable catfight over their job, ostensibly, but boring Harrison Ford, in actuality. *The Witches of Eastwick* could also be described as an anti-sisterhood movie, but that film—starring Michelle Pfeiffer, Susan Sarandon, and Cher, all obsessed with Jack Nicholson's penis—ultimately satirized the genre.

Negative sisterhood movies are now the default style for what were once romcoms and women's movies: movies consisting of women hating each other and competing with one another. What's strange is that these films are all less successful than the traditional women's movies such as *Steel Magnolias* ever were. So if you want to know how little Hollywood cares about women today, watch a negative sisterhood movie.

Everyone knows that the representation of women in movies today is bad. Even Faludi, who raged so passionately against the representation of women in eighties movies, had to admit that, in the early nineties, film roles for women had dropped so far that male characters made up two-thirds of people on-screen, and that number hasn't changed since. When Faludi returned to *Backlash*, she wrote in the new introduction to the 2005 edition: "Back in the 80s . . . were single women breaking courtship rules and taking the sexual initiative? 'You'll turn into a psycho killer and meet your maker in an overflowing bathtub!' the Hollywood mullahs decreed. Ah, the good old days." After all, she concluded, "There are some things worse than a backlash."

In 2013, women made up only 21.8 percent of the crews of the one hundred top-grossing films in the United States, and that number has remained pretty steady for the past twenty years, although the numbers get worse the higher up the credits you go. In 2014, for example, only 1.9 percent of the hundred top-grossing films released in the United States were directed by women.* It's impossible not to see the connection between that and the fact that between 2007 and 2014 women made up only 30.2 percent of all speaking or named characters in the hundred top-grossing films released in the United States. As Manohla Dargis put it, "For every 2.3 male characters who say 'Dude,' there is just one woman saying, 'Hello?!' "† But people within the industry say it is far from the complete picture and what's actually changed is what studios will allow them to do. "I love directing women but, for so long, it's just been a nonstarter," says Paul Feig, the director of female-led hits *Bridesmaids*, *The Heat*, and *Spy*. "You'd go into meetings and people would say, 'Oh, a female lead? Can't you make her male?' A movie starring a male is normal but a movie starring a woman is a gimmick, and it just didn't make any sense to me."

And this is as true of movies aimed at children as at adults. In 2006 Feig signed on to direct the children's film *Unaccompanied Minors*, about a boy and his little sister causing chaos in an airport.

"It wasn't until I got into the rewriting that I learned it was based on a real story that had happened to a girl and her sister. Again you go, 'Gosh, they just changed the lead girl to a boy—that's really aggravating!' It was never entertained that it could have been a girl in the lead. It wasn't even an issue," he recalls with a laugh of frustration. It is actually quite a common practice in Hollywood movies to change the gender of a lead character from female to male. At the Cannes Film Festival in 2015 director Denis Villeneuve said that the screenwriter of their thriller *Sicario* had been urged to change the gender of the script's female lead.

---

* Stacy L. Smith et al., "Inequality in 700 Popular Films," Annenberg School for Communication and Journalism, University of Southern California.

† Manohla Dargis, "Report Finds Wide Diversity Gap Among 2014's Top Grossing Films," *New York Times*, August 5, 2015.

"The screenplay was written some years ago and people were afraid that the lead part was a female character. I know several times [Taylor Sheridan] had been asked to rewrite the role. . . . But these guys had the guts to keep it as it was."

Ultimately, the role was played by Emily Blunt to critical acclaim.

"And this whole debate about whether female superheroes can open their own movie—just fucking do it!" adds Feig. "What is the big debate about it? Why does Wonder Woman have to be part of an ensemble? Why can't she come out of the gate in her own movie? Why are we so precious about it? To me it's not even an issue, but that's why it's so funny that it's an issue!"

The common argument in defense of the current low representation of women in movies is that studios aren't sexist—they're simply looking after the economics. So while women will see movies starring men and women, men will see only movies starring men—in other words, it's the audiences who are sexist. This problem is hardly exclusive to the film world. The books website Goodreads recently surveyed 40,000 of its members and found that readers overwhelmingly preferred books written by authors of their own gender: 90 percent of men's 50 most-read books were by men and 45 of the 50 most-read books by women were written by women. Currer Bell, George Sands, George Eliot, and Robert Galbraith didn't need 40,000 people to confirm that readers judge authors by their gender.*

Yet just as the Goodreads survey found that male and female readers alike both rated women authors more highly than male

---

* One of my favorite newspaper columns in the world is the *New York Times'* By the Book series, in which famous people discuss their favorite writers. Almost invariably, readers cleave to their own gender: Bruce Springsteen, for example, mentioned thirty-seven authors, only two of whom were women.

ones, so audiences—male and female—have repeatedly proven how much they like movies with female protagonists. Recent films featuring female protagonists including *Bridesmaids*, *Frozen*, *The Help*, *Gravity*, and *The Heat* have all been enormous successes, while male-led ones like *The Lone Ranger* and *After Earth* have flopped. In fact, the biggest box-office disasters of all time all featured male protagonists, including *47 Ronin* (Keanu Reeves), *The 13th Warrior* (Antonio Banderas), *The Lone Ranger* (Johnny Depp and Armie Hammer), *Ishtar* (Warren Beatty and Dustin Hoffman), and *Heaven's Gate* (Christopher Walken and Kris Kristofferson). As yet, no one has taken the failure of these movies as proof that men aren't funny, men can't carry a movie, or that maybe audiences just don't like to watch men.*

The fact is, women's movies—the few that still come out—are generally very profitable. They don't make as much money as many men's films, but that's because action movies (which generally star men) are bigger productions with bigger marketing pushes, but also with higher costs. In fact, Silverstein's Women and Hollywood blog found in 2013 that movies with a female protagonist that year earned 20 percent more than movies with just a male protagonist, making $116 million compared to male-led ones making $97 million, even though, out of the 100 movies they sampled, only 16 had female protagonists. But as Amanda Hess pointed out: "We still don't know whether gender equality in films would constitute a smart economic

---

* *New York Times'* Manohla Dargis pointed out that when Michael Mann's 2001 film *Ali* failed to make back its costs, his career was barely affected and he directed big-budget films for Paramount and Universal soon after. When Kathryn Bigelow's 2002 adventure film, *K19: The Widowmaker*, didn't recoup its costs, she didn't make another film until 2007 and it was funded by a French company. "Ms. Bigelow is one of the greatest action directors working today, and it's hard not to wonder why failure at the box office doesn't translate the same for the two sexes," Dargis writes in "Women in the Seats but Not Behind the Camera," *New York Times*, December 10, 2009.

choice for Hollywood, because we've never gotten anywhere close to testing that assumption."

And so one woman, who started acting in the eighties, decided to try to rectify that. "*Thelma & Louise* [which came out in 1991] was my first experience with the difference between how media respond to something and how it turns out in real life," recalls Geena Davis. "All of the press was about, 'Get ready for many more female buddy pictures and road trip films.' And then . . . nothing. Same thing happened with [1992's] *A League of Their Own*: 'Proof that women's sports movies can make huge box office!' Name all of the female sports movies since then, right? This happens every few years, with the press anointing yet another female-starring film as the One That Will Change Everything, but nothing happens."

Davis made her film debut as a rarely clothed starlet in 1982's *Tootsie*, sharing a dressing room with a somewhat embarrassed cross-dressing Dustin Hoffman. Her roles throughout that decade were remarkably, even hilariously, varied, including playing an insect's girlfriend in *The Fly*, a temptress of aliens in *Earth Girls Are Easy*, a rubber-faced ghost in *Beetlejuice*, and a mercurial dog trainer in *The Accidental Tourist*, for which she won an Oscar. She still acts occasionally today—she had a small part in 2013's *In a World*, about sexism in the movie trailer business—but, like many actresses before her, she found that studios stopped calling once she was over forty:

When I was starting out it was the era of Meryl Streep, Sally Field, Jessica Lange, and Glenn Close getting nominated for movies with spectacular female roles in them. I had heard that great parts for women drop off at forty, but I thought, These women will change everything. It won't be a problem anymore when I get there. But it didn't change. Before forty, I was averaging about one movie a year. During my forties, I only made one movie. That's a big change. But I look back on that decade when I was coming up and there were so many movies about interesting women: *Frances*, *Places in the Heart*. They were the anomaly then, which is why women were still in the minority then according to the statistics, but those movies were still made.

In 2004, while staying at home with her then-toddler daughter, Davis noticed something odd about the movies and TV shows aimed at children: there were notably few female characters, and this "absolutely floored" her: "Then something else shocked me: NO one seemed to be seeing what I was seeing: not my friends (until I pointed it out), and not the decision makers in Hollywood, either. Whenever I brought the subject up, if I happened to be meeting with a studio executive or director, to a person the response was, 'Oh no, that's been fixed.' And they would very often name a movie with one female character in it as proof that gender inequality had been fixed! That's when I knew I needed the data."

Davis ended up sponsoring the largest amount of research ever done on gender depictions in entertainment media, covering more than a twenty-year span at the Annenberg School for Communication and Journalism at the University of Southern California. Inspired by this, she then launched the Geena Davis Institute on Gender in Media in 2007. The data the research and institute uncovered appalled her: "In family-rated films, crowd and group scenes contain only seventeen percent female characters. Seventeen percent! In animation and live-action. That means the fictitious worlds that are being created for kids have only about a seventeen percent female population. Why, in the twenty-first century, would we be training kids to see women as taking up far less space in the world than men?" she asks.

Nor is it just the numbers of women who are being represented:

it's how they're represented, full-stop, says Davis. "Female characters in animated G-rated movies [U.S. equivalent of a U], made for the youngest of kids, wear the same amount of sexually revealing clothing as the female characters in R-rated [U.S. equivalent of 18] movies. Astounding, isn't it? And in research, there are no fuzzy definitions; this is not sexy appearance in a generalized way. It's specifically revealing clothing. These findings highlight how seemingly innocuous children's fare can be sending a damaging message to kids: it's teaching kids to see women and girls as less important than men and boys, and that girls should be judged on their sex appeal," she says.

The sexualization of young women on-screen is—as will surprise precisely no one—getting more extreme. In a study of the top five hundred films of 2012, 31.6 percent of female characters were featured in sexy clothes (compared to 7 percent of male ones) and 31 percent were at least partially naked (compared to 9.4 percent of male ones). Even more creepily, actresses aged between 13 and 20 are more likely to be sexualized than those between 21 and 39 (ugh—21! who would want to see such a hag naked, amirite??), and the number of near-naked female teenagers increased on-screen between 2007 and 2012 by 32.5 percent.

In 2011 women accounted for 33 percent of all characters, but only 11 percent of protagonists. In 2013 one journalist calculated that 90 percent of the film screenings showing near her in Washington, D.C., were stories about men, and the ratio would have been even worse if she didn't live in a major city. That year, women made up only 15 percent of protagonists in the biggest movies from the United States. And as *New York* magazine pointed out, it has been thus for the past twenty-five years.

Statistics don't necessarily tell the full story, of course. For a start, the figures from 1980–89 don't look much better: according to the Annenberg Public Policy Center, at the University of Pennsylvania, only 29 percent of the "main characters" in a movie were women. But as Amy Bleakley, who conducted the more recent study, points out, they did not take into consideration the context of the women's roles, such as whether they were the protagonists or near-nameless girlfriends.

"We can see that women are not on-screen anymore," says journalist Melissa Silverstein. "They are not protagonists in films and they're not leaders, and this says a lot about how women are valued in our culture."

"Women have advanced, while much of the movie industry has not," writes the *New York Times'* film critic Manohla Dargis.

The theory that women are being pushed out of movies in order to appeal to the Chinese market doesn't necessarily stand up, Davis says. After all, according to the latest report from the institute, China has a pretty good record of featuring women in its own films: in films made by China aimed at children and young people released between January 1, 2010, and May 1, 2013, 30 percent featured casts with a gender balance. In equivalent films from the United States, precisely zero films featured a gender balance. In fact, according to the study, it's not China that's the problem, but America. When looking at, again, equivalent films made by the United Kingdom, 38 percent featured a female character, 30 percent featured a female lead, and 20 percent featured casts with a gender balance. In U.S.-British coproductions, these figures plummeted to, respectively, 23.6 percent, zero, and zero.

But Davis stops short of suggesting that any kind of nefariousness lies behind this. Instead, she puts it down to something that is, in fact, worse: blitheness. "There is no plot against women in my industry; creators are simply not aware of how many female characters they're leaving out!" she says.

Bleakley suggests that the increasing reliance on violence in movies also plays a part: "Some of the more profitable movies (including PG-13) feature a lot of violent content, which historically has primarily involved male characters," she says. "[Also], most successful writers and directors are men, and they may be drawn toward telling stories through perspectives and characters they are most familiar or comfortable with—i.e., other men."

Kathleen Turner, Davis's castmate in *The Accidental Tourist*, also played an extraordinarily wide range of roles in the eighties, and this was a conscious decision on her part: "Once I have explored and created a character, I have no desire to repeat it so I automatically look for the thing that's the opposite," she says, in that voice that's only gotten more impressive with age. "So from playing a femme fatale in *Body Heat* I went to *The Man with Two Brains*, which is a takeoff on the femme fatale, to *Romancing the Stone*, which is a woman who doesn't know anything about her sexual power, then to *Crimes of Passion*, which is a woman who sells herself on Sunset Boulevard for fifty dollars. Pretty much each role is a contrast to the one before."

These days, Turner says, she sees not only fewer studio films for women ("and that's just fucking unbelievable"*) but also less variety in the roles: "For years I have been rather disgusted by the studio films coming out of Hollywood because the women are such clichés. Women in particular today are encouraged to build on their successes, by which they mean play the character that sells, and I don't know if audiences really want to see that. That poor woman, Jennifer Aniston, has been playing the same role for twenty years. I'm like, come on, honey, aren't you bored?"†

---

*An interview with Kathleen Turner is pretty much all that you want it to be. Sadly I can't print everything she told me without fear of being sued for libel by half of Hollywood. But if you ever have the opportunity to spend an afternoon with her, I highly recommend it.

†Told you.

Paul Feig agrees with Geena Davis up to a point: yes, he says, there's no nefarious plot against women in Hollywood, but women are being deliberately excluded from movies. "Right after I did *Bridesmaids*, a very successful producer said to me, 'You're going to have to be careful because you're going to be put in this niche of directing women and that's a problem.'" He continues: "You know, Hollywood is not an altruistic town. We are in business and if someone gives you a compelling business reason [for not having women in a movie], then you have to actively change that because the idea of going, 'Well, okay, I guess we can't do it!'—that's a nonstarter for me. You say, how do we solve this?"

The answer, he decided long ago, was to make big commercial movies that starred women that would be so successful that "there would no longer be an argument." But he had to wait awhile until he had enough power in the industry to do this. In 2007 his friend and frequent colleague Judd Apatow, who by then had quite a lot of power, gave him the script for *Bridesmaids* "and I fell in love with it—the idea that all these women have roles in it, it seemed like a dream to me," he says.

Bridesmaids was, fortunately, a huge success ("And thank God. I was in a terrible panic half the time making the movie thinking, If we fuck this up . . . But how terrible that there was such pressure!" Feig recalls), and on the back of that, he was able to make *The Heat*, a female buddy cop movie. When we talk, he has just finished making *Spy*, a very funny and hugely fun female spy film, starring Melissa McCarthy, Miranda Hart, and Allison Janney, three women all over the age of forty and hugely talented ("I'm a huge fan of James Bond and I just thought, Why not make it with a woman? That's interesting!") and he has just been confirmed to write and direct an all-female version of *Ghostbusters* "because that sounds really fun to me!"

"You know, if Hollywood thought monkeys starring in movies were the highest-grossing thing, then all you'd see is monkeys starring in movies. You can't look to Hollywood to fight a cause, you have to look to individual filmmakers to care and to do it well enough so that it makes money," he says. "And the success of [female-led international hit] movies like *The Hunger Games* and *Lucy* starts to open the door. Why just sit there with the door closed?"

Feig's films are probably the closest Hollywood will come today to making classic women's movies. In *Bridesmaids* and especially *The Heat*, what's at stake isn't whether a woman will Get a Man but rather the maintenance of a female friendship. *Bridesmaids* has plenty of rom with its com, and it does end with the obligatory closing-scene kiss, but the film takes pains to emphasize that the real happy ending comes from the two main female characters becoming friends again and the rest of the bridesmaids becoming friends with each other. By the time Feig made *Spy*, he had enough clout to go against the grain. The movie features a heroine explicitly rejecting the romantic ending so as to go out for dinner with her female best friend instead. None of these films has the gentle domesticity of *Terms of Endearment* or *Steel Magnolias*, but they were clearly made by someone who likes women, respects them, and finds them interesting. Feig might have to frontload his films with some gross-out gags (*Bridesmaids*) and action (*The Heat*, *Spy*) and a few too many self-deprecating jokes from Melissa McCarthy, but if that means good movies are being made that star women and get proper distribution, that feels like a trade-off worth making.

So does he think things are going to get better for women in movies?

"Oh yeah. It's so obvious that [women starring in movies] draws people to theaters and makes money. Things just have to change. They have to. People won't accept it anymore." And he's right—they won't. Ever since it was announced, there have been plenty of on-line grumblings about Feig's plans for an all-women's *Ghostbusters*, which are all about as logical and convincing as the similar grump-ings about the prospect of a black James Bond. "The Ghostbusters were always men!" "You can't just change a man's skin tone!" "What next, a gay Superman?" and so on. (It turns out that there are A LOT of adults out there who don't quite understand the difference between fictional characters and actual people.) But away from the loud and loony fringes of the Internet and right-wing media, most people accept that the current status quo about women's representa-tion in film has become just too ridiculous to be maintained, and filmmakers such as Feig have proven that there is no economic argu-ment for it to be that way.

As a rule, I can't stand remakes of eighties films, as they speak of a studio system that has no ideas of its own and completely fails to understand the joy of the original films. And yet, as an adult who just about accepts that Peter Venkman is not a real person, I couldn't be more thrilled by the prospect of Feig's film. By casting women in *Ghostbusters*, Feig not only makes the remake feel like it has something to say beyond just a desire to milk a familiar name, he is showing that women really can, contrary to current Hollywood view, carry a franchise, by giving them the best franchise film of all time. A remake of *Ghostbusters* with men would feel both sad and pointless—a remake with women feels like a hopeful glimpse into the future, one in which women are trusted with genuine event movies that celebrate friendship as opposed to catfights. With bonus estrogen and proton packs. That's my kind of women's movie.

Baby Boom

When I was a kid, I had a very clear picture of what my adult life would be like. Every day I'd stride—not walk, STRIDE—into a steel and glass office building in an Armani skirt suit, pantyhose, high heels, and a camel-colored coat, fresh from a 7 a.m. salon appointment, clutching a briefcase in one hand and a paper cup of black coffee in the other, my Ferragamo heels click-click-clicking authoritatively on the sidewalk. Walking alongside me through the giant marble entryway to my office building would be two men in Brooks Brothers suits, talking urgently about how we had to close the Del Monte deal that day. As we got out of the elevator, I'd calmly reassure them that I had everything in hand and that they really needed to relax more, then I'd stride off while they gazed after me with expressions that suggested an equal mixture of awe, loathing, and lust. When they talked about me later they'd refer to me as "Killer," my office nickname. I'd then go to my corner office, handing my coat to my secretary Tom on my way in (Tom would then bring in a cappuccino, made just the way he knew I liked it), and I'd make various important-sounding phone calls before meeting my silver-haired boss, Chesterton, for lunch at a new French place "downtown" with white tablecloths and white wine. Chesterton and I would have a father-daughter-like relationship, with absolutely nothing improper going on there: I would look up to him as a mentor and he'd look fondly upon me as the child he should have had. The afternoon would be taken up with meetings in gigantic boardrooms, where I'd close the Del Monte deal, of course, and everyone would shake their heads in murmuring wonderment at the Killer's killer instinct. Then in the evening, my camel coat and I would meet my not-quite-as-high-powered boyfriend for dinner at a darling Italian place "uptown," but we'd have to stay at mine as my personal trainer was coming over the next morning at six.

Most children take their template for adulthood from their parents. Some look to their teachers for inspiration. I took my cues entirely from eighties movies about working women, and, my gosh, there were so many to choose from. There was *Working Girl*, most obviously, in which a young woman hacks her way to the top of the corporate ladder through a combination of some smarts, a lot of deception, and even more sex (tchuh! typical woman, amirite?). But there was also *Die Hard*, in which John McLane's (Bruce Willis, of course) wife Holly (the brilliantly named Bonnie Bedelia) does something that requires her to look very serious all the time for a Japanese company. Less generally enduring but no less personally formative was the Michael J. Fox yuppie comedy *The Secret of My Success*, in which Christy (Helen Slater) pushes her glasses up on the bridge of her nose very authoritatively in board meetings in between typing important memos and having sex with her boss, which is amazing to watch as a grown-up because that's EXACTLY what my life is like now.*

Then there were all the kick-ass female hard workers who worked beyond Wall Street: Holly Hunter producing TV news in *Broadcast News*; Cher being the best damned accountant on the Lower East Side in *Moonstruck* (Cher as an accountant—now there's some out-of-the-box casting); Meg Ryan as a successful journalist in *When Harry Met Sally*; Amy Irving running a bookstore in *Crossing Delancey*; Kathleen Turner playing a successful romance novelist in *Romancing the Stone* and *The Jewel of the Nile*. But there was no movie that was more influential on my fantasies about being an adult woman than the great 1987 comedy about the difficulties of combining work and motherhood, *Baby Boom*, cowritten and produced by Nancy Meyers.

I meet up with Meyers on a warm September afternoon in London the week her latest film, *The Intern*, was being released in the United Kingdom. Like *Baby Boom*, *The Intern* features a protagonist who is a working mother (Meyers describes the two films as "companion pieces") and, as chance would have it, my interview with Meyers is my first as a working mother: three weeks to the day earlier, I gave birth to twins, my first children. So when I turn up, breast pump in ridiculous designer handbag,† hormonal head all over the

---

*Legal disclaimer: that is not at all what my life is like now. I still can't even walk in high heels, for God's sake.

†In the early days of parenthood I had a theory that if I carried around the baby stuff in a fancy bag I would feel more like me, my old self, and show I hadn't collapsed under the weight of motherhood. You'd think that someone who watched *Baby Boom* more than a million times—in which the lead character tries to kid herself in one scene that if she can push her baby in her stroller just that little bit quicker she'll prove to herself that she is on top of things—would be a little more self-aware about these kinds of misguided attempts at overcompensation.

place, utterly determined to act like nothing's changed when clearly everything has, I realize that I'm not merely interviewing Nancy Meyers—I'm pretty much a character in a Nancy Meyers movie.

Meyers has always taken pride, she says, in "telling women's stories." She herself looks strikingly like a character in one of her own films—in fact, she looks a lot like Diane Keaton, who has appeared in four of Meyers's films—and she has always talked about how she uses her own life as inspiration for her films.* More recently, that has meant making movies about fifty-something divorcées, such as *Something's Gotta Give* (which starred Keaton) and *It's Complicated* (which starred that not-a-million-miles-away-from-Meyers-herself Meryl Streep). Even though she's made only two films about this world in her very successful thirty-five-year career, Meyers has become closely associated with this specific demographic because she is, amazingly, just about the only filmmaker around with enough clout to be allowed to cater to this apparently niche (but actually extremely large and lucrative) audience. No amount of box-office success seems to convince studios that it's worth occasionally making films for fifty-five-year-old women as opposed to aiming always for their teenage sons.

"My kind of movie, one with human stories, is not the kind of film studios have wanted to make for a while. They've been making Superman, Batman, Everyman films—comic book movies, gigantic action movies, and guy comedies. And all those kinds of movies, [studio executives] think only a man can direct, as if only a man

---

* Predictably, though, critics have often used the fact that Meyers parlays her life into her work as proof that her work is somehow lightweight, or limited, or cheating, or just for women (as though women were a minority group instead of half the human race). When, say, Judd Apatow does this, however, he is praised for being "honest," "open," "accessible." Don't worry, I won't bang on about this too much—there's only so much room in a footnote, after all—but it is predictable, given that when a woman writes about herself she is being narcissistic but a man who does the same is brave.

can direct dinosaurs, or flying people, or whatever. Meanwhile my movies get called 'female-centric,' even though they star very big actors [including Jack Nicholson, Alec Baldwin, and Robert De Niro]. Studio executives make movies happen and the executive community is a boys' club. They like each other, they like to go out with each other and meet up for a drink, so being a woman in that world is hard. So it's been a dark time for personal films and comedies that didn't only star men. It was a dark time for me—it was difficult! But I hung in there and a couple of those superhero films didn't do so well and things swung back my way," Meyers says (just as her films smuggle bleak themes—infidelity, widowhood, divorce—beneath a deceptively easygoing surface, so Meyers has a knack for smiling while making rather solemn statements).

But if Meyers sounds sanguine about this, that is probably because she has been dealing with sexism in the film industry since the start of her career. While working on her first film, *Private Benjamin*, she tried to hide her burgeoning pregnancy out of concern it would cost her the job. ("Can you imagine?") Such anxiety is understandable, given that the studio had it written into her contract that she was never allowed to be on set without being accompanied by one of her male coproducers.

"I looked at this and said to my lawyer, 'Should I agree to this, this is absurd!' And of course, me in 2015 would have taken a red pen to it and said, 'That's ridiculous.' But as a twenty-nine-year-old making my first movie I laughed at it and was obviously insulted, but I didn't go to the mat about it, so it remained in the contract," recalls Meyers.

Even after Meyers had achieved huge professional success, including being nominated for an Oscar for *Private Benjamin*, film executives still insisted on treating her as if she were an intern. When she and her partner Charles Shyer would go into studios for meetings,

Meyers recalls, "they'd direct every questions to [Shyer]. Even when I'd answer, they'd then look at him to make sure it was the right answer."

"Unfortunately, some men are more comfortable talking to men. If Nancy were the director on our movies, the studio brass would be considerably more uptight," Shyer said at the time of *Baby Boom*'s release. (Shyer directed the film, Meyers produced it, and they wrote it together.) Considering only 1.9 percent of the one hundred top-grossing films released in the United States in 2014 were directed by a woman, it seems safe to say the studio brass are still pretty "uptight" about this issue. In any event, it was precisely these kinds of experiences that inspired the writing of *Baby Boom*.

Certainly there had been movies about women who work before— *His Girl Friday* and *Adam's Rib* being two of the more obvious—but *Baby Boom* was the first to look at how repulsively unaccommodating the corporate world was, and remains, to mothers. The film tapped a real nerve, and it was hotly discussed in the media at the time. Think of *Baby Boom* as the *Lean In* of its time, but with a more realistic view of the business world's limitations to accommodate motherhood than Facebook COO Sheryl Sandberg's book provided.

Baby Boom tells the story of J. C. Wiatt (Keaton), who is so successful in her job as a management consultant that she's known as the "Tiger Lady." (As will become increasingly clear here, my fantasy about adulthood was basically a bad sitcom rip-off of *Baby Boom*.) She lives with a boyfriend, Steven (Harold Ramis), who likes face packs, brief sex, and spreadsheets (swoon!). By day, she has lunches with her white-haired boss Fritz (Sam Wanamaker) and orders around evil young office upstart Ken (James Spader).* Nothing can slow the Tiger Lady down.

---

* She lives with Harold Ramis and she works with James Spader: not only is *Baby Boom* my fantasy about adulthood, it is my ultimate sexual fantasy.

Nothing, that is, except unexpectedly inheriting a baby from a dead relative. This baby, Elizabeth, is, despite being the cutest baby ever conceived, so horrific to those in J.C.'s world that she loses, in short order, her boyfriend, her partnership prospects, and finally her job, much to evil Ken's delight. So she moves to Vermont, shacks up with a hot vet (Sam Shepard*), invents gourmet baby food, and makes an absolute fortune. Her former colleagues in New York then try to buy her baby food company and she returns there to tell them where to stick it, because she still hates James Spader. She then comes back to Vermont to run her company and make out with Sam Shepard in his office, the end.

You are presumably now getting an idea of why this film made such a deep impression on me.[†‡] And not just on me. As journalist Megan Reynolds pointed out in a 2014 article, *Baby Boom* created the mold from which movies and TV shows about working mothers have been fashioned ever since, from J.C.'s power suit wardrobe to her struggles with motherhood. This has influenced all depictions of the theme since, from the good (Cynthia Nixon in *Sex and the City*) to the bad (Sarah Jessica Parker in the execrable *I Don't Know How She Does It*).

But *Baby Boom* wears its feminism more prominently on its sleeve than any of its copycat followers, certainly more than its contemporary *Working Girl*, which is just one of the reasons I prefer the former to the latter.

Working Girl is more interested in class snobbery than feminism, with the film emphasizing from the start that Tess's (Melanie Griffith) accent and non–Ivy League background are holding her

---

* Like I said, this movie is SERIOUS sexual fantasy fodder.
† Have I mentioned all the sexual fantasy stuff yet?
‡ It also helped that the town she moves to in Vermont is called Hadleyville. These things are extremely important when you're eight.

back, in contrast to her elegantly spoken patrician boss, Katherine (Sigourney Weaver). But the movie then sacrifices this potentially interesting path by turning the story into a predictable and ridiculous catfight between Tess and Katherine over the exceptionally dull Jack (Harrison Ford). *Baby Boom*, by contrast, lays its feminism out on the table from the start. The film opens with a montage of images of women going to work in New York City, clutching copies of the *Wall Street Journal* and cups of coffee. These women, the (female) voice-over says, "grew up being told to marry doctors and lawyers and instead became doctors and lawyers." These women, *Baby Boom*'s audience is told, rather thrillingly, "are the phenomenon of our time" and are "turning thousands of years of tradition on its ear."

But the film's promises of the women's movement's forward propulsion look a little sad in retrospect, considering what's come since. When I watched the opening of the first episode of *Sex and the City* back in 1998, I was delighted at how the program used strikingly similar imagery and narration to *Baby Boom*'s opening, with shots of working women marching down Manhattan sidewalks while Carrie (Sarah Jessica Parker), in voice-over, saluted these ladies who "travel and pay taxes, and spend four hundred dollars on a pair of Manolo Blahnik strappy sandals." But whereas *Baby Boom*'s tone is celebratory, *Sex and the City*'s shifts swiftly into one of baffled sadness, noting how these women are "alone." Instead of applauding women's progress, the HBO show opened with a self-flagellating apology for it. This shift is dismayingly apt considering the difference in attitudes between the women who made the show and film. Whereas Meyers proudly describes herself as a feminist ("Of course!"), *Sex and the City*'s Sarah Jessica Parker, like a wearisome number of female celebrities today, shies nervously away from the term, insisting in interviews instead that she is "a humanist." (Demi Moore and—O fallen idols!—Madonna also use that bullshit fudge.) Can't possibly alienate all those male fans of *SATC* and *I Don't Know How She Does It* with icky feminism, right, SJP?* If anyone watching *Baby Boom* today finds themselves wondering why this film feels still so relevant and why so many of the issues raised in this movie made more than thirty years ago—such as women's basic rights in the workplace in the first world—are still a problem, here's at least part of your answer. If even prominent and privileged women and modern TV shows and films made for women feel embarrassed about standing up specifically for women, then it's hardly a surprise that sexism in male-dominated systems continues to thrive.

But *Baby Boom* is not rose tinted about feminism or, more specifically, its limitations and the sacrifices forced on women who care about professional success, because this is what the whole film is about. Meyers and Shyer researched *Baby Boom* by talking to women in the corporate world about the pressures they experienced, especially regarding motherhood:

"When Charlie and I interviewed women CEOs, we found that more than a few were told by their bosses when they got pregnant that they should have abortions if they wanted promotions," she recalled at the time. Meyers, by contrast, was able to work on this movie with her family, even bringing her young daughter onto the set with her. "I went into labor [with her second daughter] in the editing suite!" she laughs. But even in this supportive setup, she still knew about the compromises working mothers face. In one instance, Meyers was late for a newspaper interview because her older daughter wanted to go to FAO Schwarz, mirroring the struggles of the lead character in her film to look professional with a baby on her

---

* Other modern female celebrities who refuse to describe themselves as feminists include Shailene Woodley, Marion Cotillard, Katy Perry, Melissa Leo, Carrie Underwood, Kelly Clarkson, and, most dismayingly of all, Björk.

hip. Never let it be said that Meyers knows not of what she writes.

Even by the eighties, the most overdebated and boring question was, Can a woman have it all? The film has as little interest in that question as any other woman with half a brain cell. So it settles the matter early on: no, a woman cannot have it all, not in the way the film originally sets out. When J.C.'s boss takes her out to lunch to discuss a partnership, he warns her about "the sacrifices you'll have to make." He continues, "A man can be a success and have a full personal life. I'm lucky—I can have it all." J.C. knows all this already and leans across the table without an iota of doubt on her face: "I don't want it all. I don't." This disparity between the sexes is not fair, the movie says, but it is the reality, and within that clear-eyed assessment of the corporate world the film has some fun mocking the institutional sexism. In one scene, two of the head honchos discuss the possibility of making J.C. partner.

"Do we have any women partners?" one asks the other.

"Mmm, down in Chicago," his colleague replies.

"Right, right—the redhead!" says the first, satisfied.

No matter how successful a woman becomes, she's still known only by her hair color.

Again, this inability to have it all, at least at the same time, was something else Meyers knew intimately and, like the film, she did not spend time fretting about it—she worked around it. When asked in one interview at the time of *Baby Boom*'s release why she was the producer and her male partner the director, she replied, "To direct a movie is an around-the-clock commitment, and now, because of [our daughters] Annie and Hallie, I just have to be home by 7:30 to feed them and put them to sleep. I think we're flexible enough that on our next project, Charlie might produce and I might direct, because I'd like to very much." Meyers did eventually move into directing when her daughters were older in 1998, with *The Parent Trap*. As chance would have it, she and Shyer, married at this point, promptly got divorced. Not all stories in the real world about women get to have a Meyers-esque happy ending.*

J.C., meanwhile, who "graduated first in her class at Harvard," as the film emphasizes, is most certainly a feminist. She explains to Steven she couldn't give Elizabeth up for adoption because the adoptive mother "called her husband 'sir.'" Later, when she reads Elizabeth a bedtime story she changes the ending of *Sleeping Beauty*: "The princess said, 'Thank you for waking me—I overslept and I have medical school today so I can become a doctor like all women can be,'" she coos to her baby. Unlike certain modern female celebrities, this is not a film that feels any qualms about showing its allegiances regarding gender politics.

Just as J.C. finds a way to accommodate feminism within the not generally feminist strictures of children's fairy tales, so the movie sets about finding a way for her to achieve professional success and personal satisfaction within the not generally feminist strictures of a Hollywood movie—and it succeeds. *Working Girl*, on the other hand, happily maintains the usual gender roles, and endorses those who do likewise. Jack is originally attracted to Tess when he spots her at a work event wearing a pretty dress: "You're the first woman I've seen at one of these things who dresses like a woman," he murmurs admiringly. Later, when he's praising Tess's intelligence to a potential business colleague, he says, "She's your man," because women wear pretty dresses but men are smart. Meanwhile, the film's humiliation of the character of Katherine begins when she starts talking about her biological clock to Jack, much to his embarrassment and

---

* Although it's worth noting that Meyers has had notably more professional success than her now ex-husband since they split. This might not be the kind of happy ending that Meyers would write, but it is one that would please her characters.

repulsion. Women should be women—but not to the point when it gets awkward for men, apparently. In *Baby Boom*, by contrast, the hot vet is utterly unfazed when he first meets J.C. and she mentions sadly how long it's been since she had sex.

Which brings us to a very key element in *Baby Boom*: J.C.'s love life. J.C. starts off with Steven, who, as an investment banker, is her professional equal. He loves that she loves her job, teasing her fondly about her addiction to work and working happily alongside her in bed. She then ends up with Dr. Jeff Cooper, a vet who is vaguely impressed by her success but generally unbothered by it. In other words, J.C.'s ambition and success are, at best, sexy and, at worst, not an issue.

This is no anomaly to *Baby Boom*. One of my absolute favorite things about eighties movies set in the workplace is that male characters repeatedly fall for women who are emphatically more successful professionally than them, and that is part of their appeal. In *The Secret of My Success*, Christy is far more high-powered than Brantley (Michael J. Fox), who still works in the mailroom, and he is entranced by her partly because she represents, not a threat, but what he wants to be. In *Moonstruck*, Cher is an accountant whereas Nicolas Cage is a baker. In *Broadcast News*, Holly Hunter is senior to both Albert Brooks and William Hurt, and they both fall for her. Pleasingly, the film emphasizes that even though she ends up with neither of them, she does not then end up alone. In *Raising Arizona*, Holly Hunter (again) is so much more successful than her doting husband (Nicolas Cage, again) that they meet when she takes his mug shot each time he's arrested. In *Romancing the Stone*, novelist Joan Wilder (Kathleen Turner) is far more successful than renegade Jack Colton (Michael Douglas), and this ultimately saves them when potential killers recognize her and profess themselves to be fans.

"Poor Michael doesn't get much credit in that movie, does he?"

cackles Kathleen Turner delightedly. Turner adds she "deliberately looked for parts that were the opposite to what I did before" in the eighties, and she succeeded, playing both a femme fatale (*Body Heat*) and a prostitute (*Crimes of Passion*), a frustrated divorcée (*Peggy Sue Got Married*), and a contract killer (*Prizzi's Honor*).

Male characters who tell their female partners in eighties films to stop working are derided. In *Coming to America*, among Darryl's (Eriq La Salle) many faults is that he thinks "my lady shouldn't work," whereas Akeem (Eddie Murphy) came to the United States specifically to find an independent, intelligent woman with ambitions beyond being his wife (although I do think it unlikely that Lisa keeps her job in a fast-food restaurant once she becomes the Queen of Zamunda). In *St. Elmo's Fire*, Alec's (Judd Nelson) dickishness is demonstrated by his lack of respect for his girlfriend Leslie's (Ally Sheedy) job. "I have to have something for myself," she tells him. "Will you just for once not use as the excuse for not marrying me, *your goddamned career?*" he snarls back, dismissing her ambitions with a sneer. Yet he's so devoted to his career that he jettisons his dreams of being a Democratic senator in order to work for a Republican. Not even the assistant principal foresaw such duplicitousness in Bender.

"In movies from the 1970s and 1980s, you see the ascendancy of women, and that's because feminism was in the ascendancy and people were interested in it," says Melissa Silverstein, founder and editor of the website Women and Hollywood. "Movies didn't cost a billion dollars to make and filmmakers were able to make movies featuring women in positions of strong leadership."

Of course, not all eighties movies were totally on board with this crazy idea of women being high-powered. Katherine in *Working Girl* won't be celebrated by feminists anytime soon, as I mentioned earlier, and let's not even get started on poor Alex (Glenn Close), the deranged book editor in *Fatal Attraction*. In *Die Hard*, John McLane visits Los Angeles, where he is nearly killed by Alan Rickman's German accent, because his wife insisted on moving there for her career. And look what THAT gets her: a destroyed office, dead colleagues, traumatized children, and a beat-up husband. FEMINISM RUINS EVERYTHING. Thank heavens her husband happens to be in town to save her from this dreadful feminist mistake, right? Just to clarify that this woman is a selfish feminist witch, she insists on going by her maiden name, which is, like, totally outrageous—the film suggests—because her husband loves her so much, despite his flaws. But by the end of the movie, Holly has learned her lesson and obediently introduces herself as "Holly McLane," and her husband grins at his newly tamed wife. Yet these hilariously over-the-top counterarguments are vastly outweighed by the eighties movies that love career women—and they certainly love them a lot more than movies do now.

It's astonishing to look around now and realize how rarely movies today celebrate high-powered women, particularly movies aimed at women. Sure, you don't see too many films like *The Secret of My Success* (or, to a certain degree, *Baby Boom*), which celebrate the glamour of the corporate world, because that life isn't seen as quite as desirable as it was in the eighties. But you also don't really see women working at all. One recent study found that for every single career that the Bureau of Labor Statistics keeps data on, from bartenders to lawyers to nurses, women are represented on-screen far more rarely than they are in reality. Business professionals, the study's author Walt Hickey noted, are especially "dramatically underrepresented on screen": "When Hollywood depicts a prestigious occupation or a job that requires substantial post-secondary education, it usually goes with a man. And while the same is often true in the real world, it kind of sucks that movies are even worse," Hickey writes.

Similarly, a 2014 study confirmed what any audience member could already see: while male characters in modern films were most likely to be identified by their job, such as "a doctor or business executive" (61 percent of male characters to 34 percent of female ones), female characters were more likely to be identified by their personal life, such as "wife," "mother," and so on (58 percent of female characters to 31 percent of males).

At best, women in modern movies have safely "feminine" and unthreatening jobs, such as Kristen Wiig playing a (deeply improbable) pastry chef in *Bridesmaids* (and a failed one at that), or Elizabeth Banks in the appalling *What to Expect When You're Expecting*, playing the manager of a baby clothing store. In the execrable *Love, Actually*, the women are all pointedly professionally inferior to their male counterparts: Hugh Grant as the PM falls for the tea lady, Alan Rickman's sleazy design exec gets off with his secretary, and Colin Firth's character falls for his housekeeper, who doesn't even speak his language. Laura Linney, meanwhile, is utterly denied a boyfriend in that film because she commits the unforgivable error of having a brother who occasionally needs her—doesn't she know she must be available to her man at all times, for heaven's sake? Hilariously, the one plotline in the film in which the woman is the professional equal of the man involves two porn stars. That's where you can really win in the job market, ladies—porn!*

As for successful women, the modern-day female character cliché, aka the Ally McBeal stereotype, is so established it is damn near a trope by now: working woman—great at work, disastrous in her personal life! There are hundreds of examples, from Sandra Bullock

---

* And to be fair to the film's writer and director, Richard Curtis, porn is the one area of the film industry where women make as much money as men, so maybe he's making some fascinatingly meta point about gender equality in the movie industry. Or, quite possibly, not.

in *The Proposal* to Bullock (again) and Melissa McCarthy in *The Heat*. Better yet, they are punished for wanting to work, like Meryl Streep and Anne Hathaway in *The Devil Wears Chauvinistic Stereotypes*, whose husband and boyfriend respectively leave them because they dare work late occasionally, and that is depicted as a fairly reasonable reaction to their selfish ways. (Hathaway's boyfriend returns to her when she quits her job. Streep, presumably, remains alone for her stubborn insistence on staying employed.)

"There aren't enough movies that show working women who are content at their job, good at their job, and good bosses. If I see one more movie where the horrible boss is a woman who is hated by her employees . . ." says Meyers with an eye roll.

In *Baby Boom*, by contrast, J.C.'s personal and professional success are inextricably linked—the movie never suggests she has to sacrifice one for the other. If anything, it's the inverse: when she's happy at work, both in New York and Vermont, she's happy in her romantic life. Whereas Steven leaves J.C. because she inherits a baby, the men in *The Devil Wears Prada* leave their partners because they have jobs, which is a far more conservative message to send to women especially given that it was filmed nineteen years later.

Even more grating is the very popular modern trope that working women succeed by sleeping their way up the career ladder. For some reason, this is a particularly popular view of female journalists in modern movies, as filmmakers seem to think the only way a female journalist could possibly get a story, or even an interview, is by sleeping with her subject, which is an intriguing insight into how filmmakers see journalists, considering how much time they spend with them. Admittedly, given that I am a journalist—and (spoiler alert!) a female one—I probably find this shtick especially strange, but it is an amazingly popular setup in modern films. Amy Schumer

in *Trainwreck*, Dakota Johnson in *Fifty Shades of Grey*,* Rosario
Dawson in *Take Five*, Maggie Gyllenhaal in *Crazy Heart*, Angela
Bassett in *Mr. 3000*, Judy Greer in *Three Kings*, Katie Holmes in
Thank You for Smoking, Bridget Fonda in *The Godfather III*: all journalists, all apparently able to get a story only by use of their Magical
Vagina (an essential part of a modern female journalist's kit, along
with Frumpy Spectacles and an Ugly Jacket). Honestly, it's amazing
that female journalists get any work done at all, considering how
much time they spend dropping their underwear. Even smart comedies that could have spiked the cliché with their female journalist
characters, such as Christina Applegate in *Anchorman* or Christine
Taylor in *Zoolander*, merely rehash it. (It is depressingly needless to
say that male journalists in movies—from the good, such as David
Strathairn in *Good Night and Good Luck*, to the evil, such as Jake
Gyllenhaal in *Nightcrawler*—get ahead in their professions without
use of their genitals.) Eighties films weren't averse to this trope themselves—who among us can forget Linda Kozlowski's performance
as a *Newsday* journalist in Crocodile Dundee, sent off on a totally
believable assignment to Australia to hang out with grizzled Paul
Hogan for no obvious reason but to sleep with him by a swamp? But
it was nowhere near as popular as it is now, and, in fact, it was often
undermined. In 1981's *Absence of Malice*, Miami journalist Megan
(Sally Field) does end up sleeping with the dodgy salesman (Paul
Newman) whom she wrote about. But this ends up jeopardizing her
job and when the film ends it looks like she might actually be fired.
And Veronica (Geena Davis) in *The Fly* learns that the downside of
sleeping with a story subject is that you might end up pregnant with

---

* One minute you're interviewing someone, the next you're chained up in their sex
dungeon—it's a situation all female journalists have experienced.

a gigantic maggot and having to shoot your mutant lover. Meanwhile, Holly Hunter in *Broadcast News* pointedly doesn't sleep with anyone in her role as a news producer (although she does have something of a soft spot for the airhead anchor played by William Hurt) and duly rises to the top of her profession.

Exactly when things shifted for women in movies is impossible to date precisely, but Melissa Silverstein knows the decade when everything changed: "It was the nineties, for sure. That's when we saw the ascendancy of the blockbuster, which led to a regression of female characters. There was also a cultural backlash in America in the nineties after the Anita Hill hearings and the Bill Clinton scandal, and suddenly we're not seeing strong women in leadership roles on-screen anymore. With movies about working women in the seventies and eighties, we saw the struggle women were going through in the workplace represented on-screen. But movies today do not reflect the reality of women's lives today, especially working women's lives, and that's what makes people so angry."

Silverstein is right about disconnect between movies and reality, because what makes this fear in modern films about working women even more ridiculous is that women are increasingly the primary money earners in America. In America in 1980, the woman earned more than the man in only 10 percent of households; by 2011, this had risen to 24.3 percent. And guess what? Most Americans are absolutely fine about this. According to the study, 63 percent of Americans said it did not harm a marriage if the wife outearns her husband, a rise of more than 20 percent since 1997.[*] And yet movies do not reflect either this reality or attitude. "This is the backlash.

---

[*] Wendy Wang, Kim Parker, and Paul Taylor, "Breadwinner Moms," Pew Research Center, May 29, 2013.

The backlash comes when women make strides. The studio convention now is that movies work better when women characters have unthreatening jobs. They say audiences think it's cuter," says film producer Lynda Obst.

"The biggest cultural struggle in America now is white men holding on to power and we see that in superhero movies—white men saving the world, with women just there to be saved," says Silverstein. "The only job available to women in movies now is being a princess, and that is not a job that is actually available."

In films today, women are rarely celebrated when they are more successful than men. "To make a woman adorable you have to defeat her in the beginning. It's a conscious thing I do—abuse and break her, strip her of her dignity, and then she gets to live out our fantasies and have fun. It's as simple as making the girl cry, fifteen minutes into the movie," one female screenwriter told the *New Yorker* in 2011.[*]

Even in one of the more successful modern films about a working woman, 2000's *Erin Brockovich*, the eponymous character was, according to her real-life counterpart, sexed up and dumbed down in the film, presumably to make her less threatening. In the movie, when her boss (Albert Finney) asks Brockovich (Roberts) how she is going to find the documents she needs in an archive, she famously replies, "They're called boobs, Ed." The actual Brockovich dismissed this version of the story: "I don't know that I had in my mind set, I'm going to come in here and show my cleavage to get these documents. I really don't think I was operating at that level. . . . So, however you dress, it's your own personal style. I don't mean to offend anybody. That's just who I am, and I don't deliberately utilize it as a tool to get what I'm looking for," she said at a National Press Club luncheon. In

---

[*] Tad Friend, "Funny Like a Guy," *New Yorker*, April 11, 2011.

other words, contrary to what the film suggested, Brockovich relied on her brains to succeed, not her bosoms.

Whereas movies from the eighties sneered at the men who tell women to quit their job to focus on their love lives, movies today fully endorse that clearly ridiculous message. The previously mentioned 2015 Amy Schumer comedy, *Trainwreck*, opens with the now rarely acknowledged proposition that a female film character, Amy (Schumer), can love her "kick-ass job" as a magazine journalist, not be in a settled relationship, and be totally happy in herself. But because this movie was made in 2015, this setup is quickly shown to be a myth. The film mocks Amy's job from the beginning, sneering at the stupid articles she writes, which embarrass even her. In contrast, the movie is cringingly in love with her boyfriend Aaron's (Bill Hader) job as a sports doctor, featuring endless starry-eyed shots of him mixing with sports (male) celebrities. This is a notably common ploy in movies made in the past two decades: by having female characters work in jobs that can be dismissed as fluffy, such as fashion journalism (*The Devil Wears Prada*), it is then easier for the movie to mock them for caring about their jobs more than their boyfriends. When Amy and Aaron fight, he is scornful about not just her job but ostensibly the entire journalistic profession as something for those "who don't even try," and she miserably agrees with him. The film's happy ending shows a now-unemployed Amy attempting a routine with the Knicks cheerleaders since this, apparently, will prove that she does "try," unlike writing for a magazine: "I just wanted to impress you," she whimpers to Aaron as she lies on the pad between the net, injured and humiliated. Yay, women! (Aaron, it should be added at this point, has done absolutely nothing to try to win back Amy. But why should he? He's an important sports doctor.) Pretty hard to imagine J.C. abasing herself like that to anyone, let alone the sexy vet, and even harder to imagine *Baby Boom* feeling like she needs to do so. So regarding the issue brought up in the chapter on *When Harry Met Sally* about whether romcoms have died because it's too hard to translate them into the world of today, it would help if modern pop culture weren't so scared of working women, because working women are a modern-day reality. After all, in Ephron's film, Sally is a successful journalist and does pretty much the same job as Jess (Bruno Kirby), even writing for the same publications, because Ephron knew there was no divide between jobs for the men and jobs for the girly girls.

For Meyers, the issue that interests her isn't even whether men and women work differently but how little things have changed for women in the workplace. One of the reasons she returned to the subject of working mothers in *The Intern*, she says, is that she wanted to show "there are huge differences [being a working mother in 2015 from being one in 1987] and also problems which have not been solved." In Meyers's more recent film, Anne Hathaway plays Jules, a high-powered founder of an Internet fashion company, and one big difference between her and J. C. Wiatt is that when she encounters sexism in the workplace, instead of trying to work around it she calls it out, "and that," says Meyers, "is absolutely a generational thing."

But the responses to her movies, she says, prove how little things have changed. Her working female characters, she says, are repeatedly described as "workaholics" by male film critics. "She's hardworking, not a workaholic. Men don't even realize they're saying these things." Then there are the repeated sneers in reviews and blogs about the lush interiors of Meyers's films, although no one ever comments on the similarly deluxe houses in James L. Brooks's or Judd Apatow's movies. Focusing on the surfaces of Meyers's movies, reducing them to catalogs, is an easy way to belittle Meyers, her audience, and the female stories she tells.

"I know why people go to my movies and it's not to look at the houses," she says simply.

In her latest film, Meyers emphatically overturns all the now-expected clichés about a working mother: Jules is not a nasty boss, she is not hated by her employees, she has a happy home life and a husband who ends up begging her not to quit her job for him.*

"I wanted to show a woman who's starting her own business and who isn't punished for being ambitious—she keeps her family. She has a stay-at-home husband and a little girl who is not suffering because her mother works. Telling women's stories is something that's really important to me because there are so many people telling those other kinds of stories," she says.

Meyers is hopeful that the representation of women in movies will improve "just because the conversation is so out there now. I've been working for over thirty years and this is the first publicity tour I've done where everyone has asked me about this. Everyone! People are talking about it."

So does she think it's gotten worse since the early days of her career?

Meyers thinks about this for a few seconds: "Well, of course, in some ways things have improved a lot. No one would write into a woman's contract that she wasn't allowed on set without a man! But in terms of getting women's stories on-screen, I don't see a lot of movies about complicated women with real problems, and studies tell you that's true. When I think back on the seventies and eighties I think of *Network, Baby Boom, Working Girl.* [And today] It was a real struggle getting *The Intern* made! No one wanted to take it on. Audiences always want to see real women characters but, I have to be honest with you, I think it's gotten worse."

---

* Despite all these admirable touches on Meyers's part, I have to admit *The Intern* is not my favorite of her films (that would obviously be *Baby Boom*). But I salute her valiant efforts here.

I didn't grow up to be Killer. I didn't even grow up to work in an office where anyone else is called Killer. In fact, I don't even work in an office—I work at home. So in my working life, it's a good day if I get dressed before 11 a.m. and remember to brush my teeth before the postman turns up—fantasies about a 6 a.m. session with a personal trainer are about as close to my reality as my once-cherished dream of owning a unicorn. But even if my life turned out to be nothing like that of the women in these eighties movies, they taught me something else, something that has stayed with me forever, which is to not apologize for working hard. Okay, Steven from *Baby Boom* might not have been perfect (did I mention the face packs?), but he loved JC's professional drive and smarts, and that's because he was an adult. She never played down what she did at work to him in order to ease his and the audience's precious male egos. If only more filmmakers today treated female characters with so much respect, and gave male audiences the credit for being able to cope with the prospect of a successful female character. It is jaw-dropping that so many films still feel the need to undermine success-ful women in their movies to the extent that the sexism on-screen is not only more exaggerated than it is in the real world, but actually worse than it was thirty years ago. After all, we women might not all be the actual Tiger Lady, or even Killer, but we all deserve at the least a partner who encourages us to be the most we can be, and audiences, male and female, should be seeing better.

Top Five Breakages of the Fourth Wall

 Eriq La Salle, *Coming to America*

Before he was punching the air in the credits to *ER*, La Salle was Darryl, the evil greasy-haired boyfriend in *Coming to America*. At the end of the movie his ex-girlfriend's little sister wants to get her paws into that greasy hair, and La Salle can only look to the audience for help.

 Jon Cryer, *Pretty in Pink*

When Duckie finally gets his happy ending at the prom, and shares it with the audience, it almost makes up for the fact that the ending doesn't make any sense at all.

 Rick Moranis, *Spaceballs*

Moranis talking directly to the audience? That's an eighties peak for me right there.

 Matthew Broderick, *Ferris Bueller's Day Off*

Nobody has yet bettered Ferris's skill at talking to the camera, and that includes Matthew Broderick.

Eddie Murphy, *Trading Places*

The moment when the evil Duke brothers are patronizing Billy Ray Valentine about commodities, and he looks dead at the camera. Total Murphy perfection.

Back to the Future

Even today, thirty-five years later, screenwriter Bob Gale can still remember the moment "vividly." It was a hot day in August 1980, and he was in the middle of promoting his latest film, *Used Cars*, a very funny satire about car salesmen starring Kurt Russell and directed by Robert Zemeckis. The promotion tour had taken Gale back to his hometown of St. Louis, and he was at his parents' house, in a suburb a little way out of the city. "One afternoon, I was digging around in my parents' basement—I don't exactly recall why—and I discovered my father's high school yearbook," he says.

Gale thumbed through it and discovered, to his surprise, that his father had been the president of his high school class. He'd never mentioned that. This made Gale think about the kids who had been involved in student government when he'd been at school, and how much he sneered at them. In fact, he'd been on the committee to abolish student government.

"I wondered, would I have liked my dad if I'd been at school with him?" he says. "Would I have even been friends with him?"

When he got back to Los Angeles, he called Zemeckis: "Bob, I think I got an idea. . . ."

Despite what most teenagers would like to admit, parents are an essential part of their life, for better or worse. But only smart teen films appreciate that and the bone-deep complications this entails: "I rag on you a lot about your family, but it's only because I'm jealous—it must feel good to have someone looking out for you like that," says the parentless Watts (Mary Stuart Masterson) to her best friend Keith (Eric Stoltz) in 1987's *Some Kind of Wonderful*.

"Uh, sometimes," replies Keith with a pronounced lack of enthusiasm.

It is nice to have someone care about you when you're a teenager—it's just a shame it has to be your parents.

You can always tell whether a teen film is good or not by how smart it is about the parents. Sure, there are some decent teen films that don't feature parents at all: *The Breakfast Club* is obviously great, *The Outsiders* is okay in a fascinating, overly stylized Coppola-in-the-eighties way.* But in the main, a teen film that doesn't have any well-written parental figures feels like a movie that was made by a studio trying to anticipate what teenage audiences want as opposed to a film capturing what teenagers are actually like.

Parents in teen films have gone through more growing pains than any adolescent. In the 1940s, when the word *teenager* was first coined, parents were the helpful patriarchs whom the teenagers aspired to become, meaning the teenage characters (often played by young Mickey Rooney or Judy Garland) would say realistic dialogue like "Oh, Dad, I hope I grow up to be just like you one day." In teen films of the 1950s and '60s, when studios realized that all these baby

---

* And I do honestly think that the moment Sodapop (Rob Lowe) steps out of the shower is what kick-started puberty in me.

boom teenagers preferred films that wholly validated them as opposed to patronized the hell out of them, parents became the representatives of conventional morality that the teenagers were rebelling against with their sexy modernity. By the 1970s, when teen films were being made by filmmakers who were young enough to have once been dubbed teenagers themselves but were now old enough to feel fondly about their youth, parents were either sentimentalized to the point of blandness (*Grease*, *American Graffiti*) or as doomed as the kids (*The Last Picture Show*, *Carrie*).

It wasn't until the 1980s that parents really came into their own. In the best eighties teen films they are invariably among the most fun characters in the movie, given many of the best lines, and played by supremely talented actors momentarily slumming it in a kids' movie and having a ball with it, such as Harry Dean Stanton all sad-eyed and sweet voiced in *Pretty in Pink*, John Lithgow enjoyably preaching fire and brimstone in *Footloose*, and John Mahoney playing a very different kind of paternal figure years before he became Frasier's dad, in *Say Anything*.* Partly this is because they assumed an entirely new kind of role in these movies, and partly it's because of the social attitudes of the time, and no other film made before or since encapsulates these changes more enjoyably than *Back to the Future*.

It is, arguably, a bit of a fudge to describe *Back to the Future* as a teen film, at least according to those who made it. "*Teen Wolf* was a teen film, but I always thought of *Back to the Future* more as a time-traveling adventure comedy sci-fi love story," says its star, Michael J. Fox.

---

* Weirdly, Bebe Neuwirth is also in *Say Anything*, playing the school's careers counselor, meaning that both Frasier's dad and Frasier's wife were in the same film together, yet without Frasier. Kelsey Grammer should call his agent.

"By the time I was cast in *Back to the Future*, I'd done a lot of eighties teen movies, like *The Wild Life*,* *Red Dawn*,† and *All the Right Moves*,‡ and this didn't feel like that to me," says Lea Thompson. "This felt more like a science fiction blockbuster."

But despite what those who made it thought, people who watched it at the time very much saw it as a teen film. By the time it was released in 1985, the teen film craze was well in swing and audiences were now very used to increasingly ridiculous genre movies structured around teenagers. Teenagers could now be karate aces (*The Karate Kid*, of course), fighters of communism (the aforementioned *Red Dawn*), or even detectives at Eton College (the completely brilliant *Young Sherlock Holmes*). So the idea of a time-traveling teenager seemed par for the teen genre course—as, in fact, it would soon become. The following year, Francis Ford Coppola's underrated *Peggy Sue Got Married*, also set in the fifties,§ was released. Four years later the utterly delightful *Bill and Ted's Excellent Adventure* arrived to cause parents of teenagers untold torment with its catchphrases and dude-speak.

"Teenage tastes now dominate mainstream moviemaking, and

---

* Cameron Crowe's fratty follow-up to *Fast Times at Ridgemont High*, featuring Christopher Penn, Eric Stoltz, and—pleasingly—Rick Moranis.

† TEENS FIGHT EVIL COMMIES! America's fate lies in the hands of Charlie Sheen and Patrick Swayze, God help us all.

‡ Tom Cruise fights to get a football scholarship to college instead of having to work in a mine with his father. If you like the mining scenes from *Zoolander*, you'll probably enjoy seeing the inspiration.

§ When looking at other eras, teen movies in the 1980s invariably celebrate the innocence of the 1950s, such as *BTTF* and *Peggy Sue Got Married*, and invariably mock the hippy revolution of the 1960s. The optimism and consumerism of the 1950s would have been easier for eighties Reaganite and Thatcherite teen audiences to grasp than the hippy rebellion of the 1960s, which would just have looked hilariously out of step with their own time, such as in 1982's *Valley Girl*, where the female lead sneers at her hippy parents' restaurant where "everything tastes of nothing."

that's where Gale and Zemeckis are working. Marty is . . . a teen idol . . . *Back to the Future* makes you feel like you're at a kiddies' matinee," Pauline Kael wrote somewhat sniffily in her review of *Back to the Future* in the *New Yorker*. (She also wrote: "I'm not crazy about movies with kids as the heroes," which must have made reviewing films in the eighties a bit of a drag for her.)

But Kael was right about one thing: Michael J. Fox, she wrote, was "exactly what the moviemakers wanted" for their star. After Gale pitched the film idea to an excited Zemeckis, it took years for the two of them to get the film made, and it wasn't until Zemeckis finally had a hit with *Romancing the Stone* that they got the go-ahead.* Zemeckis knew from the start that he wanted Fox to play Marty since Fox has the kind of boyish energy that the character needs to carry the film. Unfortunately, the actor was busy starring in the hugely popular sitcom *Family Ties* and the producers wouldn't release him for the movie. So, a little warily, Zemeckis cast Eric Stoltz. You can still find photos on the Web of Stoltz shooting *Back to the Future*, standing with Doc Brown in the Twin Pines shopping mall parking lot, wearing that now-iconic sleeveless puffa—and it just looks wrong. Stoltz is many things—ginger, soulful, eccentric—but he is neither energetic nor funny.

"Eric was more of an internal actor and he simply didn't have the extroverted comedic 'thing' that we wanted in the character," Gale recalls. And so, after six weeks on set, Zemeckis fired him. He then went back to the *Family Ties* producers to beg them to let him use their star.

"Bob Zemeckis pointed out to Gary [Goldberg, *Family Ties*'

---

* The reason Marty is given two older siblings is that Zemeckis and Gale had to keep throwing in more kids to make it seem credible that George and Lorraine got together in 1955 but didn't have Marty until—given he's a senior in high school in 1985—1967.

producer] that a lot of the scenes in the movie take place at night, so we could shoot the movie then and the TV show during the day, if I was up for it," Fox remembers. "And I was." Goldberg reluctantly agreed and Fox agreed "with a big grin."

With his naturally energetic comedy style, heightened by his manic exhaustion from filming both the show and film simultaneously, Fox holds the disparate timelines and characters of *Back to the Future* together, bouncing in his hi-tops. But he does more than that: he creates the illusion that Marty is an interesting character, one worthy of the audience's emotional investment, which, in truth, he isn't. He's barely a character at all. He doesn't have any defined personality traits besides wishing he owned a car and wanting to be back in good ol' 1985. His only role is to move the plot along and explain things to the characters and the audience. He is, as Austin Powers would say, Basil Exposition.

"Marty takes the role of what's known in story theory as 'the mysterious stranger.' He comes out of nowhere and helps the characters sort out their lives. It's a construct that's been used in countless westerns," says Gale.

Which is fine, but mysterious strangers tend not to have much in the way of personality, and therefore don't make for good protagonists. But the reason the role was so underwritten is not because the script failed—because it definitely didn't, it's a pretty much perfect screenplay—but because *Back to the Future* is not about Marty at all: it's about his parents.

Gale was inspired to write this, the most successful of all eighties teen films, when he was looking at his dad's yearbook. So it makes sense that, he says, "the pivotal character in the film is actually George McFly—he's the one who grows." To emphasize this, he and Zemeckis cast one of the weirdest and most scene-stealing actors of all time as George: Crispin Glover. "When we auditioned him, we recognized that he had an unusual quality that we thought would make the character particularly memorable. He made the part so much his own that I can't even recall what we were thinking when we wrote him, other than having some endearing awkwardness and charm like a young Jimmy Stewart," remembers Gale.

But Crispin Hellion Glover, to give him his full name, is a far stranger proposition than good ol' boy Jimmy Stewart ever was.

All the performances in *Back to the Future* are great, but they are great teen movie performances. Glover, by contrast, seems to be Method acting in his own very different, very funny movie. When we first meet middle-aged George at the beginning of the movie, cackling like a cricket chirping at Jackie Gleason on TV, his family stare at him as though he's from another planet, and it's an understandable reaction from those other actors.

"Crispin's always been interested in being an iconoclast, whereas I'm way more mainstream," says Lea Thompson. "He worked so hard on *Back to the Future* and he approached it really differently from me, more like something out of the seventies, like De Niro and Pacino and all that kind of character work."

Only Glover (and possibly Nicolas Cage*) would ever think of Method acting in an eighties teen film. These days, Glover devotes himself to veganism and making films "that reflect my psychological interests" in a chateau he bought in the Czech Republic. Not even Gale and Zemeckis envisioned a future that bizarre for George McFly in their movie's sequel.

Back to the Future is extremely funny and sweet, but the real jokes come, not from the culture clashes between 1955 and 1985,

---

* According to Molly Ringwald, Judd Nelson was, hilariously, "doing this Method thing" when they made *The Breakfast Club*. This both explains a lot and excuses nothing.

but the way the lies George and Lorraine spun in 1985 about their teenage years are unspooled when their son travels back to 1955. At the beginning of the film Lorraine insists that, as a teenager, she would "never call a boy on the phone," but in fact as a teenager she throws herself at Marty, drinks alcohol, and enthusiastically "goes parking" with him, whatever that means. The reason George gets hit by Lorraine's father's car—which then leads to the two of them meeting one another—is because he fell out of the tree outside her house while spying on her putting on her bra. When Marty takes his leave of his parents in 1955, his parting message is resoundingly aimed more at the parents in the audience than the kids. Instead of telling George and Lorraine to give their third child a car, as a more teenager-focused film might (and as Ferris Bueller definitely would), he says, "If you guys ever have kids and one of them when he's eight years old accidentally sets fire to the living room rug, go easy on him."

"Bob Z and I concluded that there's probably one horrific punishment seared into every child's memory that he—or she—can never forget. Besides, Marty would have seemed like a jerk if he asked his parents for a car, especially knowing that—in his timeline—they couldn't afford it," says Gale.

But when did looking like a jerk ever stop a teenager—at least in a teen film—grousing about how car-deprived they were? Here, more clearly than anywhere else in the film, Gale and Zemeckis were talking at least as much to the parents in the audience as the kids. And in the case of at least one parent, it worked.

On the day *Back to the Future* came out in the United States, I, age seven, decided to paint my nails in the living room. My mother told me three times to do it in the bathroom but I ignored her and duly spilt nail polish all over the rug, and I got a good spanking for it. That evening, to calm my mother down, my father took her out to see this new film, and when Marty uttered that line to his parents about setting the living room rug on fire, my mother promptly burst into tears.

This also explains the film's attitude to sex. With the exception of John Hughes's films, eighties teen films were remarkably open-minded about teen sexuality. But it's difficult to think of a film not directed by David Cronenberg that works as hard at making sex seem as unappealingly perverse as *Back to the Future*. The only vaguely sexual scenes in this film are when Lorraine unwittingly tries to seduce her own son in the car followed by Biff attempting to rape her in the same cursed vehicle. Zemeckis has said how nervous he was while writing and rewriting the script with Gale in the early eighties because at that time the nation's youth was besotted with the *Porky's* franchise: "Gosh, we're in a high school in this movie and we never went into the girls' shower!" Whereas in *Porky's* sex is the only ambition, in *Back to the Future* sex is something to be fearfully avoided, which makes sense as the film is about parents, not teenagers, and if there's anything more horrifying than a parent's suspicion that their teenage child might be having sex, it's a teenager's realization that their parents ever had sex. And yet, the film tricks teenage audiences into hoping desperately that the parents get together, because without the parents getting it on, there is no teenager. When George beats up Biff, and then when he and Lorraine finally kiss in the dance—those are the romantic points of the film, the emotional lodestars.

Actually, there is one thing more horrifying to teenagers and parents alike and that's the idea of a mother "having the hots," as Marty puts it, for her son.

"The average teen films in the [early] eighties were drinking, drugging sex comedies, and these were the films that made a lot of money. So the studios all thought our film was too soft, except for

Disney, who thought that because of the relationship between the son and the mother it was too dirty," Zemeckis said.

And to be honest, Disney had a point. This plot could easily have sunk the movie into gross-out freakiness, and would have done so without Lea Thompson's sweetness: "I remember Bob Zemeckis was so freaked out when we shot the scene when I kiss Marty because the whole movie had to change in that. The whole plot had to twist on that," says Thompson.

Of course, the real problem with this plotline, never mind the incest, is, come 1985, George would surely have been a bit worried by his youngest child's strong resemblance to that guy his wife had a crush on in high school, especially as she names their son after him. But complaining about credibility issues in a movie about time travel is surely the definition of carping, particularly a film about time travel in which a DeLorean works at all, never mind at 1.21 gigawatts.

The most popular image of parents in an eighties teen film is that of the blithe couple walking through the living room door in the final scene of the film just as their son replaces the last piece of furniture that was moved out of place during his shenanigans while they were away (see: *Weird Science, Risky Business, Ferris Bueller's Day Off*). This was certainly part of their purpose. (And not, I later learned to my cost, a lesson that exactly translated into real life. I wasn't spanked again when my parents came home from a trip away when I was eighteen to find a teenage boy wandering around in my father's bathrobe, the hall wallpaper scratched up and destroyed, and several strange teenagers working their way through the liquor cabinet downstairs, but I definitely deserved to be.) But the real role for parents in eighties teen movies is to be fixed by their kids.

In *Sixteen Candles*, Sam has to teach her father how to be a good dad again after he forgets her birthday; in *Pretty in Pink*, Andie gets her father out of his depression after his wife leaves him; in *Say Anything*, Diane Court and Lloyd Dobler teach Mr. Court about good morals; in *Dirty Dancing*, Baby teaches her father about good values; in *Footloose*, Ariel teaches her father not to be a deranged religious wingnut; in *Some Kind of Wonderful*, Keith teaches his father that teen romance is more important than going to college (not all these lessons exactly stand up to analysis by anyone over the age of eighteen). These kids are parents to their parents. Sometimes there is nothing to teach the parents: they are simply deeply flawed and the kids learn to be the grown-ups in the relationship, as in *The Breakfast Club*. In *Heathers*, which brilliantly satirizes all eighties teen film tropes, J.D. (Christian Slater) calls his father "son" and his father calls J.D. "Dad," and the result of this screwy lack of parental guidance is that J.D. blows himself and his groovy trench coat up on the school steps.

In *Back to the Future*, it is emphasized from the beginning how mortified Marty is by his weak father and drunken mother, and how disappointing they are as parents. It is only when he goes back to 1955 that he is able to teach his parents how to be the people they always wanted to be and, by extension, the parents he wants them to be. The ultimate message of all these movies is, Your parents are idiots and you are right.

"It's in the eighties that you really start to see what I call the Tyranny of the Teen, with that repeated message: your family is mixed up, and you know everything," says Steven Gaydos, editor of *Variety*. "Also, a lot of people from the world of TV commercials and family TV were starting to make movies in Hollywood, like Jeffrey Katzenberg and Michael Eisner, who knew how to sell things to young people. They realized that people over forty weren't seeing movies, so they created films that valorized young people's experience. There was less finger wagging and more 'Why are adults so weird?'"

But because these movies were asking, "Why are adults so weird?" this meant adults were made more of a central feature of teen films than ever before.

Teenagers are supposed to be rebellious: that's what movies had been saying ever since the 1950s. Teenagers in eighties films, however, had a very different kind of rebellion. Not to them did biking across the country high on cocaine appeal. Ferris Bueller skives off school to go to a fancy restaurant, the stock exchange, a museum, and a parade. Ren (Kevin Bacon) in *Footloose* wants to have a prom. Daniel (Ralph Macchio) in *The Karate Kid* wants his mother to have a nice house. Sam in *Sixteen Candles* wants to have a birthday cake. As rebellion goes, these kids make Milhouse from *The Simpsons* look like Johnny Rotten. Far from rebelling against middle-class capitalism, they are striving to be more stolidly average and middle class. Even Joel (Tom Cruise) in *Risky Business*, who would seem to be the most rebellious teenager of all when he runs a brothel out of his parents' suburban house when they go away, is actually living by his parents' ideals, as the film makes clear, because he is taking the moneymaking capitalistic lifestyle that his friends aspire to (and his parents subscribe to) to the extreme. He is rewarded for doing so when he gets offered a place at Princeton precisely because the admissions tutor is so impressed by his pimping skills (in the pantheon of films about prostitution, *Risky Business* makes *Pretty Woman* look grittily realistic). In *Back to the Future*, Marty's meddling in the past results in his parents living in a nicer house, with chicer furnishings, posher breakfast dishes, and even domestic help in the form of Biff Tannen in 1985. Marty's triumph is to lift his family up to middle-class status.

As much as teen films railed against the importance of social class in America, the teen protagonists themselves all aimed very much to be part of the mainstream middle-class world. This is part of the reason why eighties teen films still hold so much appeal to middle-class kids today: the forms of rebellion depicted in them feel eminently accessible and familiar. When life is as comfortable as it largely is today for middle-class white kids in the Western world, there's nothing, really, to rebel against without hurting themselves, so they may as well help their parents buy a bigger house. This is anti-rebellion as a form of rebellion, and its popularity in the eighties reflects this coziness and the conservatism of the decade.

Back to the Future proved to teen filmmakers that they needn't be scared of making parents part of their story. In fact, teen audiences rather liked seeing their parents humanized. Even if there has been no teen film since in which the parents are quite as center stage as they are in *Back to the Future*, many of the funniest, smartest, and sweetest depictions of parents in teen films have come in *Back to the Future*'s wake: Dan Hedaya as the terrifying litigator father in *Clueless* (so much more fun than his nineteenth-century counterpart, the profoundly irritating Mr. Woodhouse in Jane Austen's *Emma*); Larry Miller as the neurotically protective Mr. Stratford in *10 Things I Hate About You*; Eugene Levy showing those whippersnappers how comedy is done in *American Pie*; the mighty Amy Poehler as "the cool mom" in Juicy Couture in *Mean Girls*, doing her usual thing of being at once hilariously exaggerated and wholly credible.

Robert Zemeckis has said *Back to the Future* could "never" be made now—in fact, he wouldn't even bother pitching it if he were starting out as a director today because "the sophistication of the audience has regressed."* But seeing as audiences still enjoy the movie arguably more so than ever, they do not seem to be the problem here. In fact, *Back to the Future* is one eighties film that could definitely be made now—plenty of spectacle, guaranteed franchise

---

* Robbie Collins, Robert Zemeckis interview, *Daily Telegraph*, September 26, 2015.

material—and it's not too hard to imagine a studio remaking it, maybe starring Channing Tatum or some such. But Zemeckis, to his great credit, has refused to let anyone do so, making it one of the few pieces of great eighties pop culture to be unharmed by any modern rehashes, because he knows it would be a completely different film. For a start, Lorraine and George would not be at the heart of it. As much as movie marketers want to reach as many quadrants of an audience as possible, teen movies today are just about teenagers and not adults, so as to keep the focus on the most important audience members: teenagers. A teen movie in which the love story is the one between the parents would be unthinkable. More obviously, the idea of a mom trying to seduce her son in a mainstream teen movie would just never fly today because that would be too risky, too ick, too dependent on subtle acting and storytelling. Stiffler's mom seducing her son's friends in *American Pie*? Raunchy good fun. Stiffler's mom unwittingly seducing her son? No.

Hollywood is far too risk-averse for such things now. So if *Back to the Future* were remade tomorrow, Marty's challenge would be to save the world, or at least guarantee America's dominance against an evil invading country. You know, something far more accessible than dealing with one's parents.

Teen films in the 1980s taught kids three things about their parents: if they are divorced, they'll get back together for you; they will never notice when you've had a party; and they are deeply, deeply square. But George McFly and Lorraine Baines taught them something else as well: parents are weird, but they're weird just like you're weird, and no matter what the kids in *The Breakfast Club* say, someday you will be them, too, and that's why parents in smart teen films are so fun. Because while you might be able to change destiny and become a sci-fi writer instead of a bullied wimp, George McFly–style, you can't ever change that.

Top Five Eighties Steve Guttenberg Moments

Plenty of eighties stars saw their careers die out in the nineties: Molly Ringwald, Andrew McCarthy, Judd Nelson. But no one vanished quite as spectacularly as Guttenberg, the man who was ubiquitous in the eighties only to disappear entirely in the nineties. These are his greatest moments.

 5 *Short Circuit*

How much you accept Guttenberg could be a scientist for the military depends on how much you rate his acting skills.

 4 *Three Men and a Baby*

The beginning of the end for Guttenberg, I suspect, as he is totally outcharismaed by Tom Selleck and Ted Danson. Still, it's one of his best films.

 3 *Cocoon*

Why doesn't anyone watch *Cocoon* these days? It's such a lovely film full of such cool older people. Guttenberg doesn't get to do much here and is acted off the screen by Don Ameche, but that's fair enough, really.

2   *Diner*

Mickey Rourke—and Steve Guttenberg. Truly, a natural pairing! Guttenberg is sweet in this, playing the virginal bridegroom. You'd almost think watching it that he might become an actual actor one day.

1   *Police Academy*

No, I would not claim that *Police Academy 7: Mission to Moscow* is the greatest contribution to the world of film since *Citizen Kane*. But I would strongly argue that Mahoney, the cheeky police recruit, is Guttenberg at his finest.

Batman

As for every other oversensitive kid of the eighties, it was love at first sight for me and the films of Tim Burton. Which was something of a surprise because the first film I saw of his—which was also the first feature film he made—was *Pee-wee's Big Adventure*. Now, despite being very much an American child of the eighties, I did not like Pee-wee Herman. In fact, it would be fair to say that I actively disliked Pee-wee Herman. As I was seven when the film came out, I didn't quite have the ability to articulate what it was I didn't like about him, but now that I'm thirty-six I very much do: I thought he was creepy.* I might have been only a kid, but I

---

* Some snarky types out there might be encouraged to remark that later events in the life of Pee-wee's creator, Paul Reubens, who was arrested in 1991 for indecent exposure when he was caught masturbating in a porn cinema, validated my initial impression. But I would disagree most vehemently with this. For a start, now that we live in an era where a person is turned into a celebrity by appearing in a sex tape, the idea of a celebrity's career being destroyed by masturbation seems downright quaint—as quaint as the idea of porn cinemas, really. For heaven's sake, what are people supposed to do in a porn cinema if not masturbate—eat popcorn? (Public

wasn't stupid and I could see that Pee-wee was not so peewee—he was an adult.

And yet, he was an adult pretending to be a kid. That's creepy. On *Sesame Street* (my children's TV show *du choix*), the adults acted like adults, the children acted like children, and the Muppets acted like Muppets, just as God intended. There was no confusion between the ages or species, and that was how my hardened little conservative heart liked it.

But a girl in my first-grade class, Alison Schnayerson,* was having a birthday party, which involved going to see *Pee-wee's Big Adventure*. Obviously, you can't turn down an invite to a seventh-birthday party without incurring social death so, with a heart as heavy as when my mother dragged me to my weekly swimming lessons, I set out to meet my school friends at the Eighty-Sixth Street and Lexington Avenue cinema. Reader, I loved him. No, that's not right—I never loved Pee-wee Herman. But I loved it, the film, with its cartoonish overexaggerations (Pee-wee's dreams about his bike are so theatrical they are like the fantasy dance sequence, "Broadway Melody," in *Singin' in the Rain*), the heightened colors (the rich green wooden mailboxes especially appealed to me, probably because they were so far from the anonymous metallic pigeonholes we had in our apartment building), and the depiction of suburbia as a place with all sorts of nefariousness simmering beneath the manicured lawns, and worse was beyond its rosebush borders. I still thought Pee-wee himself was weird, but somehow, getting him out across America on a task, as happens in the film, made him seem slightly less creepy than he did

---

health announcement: do not eat in a porn cinema.) In fact, I'd go so far as to claim that masturbating in a porn cinema was the least creepy thing Paul Reubens did in the entertainment industry by 1991.

* Not actually her real name, but all middle-class New York girls in the eighties had names like Alison Schnayerson.

on his TV show, *Pee-wee's Playhouse*, where he just sat inside and talked to the window.* Also, he spoke less in that blaring hornlike tone in the movie than he did in the show, and that helped A LOT.†

So I liked *Pee-wee's Big Adventure*, in other words, for many of the qualities I would later recognize in all Burton's films. Burton himself said about the movie, "I could add, but I wasn't imposing my own thing on it completely. I got to take the stuff that was there and embellish it." It wasn't until he made *Beetlejuice* three years later that he got to impose a lot of himself on a film, and my initial spark of love turned into a lifelong burning affair.

Beetlejuice, which is about a couple (Geena Davis and a bizarrely miscast and visibly uncomfortable Alec Baldwin) who die and try to scare a family out of their home with the aid of the eponymous Beetlejuice (Michael Keaton), is such a weird and interesting film that I'm not even going to try to discuss it here, as it deserves its own chapter. So I'll limit myself to noting just that so many of the qualities and tropes that are now seen to define a Burton film have their roots in *Beetlejuice*: the misunderstood male loner; the soulful female outsider; the permanent black sky; the raggedy rooftops; the black and white stripes; the model village. *Beetlejuice* also has the look and tone of what would become Burton's distinctive style: cartoonish

---

* I am not exaggerating: that is literally what *Pee-wee's Playhouse* was. I think to enjoy that show you have to have an already existing or incipient love of psychedelics.

† A separate sentimental part of me also suspects that part of the movie's appeal comes from the fact that the wonderful and sadly now late Canadian comedian Phil Hartman cowrote it. Hartman appeared occasionally on *Pee-wee's Playhouse* and was a much-beloved cast member on *Saturday Night Live* in the 1990s, but he is best known in Britain as the voice of shady lawyer Lionel Hutz and cheesy infomercial host Troy McClure in *The Simpsons*. Hartman, by all accounts one of the sweetest and lowest-key guys in show business, was shot and killed by his wife in his sleep in 1998. Sorry, I know this is a terribly distracting and pretty unnecessary footnote, but some people should be commemorated at any possible opportunity.

artifice coupled with noirish comedy, plus a character with whom the movie seems to feel such a strong sense of emotional affinity that it's hard not to suspect there's some autobiography going on. In *Beetlejuice*, this character is Lydia (Winona Ryder), the angry, gothy teenager who is filled with such righteous disgust toward her boring bourgeois father (Jeffrey Jones) and stepmother (Catherine O'Hara) and their obsession with interior decoration that she rejects them to live in the Underworld—and what teenager has not fantasized about doing that at some point? Lydia's predicament is one that Burton repeats throughout his work: the freak stuck in an artificially beautiful world, echoing the frustration he felt when growing up in Burbank, California—Lydia even has Burton's skewwhiff hair and his all-black uniform. "I know people say [my work] is slightly autobiographical but if I think about it too closely I get freaked out. It's weird; I need to feel connected but also distanced," Burton said.

Kids and teenagers are pretty good at spotting phoneys, especially people who pretend they're in touch with their younger selves when they're really just putting on a baby voice. Burton, for better or worse, was no phoney. Despite being in his early thirties by the time the eighties ended, his films of that era expressed the mentality of a disaffected kid, one who felt ostracized from his school friends and family and told himself that this proved he was morally superior. And yet, he had the maturity to construct this mentality into wonderful and strange and sensitive stories. In this regard, he was very much like John Hughes, but whereas Hughes's cinematic alter ego was the righteous nerd Duckie in *Pretty in Pink*, Burton was more like gothy loner Allison in *The Breakfast Club*. I loved to read about his early, miserable years working as an illustrator at Disney, which he joined when he was twenty-one: "I was very strange back then. I could see I had a lot of problems. I was always perceived as weird. I would sit in a closet a lot of the time and not come out, or

I would sit on top of my desk, or under my desk, or do weird things like get my wisdom teeth out and bleed all over the hallways. . . . I was having emotional problems at that stage. I didn't know who I was," he said.

Already by the age of ten, I was starting to cultivate my own sense of estrangement from my peers, holding it close to my chest and stroking it jealously, like Blofeld petting his white cat. I had neither the emotional problems nor, arguably, the courage of Burton to externalize my sense of inner weirdness as much as he did, but it thrilled me to know I could watch things made by someone who, I felt sure, understood my own increasingly lonely confusion. What nineties teenagers felt about Kurt Cobain, I felt about Tim Burton in the late eighties.

I think part of the reason I and so many other former eighties kids feel such a strong affinity with Burton is that, in many ways, he grew up alongside us. Although he is about two decades older than my generation, having been born in 1958, his films seemed to go through the same life stages as us in real time: there were his childlike playful years when he started in the eighties, with *Pee-wee's Big Adventure, Beetlejuice,* and *Batman;*[*] his step into teenagehood in the nineties with his more self-consciously gothy films that celebrated outsiders and loners, such as *Edward Scissorhands,* as well as *Ed Wood* and *Mars Attacks!;* his stumble into adulthood in the 2000s, with sentimental films about the impact of the death of one's parents (*Big Fish, Charlie and the Chocolate Factory*[†]), halfhearted

---

[*] "I really liked [*Pee-wee's Playhouse*] because it really tapped into the permanent adolescence thing, and I completely connected with that," Burton said (*Burton on Burton*). When Burton made *Pee-wee's Big Adventure,* he was twenty-seven.

[†] "Even though I wasn't that close to them, [losing your parents] obviously has a huge effect on your life. I was shocked at how much I was affected," he said ("Dark Arts," *Guardian*).

attempts at big-budget films for grown-ups (*Planet of the Apes*) and kids (*Alice in Wonderland*), and a creative stasis with films apparently made on sleepy autopilot (*Sweeney Todd, Sleepy Hollow*); his eventual happy maturity, with films that featured his familiar interests (*Frankenweenie*) but without the narcissistic tendency of his youth to make films only about himself (*Big Eyes*).

As the subtitle of this book might have suggested, I'm interested in why so many movies made in the eighties could not be made today, and that is true of Burton's films—but not necessarily because of changes in the studio system and what have you (although that, too: it's hard to imagine a director with such relatively little experience getting to work on *Pee-wee's Big Adventure*, to say nothing of *Batman*). Rather, it's because Burton himself changed. He grew up, and watching the films of his I loved from the eighties onward is a little like watching the progress of my own inner life from childhood to adulthood, noting the changes but also the consistencies: "Certain images and feelings stay inside of you all your life," he said. "You think you've worked through them, but you don't, really. You just keep drawing something for a long time and it becomes part of you. Just when you've reached a new plateau in your life, it mysteriously comes again."

Burton has said that the repetition of imagery in his films merely reflects his own "limitations." But to eleven-year-old me, who had never before encountered a modern-day American director with such a strongly recognizable vision, this coherence was something else: it was art. With his films of the eighties and, later, the nineties, Burton taught me about visual style, and how the way something looks can be exciting in itself. He also taught me that a movie can capture the spiraling unhappiness I often felt inside, but still be funny about it, and the eighties film that taught me these lessons most clearly was Burton's blockbuster, 1989's *Batman*.

Like me, Burton was not a comic book fan (another personal affinity that pleased me), but we both learned to love comic book movies with *Batman*. Burton snobs (who are very distinct from Burton fans, which is what I am) sometimes dismiss *Batman*, saying it is the least Burtonesque of his films due to studio control over the film. But I've never understood that, and have often suspected that what these snobs actually dislike is that the film was so ridiculously successful in the mainstream. Burton's supporters generally come from the same demographic as the director, that is, current or former school misfits, and it's hard when one nerd sees their fellow nerd friend suddenly elevated to being the coolest kid in the playground. What a sellout, right? And I got that, I really did. I refused to buy any of the *Batman* memorabilia that flooded the world the way *Star Wars* toys did ten years earlier, because I knew Burton would never have been involved in such bland, corporate, identikit junk. But the movie itself was different.

No one, really, can argue that *Batman* doesn't feel like a Tim Burton film. All the familiar Burton motifs are there, bigger and— therefore to my eleven-year-old mind—more exciting than ever. Gotham City—always a stand-in for New York City—thrilled me, with its mix of looming architecture and rickety buildings, the worst of art deco mixed with a circus from hell. Gotham is chaotic, jumbled, and unnavigable, and everything is absolutely HUGE, from the buildings to the crime waves. It's a far cry from the idealized and sparkling New York of, say, *Breakfast at Tiffany's*, and it looked, to be honest, a lot like how New York looked to me as a kid: big and scary and confusing and exciting.

Burton's Gotham encapsulates not just Burton's style but also an attitude toward modern-day cities that runs through eighties movies. For an era that was ostensibly so upbeat about capitalism and all the possibilities it offered, eighties movies were remarkably negative about modern-day cities. Even besides the obvious examples, like *Blade Runner* and *Escape from New York*, think of the poverty and the squalor in Hill Valley 1985 in *Back to the Future* and the filth and crime in eighties New York in *Ghostbusters*. With Gotham, Burton took that trend to its climactic extreme at the end of the decade and, in doing so, established the template for how cities would be depicted in superhero films for the next thirty years.

It is a real testament to comic book artist and writer Bob Kane and Bill Finger that two of the most influential movies of the 1980s and the twenty-first century feature the same protagonist, one they created back in 1939. But it's also quite something to look back now at the early coverage of Burton's *Batman* and see how fretful critics and fans were that it would be "too dark" and "too scary" for kids. Instead, he changed the way Hollywood depicted superheroes forever, rescuing them from the bright and cheerful campness of the *Superman* movies (and Adam West's kitschy TV show) and turning them into phenomenally lucrative brooding men of mystery. Burton's influence has only deepened over the past few decades, now that superhero films are so ubiquitous and form the spine of the U.S. film industry, and compared to superhero films made in the twenty-first century the 1989 *Batman* looks like *Sesame Street*: there are colors, there is relatively little violence, and the characters don't all look absolutely miserable. There were huge protests at the time against Burton's casting of Michael Keaton as *Batman*, with fans suggesting he was too weird and too weedy to play an all-American superhero. But next to creepily intense (and Welsh! scandal!) Christian Bale, Keaton, with his crazy eyes, looks perfectly batlike.

Christopher Nolan picked up this baton again in 2005 with *Batman Begins*, saving the franchise from the camp mess Joel Schumacher made of it in the 1990s,* and he restored the dark look of the movie franchise to something more in line with its comic book origins. The impact of this shift has been enormous in Hollywood, arguably even more so than it was when Burton did it in 1989, simply because there are so many more superhero films being made now than there were two decades ago, thanks in part to the nigh-on superhero-like rise of Marvel Studios. All superhero films after 2005 became much darker as a result of *Batman Begins*'s success, from the *X-Men* to the *Avengers* to *Spider-Man*.

But I'm going to lay it on the line here and just say it: I don't like the Christopher Nolan *Batman* films. Not out of loyalty to Burton—although I admit I did think that would be why when I first went to see *Batman Begins* with a skeptically cocked eyebrow—but because they're boring. God, they're so boring, full of endless speechifying from the characters about how good and evil are two sides of the same coin, and we all wear masks, and true power is a terrible burden, and it's always darkest before dawn,† and the rain in Spain stays mainly on the plain and blah blah di freaking blah. I suspect Nolan knows this, which is why he sticks in about seventeen action sequences per minute in his films. But the scene in the museum in *Batman*, in which Jack Nicholson serenades Kim Basinger to Prince while poison-gassing everyone else, sticks in my mind far

---

* I don't think we need to talk about Schumacher's *Batman* films too much, for two simple reasons: they were made in the nineties and are therefore fairly irrelevant to our purpose here, and they are absolute garbage. When the best performance in a movie comes from Elle Macpherson, as is the case in *Batman and Robin*, you know you are in the presence of a Thanksgiving-size turkey.

† Which, by the way, isn't even true. Of COURSE it isn't darkest before the dawn—it's darkest in the middle of the night, not at 5 a.m. Sheesh!

more than any of the 10,781 action scenes from Nolan's series, because contrary to what superhero filmmakers think today, the more action scenes you include, the more diluted they become.

The only interesting thing about Bruce Wayne—a rich playboy whose power resides in his access to jazzy toys invented by others—is how he became Batman, and Burton knew this, which is why he focused on it in *Batman*, and it's why his sequel, *Batman Returns* (1992), stumbles a little, because he no longer had that storyline to mine. Nolan knows it, too, and so the first part of his trilogy, *Batman Begins*, takes that as its main plotline—and stretches it out to an insomnia-curing length of two hours and twenty minutes, padded out with seemingly endless scenes involving Christian Bale training to be a ninja in the snow. Hey, Nolan, I came here to see *Batman*—not *Kung Fu Panda*.

Burton is a much punchier storyteller, conveying what needs to be said (Bruce Wayne's a rich loner! He was really messed up over the murder of his parents!) with a single scene. His action scenes are also far, far easier to follow than Nolan's, which are a jumbled mess because too much is going on in them with too many characters. After *Batman Returns* (starring Keaton, Christopher Walken, Danny DeVito, and Michelle Pfeiffer), all superhero films became overstuffed with famous actors in the belief that audiences would be so distracted by the celebrities they wouldn't notice that the plots don't make a bit of sense. The problem with this is that it then increases the chances of the heroes themselves—always the dullest characters in a superhero film—being overshadowed by all the villains. This is not a problem in Burton's film, because Burton revels in the weirdness of Batman,* and

---

* "Part of what interested me was that it's a human character who dresses up in extremely vulgar costumes . . . [it's] the freakish nature of it, and I found it the most frightening thing" (*Burton on Burton*).

Keaton's eyes are always fascinating to watch, even when they're near hidden beneath a mask.

But Bale, while a brilliant actor, doesn't have Keaton's deranged magnetism—if anything, the mask makes him look weirdly pouchy—and giving him a stupid vocoder voice when he's Batman simply obscures Bale's charisma even more. Thus *Batman* becomes a boring, opaque drag and it often feels like the heart of Nolan's *Batman* films is not with Batman, but with Jim Gordon (Gary Oldman), the good police officer, and this is especially true in the second part of Nolan's trilogy, *The Dark Knight*. This is by some measure the best of the modern *Batman* series because it features Batman's best villain—the Joker—who is played by Heath Ledger, giving the most mesmerizing performance in the whole trilogy. But even here, I have to admit that I still think of Burton: with his cracked white face paint, skewwhiff hair, brightly colored suit, and self-description as an "agent of chaos," Ledger's take on the Joker looks an awful lot like *Beetlejuice*.

There is no point in debating who did the Joker better, Ledger or Nicholson, because they're both clearly magnificent: Nicholson's feels iconic from the moment he steps on the screen whereas Ledger's performance snarls and burrows its way beneath your skin with its creepiness. But Nicholson's Joker is ultimately more satisfying because he gets a backstory (the snappy tale of Jack the lad ending up in a vat of acid because he slept with his boss's girlfriend, played respectively by Jack Palance and Jerry Hall*) and he gets a death, when Batman's trickery makes him plummet hundreds of feet down to the pavement, landing with a smile on his face and a mechanical toy laughing in his coat pocket.

In truth, it's fortunate that Nolan doesn't bother with his Joker's

---

*Another major point in Burton's *Batman*'s favor: it has a STELLAR cast.

backstory because he'd probably have taken four hours to establish it. But the lack of a death, well . . . Nolan is oddly averse to showy dramatics, as if slightly embarrassed that he's making a film about, you know, SUPERHEROES. Compare, for example, the thrilling opening scene in which Batman is introduced in Burton's film ("I want you to tell all your friends about me." "What are you?!?!?!" "I'M BATMAN.") with Nolan's decidedly less exciting version in which he makes banter with a homeless man ("Nice coat"). So it is perhaps not surprising that in *The Dark Knight* he doesn't even kill the Joker—he just leaves him hanging upside down somewhere. But it is also less satisfying.

Nolan fans say they prefer the "realism" of Nolan's films compared to Burton's, and critics frequently cite the "gritty reality" of the movies admiringly; but, if these films were "realistic," they would consist of crowds of people standing around and pointing at Batman and saying, "Oh look! It's one of those Fathers4Justice morons! What a DICK." Also, take it from a reformed fashion writer: no man can wear a full-length cape in the real world without sparking serious mockery. But the real point is, who comes looking for realism when they watch a movie about some dude who flies through the air dressed as a freaking bat? I'll tell you who: people who are trying to pretend that they're not watching a superhero film, and trying to convince themselves that this film is Saying Something Important.

Many of the differences between Burton's and Nolan's *Batman* films can be ascribed to the different style of the directors. But that's not the full story and many of the reasons I find Nolan's *Batman* films often next to unendurable have to do with the time in which they were made.

All disaster films set in New York now look like responses to 9/11, even if they were made years before (I find 1996's *Independence Day* almost unwatchable now for that reason, not that I try to watch it too often). But it is pretty obvious that the wild rise of superhero films in Hollywood since the beginning of the twenty-first century is as much a response to 9/11 as it is to the growing importance of international audiences. Superhero films provide escapism, and they also create a self-validating narrative for an America that feels under attack by an enemy it doesn't understand.

People have been writing about how superheroes reflect American self-identity pretty much since the day after Superman first appeared in 1938. Whole dissertations are written on this subject today, with titles such as "Rethinking the American Man: Clark Kent, Superman, and Consumer Masculinity" and "Nationalism and Power: Captain America, Governmental Policy, and the Problem of American Nationalism."* You can easily widen this argument out to movie heroes in general: from the 1920s to the 1960s, American film heroes were masculine, dominant, even swashbuckling, reflecting America's self-pride after the two world wars. This attitude crumbled during the Vietnam War, and so enter, stage left—the flawed hero! This pretty much started with Arthur Penn's 1967 film, *Bonnie and Clyde*, and today, in the twenty-first century, even the superheroes are riddled with self-doubt and inner conflict. You don't need to have written an essay with a colon-laden title about Clark Kent and heteronormative masculinity to see the glut of superhero movies post-9/11, featuring tortured superheroes who are tasked with saving the world but are often misunderstood by the dull-witted masses as destructive vigilantes, as a reflection of how America sees its position in the world today.

When Alfred (Michael Caine), the loyal voice of caution, asks

---

* I did not make those titles up (how could I?). They come from *Ages of Heroes, Eras of Men: Superheroes and the American Experience*, edited by Julian Chambliss, William Svitavsky, and Thomas Donaldson (Newcastle upon Tyne, England: Cambridge Scholars Publishing, 2013). Knock yourself out with that tome.

Bruce Wayne in *Batman Begins* whether he needs to cause quite so much destruction while trying to save Gotham, Bruce smirks, "Damn good television . . . Didn't have time to observe the rules of the road, Alfred." The year this film came out, 2005, was also the year when U.S. public opinion about President Bush really began to tank. Nearly half of Americans in 2005, according to a survey by Pew Research, believed the war in Iraq ultimately caused more damage than good. Did we need to cause so much destruction? Bush scoffed at this, saying in a speech on October 7 that such concerns were ridiculous because he was dealing with a terrorist movement that wanted to "intimidate the whole world." Who has time to observe the rules of the road when dealing with "the enemy"? Certainly America's right-wing media had been echoing this sentiment for years. David Brooks wrote approvingly in 2001: "We will destroy innocent villages by accident, shrug our shoulders, and continue fighting."

The parallels between Batman and Bush post-9/11 are even more obvious with *The Dark Knight*: there's the bad guy who sends his minions out on suicide missions and blows up random buildings just to prove he can; a villain who is so unlike any others that the good guys need to break their own rules to get him, such as Batman's use of sonar to tap civilians' cell phones to fight crime (v Patriot Act, that); the fact that most people wrongly see Bruce Wayne as a screwup blessed with a wealthy daddy, and Batman as a terrorist. Indeed, even the previously road-safety-aware Alfred has come round to Bush's razed-earth point of view in this film, and he counsels Bruce that the way to destroy a villain who "just wants to watch the world burn" is to "burn the forest down." In an article in the *Wall Street Journal* titled "What Batman and Bush Have in Common," Andrew Klavan describes *The Dark Knight* as "a conservative movie about the war on terror, making a fortune depicting the values and necessities that the Bush administration cannot seem to articulate for beans." The *Washington Independent* went further, suggesting that *The Dark Knight* was, in fact, a specific endorsement of Dick Cheney, particularly in regard to its attitudes toward security, justified law-breaking, and references to "the dark side" (a favorite Cheney coinage).

At the end of the film, Batman tells the police commissioner that their acts must be hidden in a massive cover-up because the general public can't deal with the truth. The Bush administration also hid plenty of things from the American public, from the cost of the war to the use of torture. It was only in 1992's *A Few Good Men* that Colonel Jessup's (Jack Nicholson) claim that people "can't handle the truth!" was taken as proof of his dangerous megalomania; in *The Dark Knight* hiding the truth is seen as part of Batman's wise and self-sacrificing nature. As one journalist wrote in *Mother Jones*, "[*The Dark Knight* says] we need dark knights to do the dirty work to keep us safe while we can sit back and self-righteously dismiss them as going too far. . . . This film seems to laud rule-exempt leaders as the only effective weapons against our evil enemies, a message I thought Americans had finally decided to reject."

Unsurprisingly, the film's cast tried to distance themselves from such political readings of the film. Aaron Eckhart, who plays district attorney Harvey Dent, insisted "certainly that wasn't the intention" and that it "is simply good drama for good movies." But he admitted, "I agree [with the analogy] in a way. Of course [it has analogies]. When I read *The Dark Knight* for the first time, I saw a lot of political issues. You know, obviously today's culture seeped in. It's a mirror of our times."

Whether or, more likely, not Nolan meant his Batman to represent Bush and Cheney, the American media and government had been paving the way for this analogy to be made for years in their desperate search for heroes after 9/11, the more cartoonish the better. A month after the attacks, Marvel published *Heroes*, an oversize comic book featuring drawings of firemen rescuing women from the rubble, and it sold out in one day. Susan Faludi writes in *The Terror Dream*, her study of how 9/11 affected the American psyche: "The president's vows to get the 'evildoers' won him media praise BECAUSE it sounded cartoonish." One especially ridiculous American columnist compared Bush giving the 2003 State of the Union address to the moment when Clark Kent moves "to tear open his shirt and reveal the big 'S' on his chest." Another commentator, Peter Roff, wrote: "Bush punctuates his rhetoric with verbal 'Whams,' 'Pows,' 'Biffs,' and 'Whaps' to make clear who are the good guys and who are the bad guys." Roff also compared the president to the superhero the Shadow, "a man of mystery who strikes terror into the very souls of evildoers everywhere." "That," Roff writes, "is just the kind of hero America needs right now." These columns, remember, were written not for comic book–consuming teenagers, but for broadsheet-reading adults.

Nolan's *Batman* movies are aimed far more at adults than Burton's ever were. They are far more violent, with huge body counts, because who has time to observe the rules of the road nowadays, Alfred? But perhaps the most obvious difference between the two franchises is the tone. Despite Burton's reputation as a messy-haired gloommeister, his films are funny, and *Batman* is no exception. From Jack Nicholson's larkishness ("Where DOES he get those wonderful toys?" "This town needs an enema!") to Michael Keaton's dry irony ("You know, I don't think I've ever been in this room before . . ."), *Batman* is definitely a funny movie. Even when Keaton seems at his most lonely he's amusing, such as when he sneaks up behind people in his house making fun of his possessions. But he's still alone: Keaton's Bruce Wayne wanders around unseen at his parties, unrecognized by his own guests and therefore always alone. Bale, by contrast, plays Bruce Wayne as a rich asshole who turns up late to his own parties with a girl on each arm and immediately dominates proceedings by making snarky speeches.

All superhero films take themselves ridiculously seriously nowadays, and this is especially true of Nolan's *Batman* films, which are portentous and pretentious. Superhero movies now affect to provide some kind of socially and politically relevant narrative, and the political narrative in America these days is pretty demoralizing (I mentioned the bizarre anti-Occupy message of the final part of Nolan's trilogy, *The Dark Knight Rises*, in the chapter "*Ferris Bueller's Day Off*: The Impact of Social Class"). Also, studios themselves take these films so seriously because they are the tentpoles to a studio's financial year. But as Burton's *Batman* proves, you don't need to keep telling the audience how SERIOUS and IMPORTANT a movie is for it to feel like a big deal, and you don't have to act like the film is as significant as the cure for cancer for it to become a worldwide smash. Because at a certain point, someone is going to stand up and say, "Do we really want to spend our adult lives the way we spent our teenage years— looking to superheroes to make sense of our world for us? And if we do, couldn't we make these movies a bit more, I don't know, FUN?"

After *Batman*, Tim Burton made his masterpiece in 1990—*Edward Scissorhands*, the most beautiful and most explicitly autobiographical of all his feature films (Burton wrote it as well as directing it), and when I saw it, it left me so breathless I couldn't even get out of the cinema seat at the end of the film. So I stayed and watched the next screening. It combined everything I loved about his eighties films—the surreal suburbia of *Pee-wee's Big Adventure*, the desire for escape from this world of *Beetlejuice*, and the loneliness of *Batman*—but more so in this story of a miserable loner with blades for hands. I was only twelve when I went to see it and I don't know if I subconsciously recognized in it the deeply depressed adolescent I would become—one who felt so alone and longed to be hugged but hurt anyone who tried—or if I just fancied Johnny Depp. But I probably watched that film more than any other as a teenager. Today, though, I can hardly bear to look at it. To watch *Edward Scissorhands* now is like pushing on a scar that covers some still sparking nerve endings.

But just as I grew up with Tim Burton, for a while I grew out of him. Along with other childish things, I put his films away in my twenties, and it embarrassed me that I once thought of all that Hollywood gothicism as art. God, what a dork. And look! Burton was right! His films all DID look the same, mainly because they all starred the same damn actors. Was Burton perhaps unaware there are other actors in the world besides Johnny Depp? Should I track him down and whisper when he steps out of his house, "Psst! Hey, Tim! Two words: James Spader."

But thankfully, I grew out of the childish self-loathing that I mistook in my twenties for mature self-awareness, and I came back to Burton in my thirties when I went to see *Frankenweenie* (2012). It was like coming back home after a long and difficult trip away: everything felt familiar but a little different and it was comfortable but also exciting to be back in a place that, still, spoke to a small and dark corner inside me. (It also helped that *Frankenweenie* marked the beginning of Burton heaving himself out of the creative rut in which he'd labored for the past decade. Neither of us had the greatest starts to this century.) I no longer queue up to see the first performance whenever a new Burton film opens—to be honest, I don't even see every film Burton makes at the cinema these days (I still haven't ever made it through the whole of *Planet of the Apes*, and I reckon we're both fine about that). But I'll always feel extreme fondness for him for waking me up to the excitement of movies in the 1980s, and for holding my hand through the 1990s. Burton's Batman doesn't try to make a comment about sociopolitical power-playing—it's about loneliness, but done in Burton's sweet, stylish, and surprisingly subtle way. I, personally, find that a lot more moving than a two-and-a-half-hour defense of the Bush presidency. We Burton fans are weird like that.

PS. For the record, here is the official order of the *Batman* films from the past thirty years, from best to worst.

 Batman (1989, Burton)

"Simply the best! Two thumbs-up!" Tina Turner.* The best cast of any *Batman* film of all time. Jack Palance, for God's sake! Jack freaking Palance!

 Batman Returns (1992, Burton)

So much better than you remember. Christopher Walken is completely wasted but Danny DeVito as the Penguin is brilliant. His penguin funeral haunts my dreams.

 The Dark Knight (2008, Nolan)

There are too many climaxes, too many characters, and too much Bushness, but unquestionably this is a gripping film. Aaron Eckhart and Gary Oldman are good; Heath Ledger is heartbreakingly great.

---

* Possibly not an entirely true quote.

4   *The Dark Knight Rises* **(2012, Nolan)**

I can make out about 25 percent of the dialogue in this film, and the anti–Occupy Wall Street plot is insane. Still, it's better than Nolan's first one. Which is . . .

 5   *Batman Begins* **(2005, Nolan)**

The film that reminded us all that Katie Holmes cannot act and Liam Neeson and Morgan Freeman stopped even bothering to try long ago.

 6   *Batman Forever* **(1995, Schumacher)**

Sort of how I imagine a gay club on cocaine in the 1980s would look. But not in a good way.

 7   *Batman and Robin* **(1997, Schumacher)**

The movie that proved George Clooney is actually a superhero because he alone among the entire cast was able to rise like a phoenix out of the ashes of this unspeakable dreck.

The Ten Best Rock Songs on an Eighties Movie Soundtrack

10   **"When the Going Gets Tough, the Tough Get Going," by Billy Ocean, from *The Jewel of the Nile***

Not, strictly speaking, a rock song. But if you have never seen the video for this song, starring Michael Douglas, Kathleen Turner, and Danny DeVito as backing singers, well, your life is just about to get a whole lot better.

9   **"Eye of the Tiger," by Survivor, from *Rocky III***

The only acceptable song to play when you're beating up Mr. T.

8   **"Stir It Up," by Patti LaBelle, from *Beverly Hills Cop***

I love Patti LaBelle, I love this song, and, most of all, I love the moment Eddie Murphy gurns to this song at the end of *Beverly Hills Cop*.

7   **"You're the Best," by Joe Esposito, from *The Karate Kid***

Play this song before leaving the house and you will win every karate tournament that day, and that's a fact.

"Footloose," by Kenny Loggins, from *Footloose*

Seriously, how awesome must it be to be Kenny Loggins? The man's an eighties movie soundtrack legend.

 "The Heat Is On," by Glenn Frey, from *Beverly Hills Cop*

Like the Big Lebowski, I cannot stand the Eagles. But such is the power of *Beverly Hills Cop* that I cannot resist this song by head Eagle Glenn Frey.

 "Power of Love," by Huey Lewis and the News, from *Back to the Future*

MARTYMCFLY4EVA.

 "Into the Groove," by Madonna, from *Desperately Seeking Susan*

I totally agree with you—there is not enough Madonna in this book. For the moment in *Desperately Seeking Susan* when she dances to herself on a jukebox, she deserves her own chapter.

 "Danger Zone," by Kenny Loggins, from *Top Gun*

Just listening to this makes me want to ride Val Kilmer's tail.

"Don't You Forget About Me," by Simple Minds, from *The Breakfast Club*

Come on, there is just no competition. Not just the best eighties movie rock song but the best musical moment in an eighties movie. Punch the air, Judd Nelson! Punch it hard!

Top Ten Weirdest Songs on an Eighties Movie Soundtrack

 "Lethal Weapon," by Honeymoon Suite, from *Lethal Weapon*

"Love can be a lethal weapon," eh? Strictly speaking, it can't.

 "Spies Like Us," by Paul McCartney

From "Penny Lane" to "Eleanor Rigby" to this. And people say marijuana doesn't damage the brain.

 Queen's songs for *Highlander* soundtrack

All credit to the group for getting references to the movie's plot in each of their songs, even if they make no sense now. "A rage that lasts a thousand years," indeed.

 "Please, Please, Please Let Me Get What I Want," by the Dream Academy, from *Ferris Bueller's Day Off*

I feel rather guilty putting this in because it's not weird. I love it. But there is still something very amusing about a self-pitying song by the Smiths getting turned into an instrumental piece by an Australian band and rendered into a love song.

"Daddy's Girl," by Peter Cetera, from *Three Men and a Baby*

This song is about the love a daughter feels for her father. Sweet, right? Wrong! Here's the chorus: "Little baby wanna hold you tight / She don't ever wanna say good night / She's a lover, she wanna be Daddy's Girl." I love *Three Men and a Baby* but someone needs to call CPS, stat.

 "Ghostbusters," by Ray Parker Jr., from *Ghostbusters*

A classic. Also: weird.

 "Peace in Our Life," by Frank Stallone, from *Rambo: First Blood Part II*

Sylvester Stallone's brother singing about peace in a movie in which his brother bombs the world. God bless you, Stallone family.

 "Magic Dance," by David Bowie, from *Labyrinth*

David Bowie, in a mullet, singing about a magic dance to a bunch of Muppets and a baby. I love the eighties.

2   **"Oh Yeah," by Yello, from *Ferris Bueller's Day Off*, etc.**

I feel like this song was in every eighties movie, but it was actually only in two: *Ferris Bueller's Day Off* and *The Secret of My Success*. It just feels that way because it was so weird. And bonus: the band were Swiss.

1   **"The Dragnet" rap, by Dan Aykroyd and Tom Hanks, from *Dragnet***

And people say white people can't rap.

Eddie Murphy's Eighties Movies

Race Can Be Transcended

Time has not been kind to eighties comedy superstars. John Belushi is long dead, Harold Ramis is recently dead, Martin Short has largely faded from view, Dan Aykroyd is only spotted these days flogging vodka, the brilliantly gifted Steve Martin moved over to romantic leads with somewhat mixed results,* Chevy Chase appears to be engaged in a full-time job of generating negative publicity about himself,† and Steve Guttenberg was last spotted doing a Christmas

---

* *L.A. Story*: brilliant. *Shopgirl*: kill me.

† Choice Chevy Chase anecdotes from over the years: in 1996 he made a guest appearance on *Saturday Night Live* and, among other things, told a female writer, "Maybe you can give me a hand job later" (*Live from New York*, Tom Shales and James Andrew Miller); no one who works with him has a good word to say about him ("Chevy has a reputation for being a dick, and that reputation is earned," said Dino Stamatopoulos, who costarred with Chase on the sitcom *Community*); even Will Ferrell, who is widely agreed to be one of the nicest men in comedy, described Chase, whom he reveres, as "the worst host [of *Saturday Night Live*] . . . maybe he took too many back pills that day" (*Live from New York*, Shales and Miller).

play in a London suburb.* Truth be told, the eighties comedy legends have struggled for longevity at least as much as the eighties teen
stars, who all seemed to disappear into outer space on the stroke of
midnight December 31, 1989. In fact, of all the comedy legends to
emerge in the eighties, the only one still standing with any real current critical credibility is Bill Murray.

And that's great—I love Murray. Murray is one of my favorite
things (Venkman) in my favorite movie (*Ghostbusters*, as I might
have already mentioned) of all time. He's also my very favorite thing
(Jeff the roommate) in one of my most-watched films (*Tootsie*) of all
time. *Caddyshack, Tootsie, Stripes, Ghostbusters, Scrooged*: there is no
doubt, Murray had a very good eighties. But back in 1989, if you'd
asked anyone on any street in any Western country which American comedy star they reckoned would still be revered in twenty-five
years' time, you would have got one universal answer, and that answer would not have been Bill Murray. It would, instead, and quite
rightly, have been the man who remains the biggest comedy star of
all time, and the one to whom time has been comparatively the most
cruel: Eddie Murphy.†

Public attitudes toward Murray and Murphy exemplify how
short people's memories are. No matter how good Murray's eighties
were, the reason he is still adored today is that he has made some
very smart career moves in the past fifteen years. With the noted
exception of *Groundhog Day* (which is really just a mystical update
of *Scrooged*, for the record), Murray, like most eighties comedians,
had a pretty patchy 1990s.‡ He made films like the laughably miscast

---

* Well, Guttenberg was a comedy superstar in MY world, okay?
† ". . . and Steve Guttenberg!" nine-year-old Hadley.
‡ Suggested essay: "The nineties were to eighties comedians what the eighties were to
seventies musicians. Discuss."

Mad Dog and Glory[*] and *The Man Who Knew Too Little*, in which he starred alongside such unlikely British costars as Richard Wilson and, er, Dexter Fletcher. Someone presumably thought this might be Murray's *A Fish Called Wanda*. It was not.

Things would very likely have continued in this vein had he not been rescued by Wes Anderson, who, with *Rushmore* (1998) and *The Royal Tenenbaums* (2001), reminded the world that Murray is, in fact, a wonderful dramatic actor.[†] Anderson's friend Sofia Coppola took note and cast him in 2003's *Lost in Translation* as the jaded celebrity bored by money and Japanese people, and lo, suddenly, it became a truth universally acknowledged that there is not a person on the planet who does not worship at Murray's altar. Murphy, on the other hand, is a different story.

Most people born before 1980 think of Murphy with the kind of bemused, embarrassed disappointment one feels about a cousin who once seemed so cool only then to grow up and become a tedious old fart who works in PR and gets drunk every Christmas and makes homophobic jokes.[‡] Murphy, it is widely agreed, hasn't made a decent comedy in almost twenty years, having opted for the grim career of a sellout consisting of fat suits, kiddie franchises, and movies so bad you can only hope he was paid $30 million for his time.

And this is really not fair. Sure, Murphy's wasted a lot of years in unwatchable dross like *Holy Man* and *The Adventures of Pluto Nash*,

---

[*] In which Murray plays a mafioso and Robert De Niro plays an everyman nebbish. Sure, that makes sense, right?

[†] Although some of us are getting a little tired of Murray playing the same role of the cuckolded husband in Anderson's films, and miss the manic Murray of the eighties and wish he didn't always have to play a jaded cynic now. But that's a subject for another day.

[‡] Although, ironically, when Murphy made homophobic jokes in the eighties—which he did A LOT, and later apologized for—the only people who protested were gay people.

one of the biggest box-office disasters of all time. But he has also made some excellent movies in (relatively) recent years: in the very funny Steve Martin 1999 comedy *Bowfinger* he is completely brilliant playing both a Hollywood superstar and the superstar's dopey brother, and he absolutely should have been nominated for an Oscar for it. But the Oscars, of course, don't do comedy so instead, in classic Oscars style, Murphy got nominated for a later and less deserving but still good performance in the otherwise pretty mediocre *Dreamgirls* (2006). As Jimmy Early, the heroin-addicted, washed-up soul singer, Murphy proved to audiences that he can do dramatic acting, but in doing so he also reminded them how spectacularly lazy he has otherwise been in his later career, which presumably wasn't quite his intention.

Having said all that, don't, for heaven's sake, underestimate *Shrek*. Without Murphy's charming voiceover work as Donkey, that film would have just consisted of Mike Myers grunting about in a Scottish accent, and no child (or parent) wants to sit through that. *Shrek* would have barely been a movie were it not for Murphy, let alone three movies. Moreover, for all the sneers (mine included) lobbed at Murphy for making franchise movies for kids, like *The Nutty Professor*, *Daddy Day Care*, and *Doctor Dolittle*, no one has done it as successfully as him: altogether, those films, including their sequels, made $3.5 billion worldwide, which can't be described as a career failure.

But not even I fancy expending too much time and energy defending Murphy's post-1989 career, particularly compared to Murray's. As I said, the man has been pig-ass lazy.* What I will do,

---

* And he knows it, and what's more, he doesn't care. Murphy: "I'm never gonna go, 'I want to do this role because it's a challenge. I might not be able to pull it off, that's why I'm excited about doing it.' For someone to sit on the outside, talking about, 'They need to push themselves,' it's so ridiculous. Push myself? I've had a whole fucking

though, is argue to the death that Murphy's eighties career more than compensates for a million *Pluto Nash*es. Eddie Murphy deserves so much more respect than he is accorded, first, because he was once the most exciting person to watch on-screen in the world. Just thinking of his grinning face in his eighties movies makes me smile. And second, because he made America believe, for the first and maybe only time in history, that race can be transcended.

In order to understand just how incredible it is that a black man became the biggest movie star of the eighties, we need to look at just how much racism eighties mainstream movies felt was A-OK. As chance would have it, I have watched a lot of eighties mainstream movies and here, in a handy list form, are some examples of the typical kind of racism to be found in them:

1. Wacky Asians
    Sixteen Candles (1984): Despite *Sixteen Candles* being a John Hughes teen movie, he was more in his slapstick *National Lampoon* mode as opposed to his soulful *Breakfast Club* gear. An exchange student from an unidentified Asian country called Long Duk Dong (ha ha! Asian people have funny names!) comes to stay with Molly Ringwald's family. He is obsessed with sex ("No more yanky my wanky!") and, of course, embarrassingly nerdy (Asians—amirite?!). His every entrance on-screen is announced by a background gong, like something out of an old Tintin comic now banned by school libraries. Twenty-four years later, National Public Radio described Long Duk Dong as "one of the most offensive Asian stereotypes Hollywood ever gave America."

---

career already, these are the gravy years. I have more than distinguished myself in the movie business." Brian Hiatt, "Eddie Murphy Speaks," *Rolling Stone*, November 2011.

2. Scary black people who teach white kids about real life

    Adventures in Babysitting (1987): This film is adorable. It exemplifies so many of the best things about eighties teen films—the sweetness, the silliness, the innocence. However, it also exemplifies one of the worst things, which is using black people as a signifier for danger. Here, for reasons that need not be overly elucidated, babysitter Elisabeth Shue must leave the safety of the white suburbs and travel into the ghettoized city, where she encounters all sorts of dangerous black people, ranging from car thieves to gangs to fans of blues music who force her and her youthful charges to sing some bebop. See also: the black prostitutes in *Risky Business* and *St. Elmo's Fire*, the black dudes in the bar in *Weird Science.**

3. Blacking up

    Soul Man (1986): When I tell people today that my sister and I actually rented this film from the local video shop back in 1987, I can see them looking at me the way I used to look at my grandfather when he talked about growing up in a time of segregated public bathrooms. Seriously, who knew people were still alive today who lived in such racist times! In this career killer of a film, C. Thomas Howell plays Mark, a spoiled white guy whose father, for no obvious reason other than to serve as a handy plot device, tells him he has to pay his own

---

* John Hughes was especially bad at portraying ethnic minorities. Aside from *Sixteen Candles* and *Weird Science*, there was 1983's *National Lampoon's Vacation*, which he wrote. In this film, the Griswold family get lost in the ghetto, which is populated by scary profane black people, and they promptly have their hubcaps stolen, because that's what black people are like. "I wonder if these guys know the Commodores," the Griswold son (Anthony Michael Hall) muses. "I'm not going to pretend I know the black experience," Hughes said in an interview with the *New York Times* in 1991, and that is fair enough. Unfortunately, he did seem to think he knew the black experience, and it was an experience consisting of thieving and jive talk.

way through Harvard Law School. Mark hits upon the idea of posing as a black student in order to score a scholarship— because everyone knows it's super-easy to get a scholarship to Harvard if you're black. They basically give them out to "the brothers," as Mark would say. So Mark takes a load of tanning pills and carries out this foolproof plan and stupid ethnic stereotypes ensue, all with a white actor in blackface for an entire movie. Perhaps the weirdest thing about *Soul Man* isn't that it was made at all, but that the black female lead, Rae Dawn Chong, ended up marrying Howell. At least one person wasn't totally repulsed by his blackface makeup. Also popular: Asianing up (the very white Fisher Stevens doing a "comedy" Indian accent in *Short Circuit*).

4.   Black people as comedy slaves

      The Toy (1982): Again, a movie I am amazed was made in my lifetime. In this film, Richard Pryor plays a poor black dude who is bought by a rich white dude to act as a toy for his spoiled brat of a kid. That's right: a black man as a white kid's toy. We can all only hope that Pryor was smoking a freak ton of crack when he signed up to make this one.

5.   Scary Asians

      Indiana Jones and the Temple of Doom (1984): We've looked at wacky Asians; now let's look at scary Asians. Eighties movies are full of menacing, mystical, and, yes, inscrutable Asians: *The Golden Child, Big Trouble in Little China,* and, on TV, pretty much every episode of *The A-Team*. Until George Lucas decided in 2008 that, after trashing the legacy of *Star Wars* with his utterly pointless prequel trilogy, he would now decimate people's memories of Indiana Jones with the appalling *Indiana Jones and the Kingdom of the Crystal Skull* in 2008, the worst *Indiana Jones* film was undoubtedly *Temple of Doom.* Here Spielberg bravely but unwisely decided to swap his usual villains, Nazis, for a blood-drinking Indian cult. Now, this is weird enough, but even worse is the portrayal of what wealthy Indians eat, which is living snakes, giant beetles, eyeball soup, and monkey brains. Ha ha ha, Asian people are GROSS. Happily, Spielberg returned to the Nazis in the next *Indiana Jones,* and that's probably the only circumstance in which I would use "happily" and "returned to the Nazis" in a single sentence.

6. Wise Asians

   The Karate Kid (1984): I imagine Mr. Miyagi (so wise! so inscrutable! so asexual!) isn't on the Japan Society's Board of Noted Cultural Figureheads, but at least he isn't played for laughs. Well, except for when he fails to catch a fly with his chopsticks—how all Japanese people spend their evenings, you know. What a LOSER.

7. The camp black comedy character

   Eighties movies were undeniably, heartbreakingly homophobic. But the popularity of camp black characters in eighties movies also reflects the era's racism. By rendering a black character, such as *Mannequin's* Hollywood Montrose (Meshach Taylor) comically, over-the-top camp, the film both desexes him and essentially minstrelizes him, turning him into an exaggerated self-parody at whom audiences can laugh.*

In fact, we can just look at Murphy's own early movies to see

---

* Not that camp white gay characters from eighties movies were exactly paragons of GLAAD's ideals. It's a tight competition but I think the most laughably awful one here is Ron (Matthew Laurance) in *St. Elmo's Fire,* Demi Moore's gay neighbor who works as an interior designer (obviously) and swans around holding a cocktail glass, as the gays do, you know.

what he was up against in this decade. In *48 Hours*, Murphy's first film, he plays Reggie, a convict who is teamed up with Jack, played by Nick Nolte, a charmingly gruff cop, and by "charmingly gruff" I mean "totally racist." Here are just some of the names Jack calls Reggie TO HIS FACE:*

"Watermelon."

"Spearchucker."

The N-word.

Truly, nothing makes a film's protagonist more adorable than some good ol' racism. It is worth noting that Jack is the lead in the movie and Reggie is his sidekick—it's just because Murphy is so charismatic that the movie seems like it belongs to both of them. It's Jack who has the personal life, and it's Jack who has the emotional journey in the film; Reggie is just there to serve the plot. So here we have a movie protagonist, whom we're supposed to like, being openly racist, in 1982. When Jack later apologizes to Reggie for saying those things "I shouldn't have said," this is depicted as proof of his inner sensitivity beneath his gruff (read: "racist") shell, and how he is actually more perceptive than the other cops who just see Reggie as a "con"—although no one in the film other than Jack uses racist slurs about him. *48 Hours* is one of the most influential cop movies ever made, and its pairing of unlikely guys, one white, one black, was copied so extensively in the eighties (*Lethal Weapon*, *Die Hard*, *Miami Vice*) and later (*Men in Black*), it's easy to forget just how original it once was. But not one of the movie's many copies took inspiration from Jack's racist language, and for a goddamn reason.

Decades later, Murphy spoke about the racist language in *48 Hours*:

---

* Obviously, calling him these names behind his back wouldn't be great, either, but watching him say them to Murphy's face is physically painful.

You know why it worked then and the reason why it wouldn't now? My significance in film—and again I'm not going to be delusional—was that I'm the first black actor to take charge in a white world on-screen. That's why I became as popular as I became. People had never seen that before. Black-exploitation movies, even if you dealt with the Man, it was in your neighborhood, never in their world. In *48 Hours*, that's why it worked, because I'm running it, making the story go forward. If I was just chained to the steering wheel sitting there being called "watermelon," even back then they would have been like, "This is wrong, wrong, wrong, wrong!"

And he's right, to a certain extent: Murphy positively chews up the screen in this movie, which is no easy thing to do when you're acting alongside a certified ham like Nolte doing his usual gruff-old-goat Nolte thing. Murphy absolutely dominates the film, and this in turn renders the abuse, according to him, less appalling. But he's slightly mixing up cause and effect. Murphy is making the movie go forward, but no one thought that would be the case when he was cast. In fact, Richard Pryor was originally envisaged for the role and, for all Pryor's undoubted gifts, he was never able to break out of the limited (read: racist) boxes in which he was put in films (see the aforementioned *The Toy*). So the fact remains that Murphy's first big film was one in which the sympathetic protagonist is a big ol' racist—and he triumphs over him. Readers who like metaphors are encouraged to make their own connections here.

In Murphy's next film, the still completely delightful *Trading Places*, he plays Billy Ray Valentine, a poor black con artist who switches places with a wealthy white dude called Louis Winthorpe III (Dan Aykroyd). Here, when Mortimer Duke (Don Ameche) uses the N-word about Valentine, this is depicted as proof of his evilness, and it's what motivates Valentine to take revenge. However, the other good male protagonist in the film, Louis, does have a tendency to refer to Valentine as a "negro," much to Valentine's understandable irritation. Strangely, though, Valentine seems totally fine when Louis later blacks up when he adopts the disguise of a Jamaican stoner in order to trick the guy who played the evil principal in *The Breakfast Club* and the stupid police chief in *Die Hard** (do try to keep up).

"That was very controversial, even back then, and [the studio heads] Barry Diller and Ned Tannen hated that we did that," says *Trading Places'* director, John Landis. "But the point is, that it's supposed to be ridiculous and pathetic, and it is. Danny can do a very good Jamaican accent, but he's doing a terrible one here." And this is true—but again, it does mean that we have a mainstream movie featuring a protagonist employing an offensive black stereotype that would not even be used by villains in movies today. But I do have some sympathy with Landis when he adds, referring to the ending of *Trading Places* in which the bad guy is trapped in a cage with a gorilla, "I was fascinated that [studio heads] were outraged by [the black face] but not some guy being fucked in the ass by a gorilla."[†]

Murphy's career began when he was turned down at the age of nineteen by *Saturday Night Live* in 1980. Even though *Saturday Night Live* prided itself on being ever so cutting-edge, the show had yet to be convinced that its audience could handle more than one black cast member at a time, and when Murphy turned up he was told that Robert Townsend had already been cast and so the role of "the black guy" was filled. Instead, Murphy was halfheartedly

---

* Paul Gleason, the go-to man in the eighties for stupid villains.
† I should probably stress again at this point that I completely adore this film and watch it at least three times a year.

assigned as a featured player, as opposed to a regular cast member. After a year and a change of boss, Murphy's talent and popularity were simply impossible to ignore and so he was promoted—and he promptly saved the TV sketch show.

"If not for Eddie's talent and popularity, *SNL* would probably have died in the early 80s," Tom Shales and James Andrew Miller write. And if that had happened, comedians who got their start on *SNL* after Murphy's era, including Chris Farley, Chris Rock, Mike Myers, Will Ferrell, Tina Fey, and Amy Poehler, might well have never been launched. Many, many comedians today stand on Murphy's shoulders.

Being "the black guy" was pretty much par for the course for black actors in America in the early 1980s. "The status of the black person in pop culture in the early eighties reflected a kind of tokenism on some levels," says Mark Anthony Neal, a professor of black popular culture at Duke University. "You look at TV shows that started up then, such as *The Facts of Life* [in which one black girl is at a posh all-white girls' boarding school] or *Diff'rent Strokes* [in which two poor black boys are adopted by a rich old white man], and you have token black bodies in strange, white situations. I think many black audiences appreciated the move away from the blaxploitation images that were very popular in the seventies, but I think there was also concern that a lot of the characters you saw were not fully rounded at all."

Being "the black guy" on *SNL* was about as thankless a job as it sounds. Garrett Morris, the first black cast member, was, according to original cast member Jane Curtin, "treated horribly, horribly—by the writers, by some of the performers, and by Lorne [Michaels, the show's creator]," which is demonstrably true. During his *SNL* tenure Morris was repeatedly humiliated in sketches that did more than border on racist: he was made to wear a monkey suit and one time the writers wrote a parody commercial for him in which he advertised a toothpaste called Tarbrush to darken black people's teeth (Lorne Michaels cut it from the show after seeing it in rehearsal, although, according to Morris, two black technicians walked out in protest that it was even considered). For his part, Morris said he built "the only nonwhite chair in that whole thing, and I shed blood for that." It cost him more than blood. The comedian became so depressed about his situation, and so bored from being underused by the writers, that he started freebasing.

Even after Murphy proved that "the black guy" could be a real asset to the show, *Saturday Night Live* continued to treat black cast members as mere tokens, there to impersonate black celebrities and little else. Damon Wayans (on the show from 1985 to 1986) got so annoyed with the program he started wearing sunglasses inside and telling people, "It's too white in here, it hurts my eyes." Eventually, he sabotaged a skit while on air and was duly fired and soon after established *In Living Color*, a comedy sketch show featuring mainly black comedians. Chris Rock (*Saturday Night Live* cast member from 1990 to 1993) also got frustrated with "this weird, Waspy world of a show"—and that was in 1993, thirteen years after Murphy arrived.

This was the world in which Murphy got his start. And yet, despite all these seemingly insurmountable hurdles, he became *SNL*'s biggest breakout star of all time. But as Bill Simmons points out, "Eddie never catered to *SNL*'s white audience, that's for sure." His jokes were about specific African-American tropes and icons, from the ghetto to James Brown to, most famously, his imitations of Stevie Wonder. He broke through *SNL*'s white ceiling, and the lagging racism of America in the eighties, not by being reductive or offensive about black people, but simply by being so incandescent that no one could resist him.

"He was young and he was tuned into what was happening in

young black America, and he wasn't Cosby, but he wasn't Richard Pryor," says Neal. "You never got the sense that he was whitewashing who he was, or what his experience was."

Murphy looked up to both Cosby and Pryor as mentors, and a large part of his success came from synthesizing the lessons he learned from them: he wasn't quite as dangerous as Pryor, but nor was he as conservative as Cosby. In his stand-up, he talked about working-class black experiences, like Pryor did, but not in a way that would alienate white audiences, as Cosby feared. His mentors, perhaps unsurprisingly, had some reservations about his tactics. Cosby, according to Murphy's very credible account in his 1989 live show, *Raw*, thought Murphy used too much dirty language. Pryor wrote: "I never connected with Eddie. People talked about how much my work influenced Eddie, and perhaps it did. But I always thought Eddie's comedy was mean. I used to say, 'Eddie, be a little nice,' and that would piss him off."

But despite his predecessors' reservations, he was more successful than they ever dreamed of being. "Eddie was making jokes in high school when he was sixteen, he was playing in comedy clubs at eighteen, he was on *SNL* at nineteen, he was a movie star at twenty, and he was a superstar by twenty-two. He was just an unbelievable meteorite," says John Landis.

He is also, as Bill Simmons points out, the only cast member of *SNL* to break into movies properly while still on the show. Even before *48 Hours* had been released, he was cast in *Trading Places*, a film that had originally been envisioned for Richard Pryor and Gene Wilder but, as the film's director John Landis delicately puts it, "Richard unfortunately set himself on fire, so the project went on hold." When the studio previewed *48 Hours*, test audiences went completely nuts for Murphy. Studio boss Jeffrey Katzenberg called up Landis, best known then for directing *Animal House* and *The Blues*

Brothers, the movies that launched former *Saturday Night Live* comedian John Belushi, and asked him to repeat this trick with Murphy, and Landis agreed. So, for the second time, Murphy was cast in a role that had been Pryor's, and, unlike Pryor, Murphy was smart enough to know that his success depended on him staying clean.* In Hollywood's eyes, Murphy was taking over from Pryor as "the black guy."†

Unfortunately, Paramount "hated everyone" else Landis cast. They didn't want Aykroyd because Belushi had just died and Aykroyd's last film, *Doctor Detroit*, had flopped. "So conventional wisdom was that it was over for Danny. It was like when Dean Martin and Jerry Lewis broke up, everyone was like, 'Poor Dean Martin, we'll never see him again.' But I cast him anyway and the studio was furious but I said, 'I'm sorry, you gave me final cut and that's who I want,'" recalls Landis. "People forget what a good actor Danny is. Winthorpe has nothing to do with Elwood [his character in *The Blues Brothers*], they're on a different planet from one another. If you give Danny direction he's great; if you leave him to his own resources, you get this strange Danny thing. But such a brilliant guy, really smart and funny."

---

* Murphy: "I've never actually even physically had cocaine. When I was 18, I was down in the Blues Bar with Belushi and Robin Williams, everybody was partying, I was like 'No.' Every now and then, I'd think about that moment, too, because I was around those guys, it was easy to party, and how everything would have changed. I know if I fucked around with that, I would have been all the way in. I'd have made a million headlines. There would have been no success, the story would have stopped in the Eighties." Hiatt, "Eddie Murphy Speaks."

† Murphy later said in an interview with Spike Lee: "Richard doesn't like me. . . . There's this thing where Richard feels that the reason his shit is the way it is, is because I came along and fucked his shit up. He really believes that. . . . It's really weird to find out that your idol hates you and shit" (Spike Lee, "Eddie," *Spin*, 1990). On the one hand, Pryor is right, Murphy did take his place. There was room for only one black man at the table back then. But on the other, it wouldn't have been so easy for him to do so if Pryor hadn't been setting himself on fire while freebasing crack.

The studio was even more outraged when he cast Jamie Lee Curtis, then known only for horror movies, as Ophelia, the kindly prostitute. "The script is wonderful but the big flaw in it is Ophelia, the hooker with the heart of gold, which is a total Hollywood cliché and a false character. So I knew I needed someone special to play her and when I met Jamie I could immediately see how funny and smart she is, and very sexy in a totally unorthodox way," says Landis.

Paramount, though, was so unimpressed by Landis's choice to hire "a B-picture actress," as studio boss Barry Diller put it, that they docked $2 million from the film's budget.

For the role of Coleman the butler, Landis desperately wanted to hire British comedian Ronnie Barker, as Landis was "a huge fan" of the British show *The Two Ronnies*. However, Barker told Landis that he never worked "more than twenty-five miles from home," so Denholm Elliott was hired instead. Finally, Landis wanted to include some old Hollywood in the cast, so he hired Don Ameche and Ralph Bellamy as the wicked Duke brothers. "And they were so supportive of Eddie, so good to him, who, you gotta remember, was still only about twenty when we made this, and the two of them were huge Hollywood legends who had been working for fifty years," says Landis. "I remember one day we were shooting the scene when Eddie's in the back of the Rolls-Royce with Don and Ralph and I have headphones on outside to hear them. Don says, 'You know, this is my ninety-ninth motion picture.' And Ralph says, 'That's funny, this is my hundredth feature film,' and Eddie shouts, 'Hey, Landis! Between the three of us we've made 201 movies!'" Murphy was, Landis recalls, "so happy when we were making *Trading Places*, just bouncing off the walls and so, so gifted. He just popped on-screen."

Murphy has said that the reason his eighties movie characters feel so real is that "[f]rom the very beginning, I always tried to make dialogue flow comfortably, I always did that to make it seem more authentic." However, he barely improvised in *Trading Places*. Even the scene when he pretends to be a blind Vietnam vet, which feels so much like a Murphy riff, was "all on paper." "*Trading Places*, John Landis movies, period—it looks like a bunch of improvisation, but John Landis is on you more than any other director I've ever worked with. He'll tell you how to read the line, and if he wants you to do a physical stunt, he'll show you. He really gets in there and you're like, 'This motherfucker,'" Murphy said.

Landis laughs at this: "Well, that's not exactly true, Eddie does improvise. I'm pretty specific, but there were times when we did improvise. One of my favorite lines in the movie was improvised. In the script [in that scene] when he's hassling the woman he says, 'Once you've had a man with no legs there's no going back. We can make it, baby, me and you.' But I just let the camera keep rolling and he then shouts out, 'Ain't you never seen *Porgy and Bess*?' That was Eddie."

During all this, Murphy was still making *SNL*. "I only had Eddie three days a week, because of *Saturday Night Live*, just like I'd only had Belushi two days a week when we were making *Animal House*," says Landis. But this would soon not be the case. *48 Hours* came out when they were still shooting *Trading Places* and audiences went insane for Murphy. When *Trading Places* came out in the summer of 1983, it was clear that Murphy was a star, and about five minutes after it arrived in cinemas, he quit *Saturday Night Live*, and it was at this point that Murphy began to transcend race.

Mickey Rourke was the first prospective Axel Foley, but he dropped out. He was then followed by (good Lord) Sylvester Stallone, who rewrote the script as a straight action movie, but he left the project two weeks before filming and made *Cobra* instead. So Jerry Bruckheimer and Don Simpson quickly hired Eddie Murphy for the role, and, in doing so, made the film the biggest hit of 1984 and one of the biggest hits of all time. Murphy is at his absolute comic prime in the film: in the scene in which he bluffs his way into getting a room at a swish Beverly Hills hotel, he goes from sweet to exaggeratedly angry to deadpan in the space of two minutes without even moving his body, and his reaction to being told the price of a room at the hotel remains one of the coolest double takes ever committed to film. Few actors—comic or otherwise—can convey so subtly so many conflicting emotions on their face, in this case, shock, trying not to look shocked, and a growing hysteria about being in Beverly Hills.

He stuck in one or two jokes about his race in the movie, including in the hotel scene, but otherwise there is hardly any reference to it whatsoever, which seems both sweetly innocent and frankly incredible considering this is a movie about a black guy running around Los Angeles in the eighties with a gun. Yes, Foley is supposed to be an outsider in Beverly Hills, but, according to the script, it's the fact that he's from Detroit that signifies his interloper status, not his race, although Murphy's race does compound that impression. (It's notable that the only other black person in the movie is Foley's boss back in Detroit. Is everyone in Beverly Hills white?[*]) For the first time in his career, Murphy's race did not define his character, and that this was allowed to happen is a testament to Murphy's superstardom, and Bruckheimer and Simpson's forward thinking.[†]

---

[*] Yes.

[†] A decade later, they would, again, recast a film written with white actors in mind with black stars. *Bad Boys* was originally supposed to star Dana Carvey and Jon Lovitz, of all the dweebs in the world. But they were then wisely swapped for Will Smith and Martin Lawrence. Bruckheimer and Simpson were impressively adaptable in their thinking about masculinity, a theme that defined all of their work together. It's very easy to imagine a Bruckheimer and Simpson *Beverly Hills Cop* starring Rourke, or even Stallone—that they cast Murphy, and therefore totally changed the tenor and ratio of machismo to comedy, shows how open-minded they actually were.

Whereas in *48 Hours* the black character is very much second-in-command to the white cop, in *Beverly Hills Cop* Axel is the leader of the pack of white cops, who don't just rely on him to catch the bad guys; they need him to show them how to behave in a bar. This wasn't just the first time a black cop was depicted as being both professionally and socially superior to his white colleagues—it is the only time, until *Training Day* (2001), in which Denzel Washington is in charge of Ethan Hawke, and even in that film Hawke eventually triumphs over Washington. "There's this little box that African-American actors have to work in, in the first place," said Murphy. "And I was able to rise above it."

But even in *Beverly Hills Cop,* there was a notable restriction placed on Murphy: his on-screen romance. The only woman in the film is Jenny (Lisa Eilbacher), who is white. When Stallone rewrote the script, Axel and Jenny are romantically involved, which completely makes sense in the universe of the film. But in the version shot with Murphy, Axel seems utterly oblivious to Jenny, even though the character keeps throwing herself at him, reclining on his bed, following him on stakeouts for no reason whatsoever other than to be annoying in that way only women in male-led action films ever are. There is no need for the Jenny character to be in this movie—she serves less than zero function—and while I don't mean to suggest that if a woman is in an action movie then the least she can do is sleep with the male lead, that is nonetheless very clearly why she was in the story in the first place. But because Murphy is black and Lisa is white (to have cast a black actress as well as a black lead would have made this mainstream action movie "too black," presumably), no romance can happen between them.

Instead, in both *Beverly Hills Cop* and its 1987 sequel, Axel is rendered completely asexual, and deliberately oblivious to white women, even when one of those white women is Brigitte Nielsen, for God's sake. This is to make him seem "safe" to white audiences, especially white male audiences: "See, this isn't one of THOSE kind of black guys—this is a good black guy! Sure, he's fun and knows where all the strip clubs in town are, but he's also the kind you can trust not to touch a white woman, even if she's lolling across a bed when alone in a hotel room with him!" the movies say.

In this regard, Axel is pretty much the opposite of the image Murphy went out of his way to portray in the hugely successful films of his stand-up that sandwich the decade, *Delirious* (1983) and *Raw* (1987), in which he prowls around the stage in head-to-toe leather: "If I took Brooke Shields to the Grammy's, y'all would lose your mind," he riffs in *Raw*. "Because y'all know Brooke would get fucked that night."

The few love interests Murphy is allowed on-screen are black women,* and audiences are never allowed to see them actually having sex, from *48 Hours* to *Coming to America*. In Murphy's film after *Beverly Hills Cop*, *The Golden Child*, he is allowed to kiss a "Tibetan" woman on-screen (actually played by the Chilean-Iraqi-Irish actress Charlotte Lewis, but not strictly Caucasian, and that's all that matters here), but no more. Even in the last scene of *Trading Places*, when Billy Ray, Louis, Ophelia, and Coleman have escaped to an unidentified paradise island, Coleman's girlfriend appears to be Tahitian and an island native, which makes sense, but Billy Ray's girlfriend is definitely, pointedly black. It's not that I'm so desperate to see Murphy have sex on-screen (and as anyone who has seen 1992's *Boomerang* knows, Murphy's enthusiasm in a sex scene can make a little go a very long way), or to see him hook up with a white woman. But it's pretty extraordinary to see how nervous eighties

---

* And notably much lighter-skinned than him, to boot, particularly in *48 Hours* and *Coming to America*, reflecting yet another racial stereotype.

filmmakers were about letting a young, attractive black man on-screen seem in any way sexual to mainstream white audiences. Tom Cruise, Tom Hanks, hell, even Dan Aykroyd were allowed to have on-screen sex lives in the eighties—but not Murphy.

The Golden Child is the second film in which Murphy's race is irrelevant to the character. There is absolutely no reason why Chandler Jarrell, private investigator for lost children, should be black, and there is no reference to it in the film, which is not surprising as Mel Gibson was originally slated to star in this film, which was conceived as a shameless rip-off of the *Indiana Jones* movies (which, themselves, are hardly a black film franchise). But Murphy was given Gibson's part and he had proved by now that he had transcended race, an achievement that would feel a little more triumphant if Murphy didn't look quite so bored on-screen during the whole of this movie. Although, to be fair to him, *The Golden Child* is a completely ridiculous movie, one that makes so little sense it's like watching a film that was dubbed into a foreign language and then redubbed into English. Although it's not quite as ridiculous as the hat Murphy wears for the whole film.

Murphy was by now one of the biggest superstars alive. He was so popular, in fact, he was able to release the delightfully stupid single "Party All the Time" in 1985, with an extraordinarily be-weaved Rick James—and it still reached number two in the *Billboard* chart, denied the top spot by Lionel Ritchie's "Say You, Say Me." The man believed he could do anything, and American audiences agreed. But times were about to change, again.

Murphy's feelings about having a social responsibility as a black actor have never been that hard to fathom: he's resented it. "I know because of the level of my celebrity I have been forced—I am being forced—to be a politician in a manner of speaking. And what happens, although I know I have a responsibility politically, ultimately I am an entertainer, I am an artist first and foremost. And you accept the responsibility, but the artist part of you resents the fact they don't just give you the freedom to just be an artist," he said in 1990. Murphy was very aware that he was the successful "black guy" in Hollywood, and with that came the awareness that in order to maintain his position, and to keep transcending race, he had—to a certain extent—to play along.

Which is not to say he didn't occasionally speak up—but, unlike Richard Pryor or, later, Spike Lee, he would do so with a smile on his face so some people might miss the punch. In 1988 he presented the Best Film Award at the Oscars and when he got up onstage he told a palpably confused audience that he initially declined the offer to present because the Academy "haven't recognized black people in the motion pictures. . . . Throughout sixty years Hattie McDaniel won the first [Oscar], Sidney Poitier won one, and Lou Gossett won one."

He paused a little at this point, as though going off script: "I'll probably never win an Oscar for saying this but, hey, what the hey I gotta say it!" He shrugged with a laugh. "Actually, that might not be any trouble because the way it's going we only get one every twenty years so we ain't due until 2004 so by this time this will have all blown over."*

But, he said onstage, his agent said, "You can't snub the Academy." So he went, even though he believed that "black people [were still made] to bring up the rear of society." If he hadn't come, then he simply would have been absent, but this way at least they noticed his speech.

"I don't think you can beat the system," Murphy said two years later. "I think you can be successful within the system."

---

* Murphy was almost right: the next African-American actors to win an Oscar were Denzel Washington and Halle Berry, both in 2001.

He argued with Spike Lee, who criticized him for not insisting on having more black actors and crew members in his movies. Murphy felt, probably rightly, that if he took this stand his career in the studio system would be jeopardized and then there would be no black actors in the mainstream A-list in Hollywood at all. "The scariest thing about you to me," he said to Lee, "is that every black person who really stood up and said, 'Fuck it, I'm about this,' got dissed, filled, fucked over—everybody from Dr. King to Ali, you know?"

But things were shifting in African-American film with the rise of the independent industry. By the late 1980s, Spike Lee had released *She's Gotta Have It* and was making *School Daze*, two independent movies emphatically about African-Americans and African-American experiences. Murphy, however, felt "I am very black and I have a very strong black consciousness, but I am about gradual change and dialogue that is much more civil." What this meant was not making an assertively black film, but a big, glossy Hollywood movie that happened to feature African-Americans. Succeeding within the system, in other words.

"Eddie called me up and had this idea about an African prince who has an arranged marriage, but didn't want it. So he comes to the United States to find a liberated woman of his equal," says Landis. "He really had no story other than that, and so I went home and told my wife, and she got incredibly excited. She said, 'John, don't you understand? It's Cinderella! It's Sleeping Beauty! It's a fucking fairy tale—from Africa!'"*

Landis started to plan the story about an African prince, Akeem (Murphy), who, along with his best friend Semmi (Arsenio Hall), comes to America to find his regal bride. He heads to—where

---

*Landis's wife, costume designer Deborah Nadoolman Landis, was right to be excited: she ended up getting nominated for an Oscar for her work on *Coming to America*.

else?—Queens, where he works in a fast-food restaurant, McDowell's, and falls in love with the owner's daughter while pretending to be a pauper. The film includes still hysterically funny and knowing references to African-American culture, including the advertisements for "Soul Glo," a horrible product that makes Afro hair shimmer, and god-awful black soul singers fronting bands with names like "Sexual Chocolate." It also gave roles to established African-American actors, such as James Earl Jones, and launched a then totally unknown Samuel L. Jackson.

"As I planned the story, I got very excited, but for reasons I wouldn't discuss for twenty years," says Landis. "I suddenly realized, The plot will have nothing to do with their color! So it was essentially a black movie but it's not—it's not about their color, it's a fairy tale. It's a romantic comedy, and the storytelling itself is very conservative and traditional, and it looks like a traditional Hollywood movie—these were all my intentions. It's the movie of mine that made the most money. Around the world, it's made almost one billion dollars. It was a huge hit, and, importantly, a huge international hit. But the great success of that movie is that it's an African-American movie and [white] people don't really notice, and that's very satisfying to me."

This, though, was precisely the sort of thing that Spike Lee objected to: he didn't want covert success, or success within a white framework, and he certainly didn't see the point in making an African-American film if no one knew it was one. Whereas Murphy believed his success was the statement, Lee argued there was no statement without a specified message. This is the trade-off that all minorities face in the search for success: in order to achieve mainstream success, how much are you willing to risk leaving behind your core audience?

According to Duke's Mark Anthony Neal:

In the early days black audiences appreciated Murphy's presence onscreen. But when you start to see some of the tensions in the late 1980s, particularly around films and the tension between him and Spike Lee, and folks that were looking for quote unquote more authentic and even political black filmmaking that resonated especially for a hip-hop generation, Eddie Murphy got left behind. He was doing something else. It's really not until the nineties that he did *Boomerang* that he begins to reclaim some of what he had lost in terms of a black following. But this was something that befell that whole 1980s crossover generation. Michael Jackson struggled with that, losing a core black audience because he had crossed over so much, Whitney Houston got booed at the 1989 Soul Train Music Awards; obviously what Eddie Murphy was doing was in there, too.

Murphy knew this and struggled with it, uncertain what to do and horrified that the people he thought he was representing were rejecting him. "You get these black people, it seems like they turn on you," he said to Spike Lee. Coupled with that, he was increasingly bogged down in the weird claustrophobia that comes with extreme fame, cut off from the real world and surrounded only by his tight, adoring coterie,* and simultaneously filled with resentment toward his critics, with whom he felt he could do no right. "If I was rubbing you the wrong way, at the core of it was some racist shit: 'Look at this arrogant nigger, two thumbs wayyyyy down!'" he said with a laugh in a 2011 interview, recalling the late eighties. "Then I wasn't

---

* You need only to look at the backstage shots of *Raw* to see how Murphy kept himself so closely nestled within his entourage, protecting himself from any outside influence or interference.

helping either. I wasn't giving no humble pie: 'Fuck y'all, suck my dick, motherfucker!' "

He is utterly wonderful in *Coming to America* but, Landis recalls, "he was less joyful, much less joyful, than the person I made *Trading Places* with five years before." So much less joyful, in fact, that he tried to beat Landis up one day on set and grabbed him by the throat. "To this day, I don't know what happened," says Landis. "We were shooting in McDowell's on Queens Boulevard, and it was snowing heavily outside. I was talking to someone and Eddie grabbed me from the back and put me in a headlock, and I was like, 'What the fuck was that?!' I was furious! And he was furious with me! And I grabbed the script girl's notebook and I shouted at Eddie, 'Here, shove this up your ass!' and I stormed off the set."

Eventually, Landis angrily returned to the movie set and went to see Murphy in his trailer. "I go in and it wasn't even a confrontation, it was just Eddie venting. He was very angry at his family, I don't know what was going on, and he was very angry at me, saying I was treating him the same as everyone else. He said, 'I'm the star, you're not giving me enough.' I don't know what the hell . . . Eddie said, 'I'm going to have you fired,' and I said, 'Okay, but let's finish the day.' "

So they finished shooting the scene in which Murphy's character, Prince Akeem, meets Patrice (Allison Dean) at McDowell's, and she invites him to a basketball game—no one watching this sweet, funny scene would guess that Murphy was raging inside, or that the director was furious at him. Murphy went home that night and, usually teetotal, had some alcohol: "I went back to the house and Arsenio got me drunk. . . . I can't drink," he said.

Landis went home that evening, similarly enraged, because he fully expected to be fired from the movie. "So [studio boss] Ned Tannen calls me and says, 'Listen, John, Eddie called and is very, very upset. But we told him he has no power to fire you, we've seen the dailies, this is his best work, he's an idiot so we said, Eddie, here's the choice: we fire John and shut down the movie and sue you for the production costs, or we continue.' I was really shocked!" Landis recalls.

The next day, he returned to the set and went to talk with Murphy.

"So I go see him and—this is a terrible story but it's true—and he said, 'All right, we're going to finish the movie but we are no longer friends.' And I said, 'Deal!' So we did the movie, but we didn't talk off set at all."

Despite his anger about the film, Murphy later said that he did his best acting in *Coming to America*. The scene he specifically cited as being his biggest source of pride is the famous barbershop scene, in which he, along with Arsenio Hall, played multiple characters, including an old white Jewish man ("Like a boid!").

Landis remembers:

Those characters were never supposed to be played by Eddie and Arsenio. In fact, we'd already hired actors to play them. But one night I saw a black filmmaker—I won't say who—on television talking about his new movie, and he said something really shocking to me. He was talking about minstrel shows, and he said blackface was created by "Old Jews who wanted to play young black men." Obviously he was referring to Eddie Cantor and Al Jolson—but does he know anything about the history of blackface? So the next day I came into work and said, "Eddie, can you do a Yiddish accent?" And he said, "I don't know." And I said, "Well, I know you can, you can do anything." And he said, "Well, how will I look?" So I had Rick [Baker, the makeup artist, who was nominated for an Oscar for his work here] make him up and Eddie was so thrilled.

Landis then shot the barbershop scene using cutaways, with Murphy's comedian brother Charlie acting as a double in some scenes.

"From that point on, as soon as Eddie saw what Rick Baker could do, he was like, 'I want to play the barber!' And Arsenio said, 'I want to play the preacher!' And we had to pay off all the actors we hired."

This use of disguise in movies, which Murphy would then employ repeatedly for the next two decades, was a means for him to escape the pressures and demands he felt from critics and audiences, both black and white.

"From then on, whenever you look at Eddie's greatest performances, they're always in disguise, and it's interesting. If you look at the *Nutty Professor* remake, when he's in the fat suit, he's brilliant, when he's the other guy, he's not that interesting. And in *Bowfinger*, when he plays the movie star he's not that interesting, but as the brother he's dazzling. It's strange, but it somehow frees him and he's brilliant at it," says Landis.

Coming to America marked the end of Murphy's triumphant movie run, and a large part of this is because it was around this time that Murphy got tired of being funny: "I think you got tremendous pressure on you, Eddie. Because every time you open your mouth, people want to laugh. And that's crazy," Spike Lee said to him in 1990.

"And they want it to be as funny as the last time I said something," Murphy replied, almost certainly with an eye roll.

Maybe Murphy was sick of the pressure to be funny. Maybe it got too easy. Or maybe to be funny requires being aware of what life is like in the real world, and Murphy was now lost in the orbit of a superstar, cloistered up in his big homes with his gang. Whatever the reason, it wasn't a bad idea of Murphy's to try to break into drama;

for the few comedy actors who made it into the nineties, moving into drama was the way they achieved this: Tom Hanks, most obviously, and, later, Bill Murray. Unfortunately, Murphy's talent for picking stinkers in drama was almost as refined as his skill at picking successful comedies. He wrote, starred in, and directed 1989's *Harlem Nights*, which he admitted soon after was an absolute mess, and thereafter began his fallow run in the nineties, with only *Boomerang* alleviating the dreariness.

In 1993 John Landis got an unexpected call: Sherry Lansing, who then ran Paramount, told him that Murphy was going to make *Beverly Hills Cop* III, and he had asked for Landis to direct it. Landis was astonished: he and Murphy hadn't spoken since their fight on the set of *Coming to America*, five years earlier. But a bigger surprise was in store for him.

"Eddie didn't want to be funny, so that made it a strange experience," he says. "He was very jealous of Denzel Washington and Samuel Jackson, and he wanted to be an action star so he would go out of his way to avoid a joke, and I gave him so many opportunities. That became a very demoralizing movie to make. Luckily it made a lot of money, but it's a weird movie, because it isn't funny."

By now, Murphy was looking extremely out of step with the times. Although he increasingly made movies with largely African-American casts (*Harlem Nights*, *The Distinguished Gentleman*, *Boomerang*), they were not the kind of movies about African-Americans that were in vogue. Spike Lee's *Do the Right Thing* came out in 1989, followed by John Singleton's *Boyz n the Hood* and Mario van Peebles's *New Jack City*, both in 1991, and these films were a far bigger part of the zeitgeist than anything Murphy was making then. He was still making glossy Hollywood products, but audiences and critics were more interested in politically aware films. Murphy's run—one unparalleled by any comedian, white or black, ever since—was done.

In terms of the representation of African-Americans in movies, no other decade saw as much progress, and as quickly, as the eighties. Going from Nick Nolte calling Murphy a "spearchucker" in 1982 to Spike Lee's *Do the Right Thing* getting nominated for Oscars in 1989 is an incredible leap, and the person who made this happen was Murphy.

"Hollywood had to be convinced that black stars could be bankable," says Neal. "Pryor started that a little bit in the seventies but it really went full tilt in the eighties with Murphy. He was the necessary step in getting stories featuring black people to the mainstream. Now folks like Denzel Washington and Halle Berry can open movies, and it was Eddie Murphy who allowed for that to occur."

The irony for Murphy, though, was that in carving this path for others, he made himself look redundant. He was no longer "the black guy." There were other black guys, from Samuel L. Jackson to Laurence Fishburne to Denzel Washington, and he's the one who made the space for them.

"His films introduced or featured many black stars who later became stars, such as Arsenio Hall, Chris Rock, Halle Berry, Damon Wayans, Cuba Gooding Jr., and others. He did not 'pull up the ladder' after himself," adds Anna Everett, professor of film and media studies at the University of California, Santa Barbara.

What Murphy achieved in the eighties is more than any black actor had done before him or has done since, and the proof of that is that no one has been able to move the representation of African-Americans in Hollywood pictures significantly further forward since Murphy's era and the immediate years after.

"We haven't fully realized the promise that was hinted at with *Do the Right Thing* in 1989 and *Boyz n the Hood*," says Neal. "Then we saw black films by black independent auteurs getting nominated for Hollywood awards. But that kind of promise has not been sustained."

In Hollywood movies nowadays, black actors are still largely cast as the convict, the slave, the outsider, or shunted into secondary roles, like a judge or a police chief.* No movie with an all-black cast, from 1993's *What's Love Got to Do with It* to 1995's *Waiting to Exhale* to 1998's *How Stella Got Her Groove Back* to the work of Tyler Perry in the past decade, has ever achieved the kind of mainstream, pan-racial, and commercial success that *Coming to America* did.

Most tellingly of all, no black actor since has come even close to Murphy's success. "Eddie's movies have grossed over $6.5 billion worldwide before adjusting them for inflation. Will Smith's total: $5.735 billion. Denzel Washington's total: $2.788 billion," Bill Simmons writes. "I'm just sayin'."

But this is perhaps not a surprise considering how few roles there are in films for black actors, still. In 2014, for example, 73.1 percent of all the speaking or named characters in the top one hundred movies were white.

Eighties comedies are, for me, the height of comedy, in that they're silly without being stupid, they're sweet without being slushy, they're funny without being mean, and they understand the importance of a good script above all, and Murphy's eighties films, especially *Trading Places*, *Beverly Hills Cop*, and *Coming to America*, exemplify all those qualities. No one was funnier in the eighties than Eddie Murphy. Goddamn, that man was funny. He could swear like opera singers can sing and he would say more with his eyes in two seconds than other comedians manage with their voices in a year. No comedian before or since was more charismatic on-screen than

---

* And depictions of Asian men have hardly improved since the eighties, either. The screaming Asian gangster in *The Hangover*, played by Ken Jeong, is a direct descendant of Long Duk Dong.

him. Murphy is the case in point that for a black man to be on a par with his white contemporaries, he has to be ten times better than them.

Murphy was a million times better than anyone else so he succeeded above everyone. Maybe he just made it all look so easy in the eighties and that's why he doesn't get the credit he deserves today.

"No matter what you do, that shit is all getting turned into gobbledygook. In two hundred years, it's all dust, and in three hundred years, it ain't nothing, and in a thousand years, it's like you wasn't even fucking here. But if you're really, really lucky, if you really did something special, you could hang around a little longer," Murphy said recently.

Murphy's achievements will hang around longer.

I've never tried to interview Murphy, partly because he eschews almost all press these days, but mainly because I suspected that the rule "Never meet your heroes" was especially apt in regards to Murphy. It had been a long time since I'd read anything about him in which he didn't come across as a jerk, and while I didn't blame him for that—it's hard to retain human decency if people have been calling you a genius since the age of twenty—I didn't especially want to experience it for myself. I've been a journalist for sixteen years and interviewed so many artists who turned out to be complete jerks, and the result was that I could never watch, read, or listen to any of their work, which I'd previously loved, again. I couldn't bear for that to happen with Murphy, and I'd rather remember him grinning as Axel Foley, or looking so excited to be in *Trading Places* that he seemed ready to jump through the camera, than the tough-faced Hollywood near recluse he'd become.

But a few months after I sent this book off to my British publisher in 2015, my editor at the *Guardian* sent me back out to Los

Angeles to cover the film awards season, again. As I walked out of one movie shindig—jet-lagged, stressed about British newspaper deadlines, and riddled with morning sickness—I looked to my left, and there was Murphy. He was tuxedoed-up, his arm protectively around the back of his girlfriend, Paige Butcher, and walking alongside another man who I guessed was a member of his entourage. His face was hardened by age, a little, and maybe from having been too famous for too long. But he was, undeniably, Murphy, and it is the literal truth to say I nearly threw up on my shoes, and that had nothing to do with pregnancy. I followed behind him in a daze for a few minutes, staring at his back like some deranged stalker, as we walked into the banquet room. "Talk to him," my stupid id hissed. "You will never forgive yourself if you don't." He was standing by a table and his girlfriend had gone off somewhere. Murphy seemed to be by himself. I seized my chance.

"Mr. Murphy, I just wanted to say—" I started, and realized, too late, that I had no idea what I wanted to say. All my journalistic experience vanished in the bright light of my starstruck state. I was completely tongue-tied. Murphy looked at me with the boredom and disdain of a man who had been harassed by strangers every two minutes for almost two-thirds of his life, strangers who wanted something from him—a connection? validation?—that even they didn't understand. He walked away from me in midsentence and I stood there, humiliated and suffused with self-loathing. Exactly what I hadn't wanted to happen, had happened.

"Hey, you okay there?" said the guy who I thought was Murphy's entourage pal. I shrugged.

"Come here, let's have a selfie," he said.

Too embarrassed to do otherwise, I handed over my phone to him and he took our picture. It was only when I looked at the photo later when I got back to my hotel that I realized it was Kevin Hart, one of the biggest comedians working today. I look so much sadder in the selfie than nice Hart deserved.

Like I said, I've had disappointments in the past. I can't watch any movies starring Robert Downey Jr., for example (long story, neither the time nor the place), or read books by a certain author whose writing I once adored but whose name I can't even bear to type anymore. But I was more disheartened after my encounter with Murphy than I'd ever been before, and I knew there was only one way to cheer myself up. When I got back to my hotel, I picked up my iPad, on which I keep my five favorite films. I settled into bed, fired up the one that always made me laugh, settled back against my pillow, and was soon happily hooting and snorting away. The movie was, of course, *Trading Places*. At the risk of suggesting my personal taste reflects everyone's taste (although Lord knows I have seized that risk in the past without a second thought), the thing about Murphy is that the work—the best of his work—has always been bigger than the man, because talent that bright outshines any objections anyone can have with him personally. So yes, Eddie Murphy broke my heart a little—but he then healed it, too. Sometimes, that's the most you can ask of your idols.

Top Eighties Quotes

I've been so restrained—so far. Cut a lady some slack now, okay? These are the top twenty, and I quote them all, aloud or in my head, on a weekly basis. I've also made separate categories for the three most important movies of the decade in terms of quotes and, quite possibly, in terms of everything, ever.

20 "I'm too old for this shit." (*Lethal Weapon*)

19 "You are evil, and you must be destroyed." (*Steel Magnolias*)

18 "Any girl that did that to me I would not be too JAZZED to hold on to." (*Pretty in Pink*)

17 "You think what you want about me—I'm not changing. I like me." (*Planes, Trains and Automobiles*)

16 "You have chosen . . . wisely." (*Indiana Jones and the Last Crusade*)

15 "I love you." [Slap] "Snap out of it!" (*Moonstruck*)*

---

* Also from *Moonstruck*, I would like to give special mention to "Chrissie, over on the wall—bring me the big knife," because I love that scene so.

14 "Fuck me gently with a chain saw, do I look like Mother Teresa?" (*Heathers*)

13 "Looking good, Billy Ray!" "Feeling good, Louis!" (*Trading Places*)

12 "You know what I am? I'm your worst fuckin' nightmare—I'm a nigger with a badge." (*48 Hours*)

11 "Shame on you, you macho shithead!" (*Tootsie*)*

10 "The royal penis is clean, your highness." (*Coming to America*)

9 "If you build it, he will come." (*Field of Dreams*)

8 "Strange things are afoot at the Circle K." (*Bill and Ted's Excellent Adventure*)

7 "If Jesus came back and saw what's going on in his name, he'd never stop throwing up." (*Hannah and Her Sisters*)

---

*Also, special credit to "Dr. Brewster has tried to seduce several nurses in this unit, claiming to be in the throes of an uncontrollable impulse. Do you know what? I'm going to give every nurse on this floor an electric cattle prod and instruct them to zap them in his badoobies. Ruby? Hi, you wanna open the Yellow Pages under the section, Farm Equipment Retail. . . ."

6 "When you grow up, your heart dies." (*The Breakfast Club*)

5 "Roads? Where we're going we don't need roads." (*Back to the Future*)

4 "Your ego is writing checks that your body can't cash." (*Top Gun*)

3 "I gave her my heart and she gave me a pen." (*Say Anything*)

2 "Human sacrifice! Dogs and cats living together! Mass hysteria!" (*Ghostbusters*)

1 "Nobody puts Baby in the corner." (*Dirty Dancing*)

Top *Ferris Bueller's Day Off* Quotes

5 "I asked for a car, they gave me a computer. How's that for being born under a bad sign?"

4 "The sportos, the motorheads, geeks, sluts, bloods, wastoids, dweebies, dickheads—they all adore him. They think he's a righteous dude."

3 "I weep for the future."

2 "Bueller . . . Bueller . . . Bueller . . ."

1 "Life moves pretty fast. If you don't stop and look around once in a while, you could miss it."

Top *The Princess Bride* Quotes

5 "Never go in against a Sicilian when death is on the line! Hahahahahaha!" [Dies]

4 "No more rhymes now, I mean it!" "Anybody want a peanut?"

3 "Inconceivable!" "You keep using that word. I do not think it means what you think it means."

2 "As you wish."

1 "Hello. My name is Inigo Montoya. You killed my father. Prepare to die."

Top *When Harry Met Sally* Quotes

No, I did not include "I'll have what she's having." It is the most famous but there are too many better quotes.

5 "Someone is staring at you in Personal Growth."

4 "I'm going to be forty!" "When?" "Someday!"

3 "It's amazing. You look like a normal person but you are actually the Angel of Death."

2 "Thin. Pretty. *Big* tits. Your basic nightmare."

1 "You're right, you're right, I know you're right."

Epilogue

On April 27, 2013, director Steven Soderbergh walked up onstage and gave a speech at the San Francisco International Film Festival about what he saw as the state of cinema. Now, as he was the leading force behind the rise of independent filmmaking in the late eighties with the release of *Sex, Lies, and Videotape*, Soderbergh focused largely on the crushing of the independent film sector. But as he is also the man who has proven studios can make stylish and interesting commercial films, such as *Out of Sight*, *Ocean's Eleven*, and *Magic Mike*, he also had some thoughts about how studios are crushing the movie business as a whole:

> Speaking of meetings [at Hollywood studios], the meetings have gotten pretty weird. There are fewer and fewer executives who are in the business because they love movies. There are fewer and fewer executives that know movies. So it can become a very strange situation. I mean, I know how to drive a car, but I wouldn't presume to sit in a meeting with an engineer and

tell him how to build one, and that's kind of what you feel like when you're in these meetings. You've got people who don't know movies and don't watch movies for pleasure deciding what movie you're going to be allowed to make. That's one reason studio movies aren't better than they are. . . .

Well, how does a studio decide what movies get made? One thing they take into consideration is the foreign market, obviously. It's become very big. So that means, you know, things that travel best are going to be action-adventure, science-fiction, fantasy, spectacle, some animation thrown in there. Obviously the bigger the budget, the more people this thing is going to have to appeal to, the more homogenized it's got to be, the more simplified it's got to be. So things like cultural specificity and narrative complexity, and, God forbid, ambiguity, those become real obstacles to the success of the film here and abroad. . . .

If you've ever wondered why every poster and every trailer and every TV spot looks exactly the same, it's because of testing. It's because anything interesting scores poorly and gets kicked out. Now I've tried to argue that the methodology of this testing doesn't work. If you take a poster or a trailer and you show it to somebody in isolation, that's not really an accurate reflection of whether it's working because we don't see them in isolation, we see them in groups. We see a trailer in the middle of five other trailers, we see a poster in the middle of eight other posters, and I've tried to argue that maybe the thing that's making it distinctive and score poorly actually would stick out if you presented it to these people the way the real world presents it. And I've never won that argument. . . .

Now, I'm going to attempt to show how a certain kind of rodent might be smarter than a studio when it comes to picking projects. If you give a certain kind of rodent the option of hitting two buttons, and one of the buttons, when you touch it, dispenses food 40 percent of the time, and one of the buttons when you touch it dispenses food 60 percent of the time, this certain kind of rodent very quickly figures out never to touch the 40 percent button ever again. So when a studio is attempting to determine on a project-by-project basis what will work, instead of backing a talented filmmaker over the long haul, they're actually increasing their chances of choosing wrong. Because in my view, in this business, which is totally talent-driven, it's about horses, not races. . . .

The most profitable movies for the studios are going to be the big movies, the home runs. They don't look at the singles or the doubles as being worth the money or the man hours. Psychologically, it's more comforting to spend $60 million promoting a movie that costs $100 million, than it does to spend $60 million for a movie that costs $10 million. I know what you're thinking: If it costs 10 you're going to be in profit sooner. Maybe not. Here's why: OK, $10 million movie, $60 million to promote it, that's $70 million, so you've got to gross $140 million to get out.* Now you've got a $100 million movie, you're going to spend $60 million to promote it. You've got to get $320 million to get out. How many $10 million movies make $140 million? Not many. How many $100 million movies make $320 million? A pretty good number, and there's this sort of domino effect that happens too. Bigger home video sales, bigger TV sales . . .

The sort of executive ecosystem is distorted, because executives don't get punished for making bombs the way that filmmakers do, and the result is there's no turnover of new ideas,

---

* Soderbergh explained earlier in his speech that exhibitors take half the gross; therefore a movie needs to make twice what it cost in order to break even.

there's no new ideas about how to approach the business or how to deal with talent or material. But, again, economically, it's a pretty straightforward business. Hell, it's the third biggest export that we have. It's one of the few things that we do that the world actually likes. . . .

Taking the 30,000-foot view, maybe nothing's wrong, and maybe my feeling that the studios are kind of like Detroit before the bailout is totally insupportable. I mean, I'm wrong a lot. I'm wrong so much, it doesn't even raise my blood pressure anymore. Maybe everything is just fine. But . . . admissions. This is the number of bodies that go through the turnstile, ten years ago [in America]: 1.52 billion. Last year: 1.36 billion. That's a 10½ percent drop. Why are admissions dropping? Nobody knows.

Movies are filled with clichés, and so are books about movies. Probably the biggest cliché of all in a film book is to bemoan that movies aren't as good as they used to be. Well, I love eighties movies so it seems apt that I should run to the cliché.

I quoted Soderbergh's speech at some length because it seems to me that when you have a phenomenally successful studio director—as opposed to, say, a thirty-something woman in her bathrobe writing a book about her *Ghostbusters* obsession—saying that movies are getting worse, and for specific, very real reasons, he probably has a point. At the risk of sounding like Mad Ol' Granny Time, sitting in my rocking chair and reminiscing about the glory days of art when people made PROPER movies like *Twins* and *Weekend at Bernie's*, clearly the movie business is very, very different from what it was thirty years ago, and that is reflected in the movies it makes. It is simply impractical now for studios to make movies that aren't (seemingly) guaranteed bankers. No longer is there the model that a studio would make one, maybe two big blockbusters a year and that would support smaller, weirder projects like *Field of Dreams*; now the whole business model is predicated on tentpoles. In 2013 George Lucas predicted that cinemas would soon be reserved for the special and few blockbusters, and they would be seen as a luxury pastime, like the theater: "You're going to end up with fewer theaters, bigger theaters with a lot of nice things," he said. "Going to the movies will cost 50 bucks or 100 or 150 bucks—like what Broadway costs today, or a football game."

To a small degree, this is already happening, with big block-busters going to IMAX theaters. Studio movies have become too expensive to make, market, and distribute, and too dependent on foreign markets, and so they increasingly feel like monolithic identikit juggernauts, because that's what they are. The formula is safely conservative.

Ah, but what about the independent sector? you cry. Indeed, many of the best films of the past twenty-five years have come from the independent sector, from 1994's *Pulp Fiction* to 2001's *Mulholland Drive* to 2014's *Boyhood*. In fact, some of my favorite movies from the eighties were produced independently, from *Dirty Dancing* (obviously) to Spike Lee's wonderful *Do the Right Thing*, which still looks extraordinarily modern almost thirty years after it was made.

However, it has never been harder to get an independent movie released, despite all the advances in technology that have rendered them, ostensibly, cheaper to make. Soderbergh said:

In 2003, 455 films were released. Two hundred and seventy-five of those were independent, 180 were studio films. Last year 677 films were released. So you're not imagining things, there are a lot of movies that open every weekend. Five hundred and forty-nine of those were independent, 128 were studio films. So, a 100 percent increase in independent films, and a 28 percent drop in studio films, and yet, ten years ago: studio market share 69 percent, last year 76 percent.

You've got fewer studio movies now taking up a bigger piece of the pie and you've got twice as many independent films scrambling for a smaller piece of the pie. That's hard. That's really hard.

But this doesn't mean that good storytelling is dying. Far from it.

No one is sitting around now and claiming this is "the Golden Age of American Movies." Instead it is roundly agreed to the point of cliché to be the Golden Age of American TV, illustrated by the success of prestige box-set shows such as *The Sopranos*, *Sex and the City*, *The Wire*, *Mad Men*, *Breaking Bad*, *Orange Is the New Black*, and *Transparent*. All these shows were made by cable networks such as HBO and AMC, and streaming platforms like Netflix and Amazon Prime. This is where filmmakers and screenwriters can experience the luxury of making stories that aren't intended to appeal to everybody, and where they can write stories about women, abortions, sex, and older people. Shortly before Soderbergh made the above speech, he released his film about Liberace, *Beyond the Candelabra*, on HBO because "the feeling amongst the studios was that this material was too 'special' [that is, gay] to gross [the necessary] $70 million."

Filmmaker Jill Soloway has worked in theater and TV (she was the co–executive producer of *Six Feet Under*) and had made well-regarded independent films, including *Afternoon Delight* (2013), for which she won the Directing Award at the Sundance Festival. But when she got that award, instead of celebrating it, she immediately started worrying how she could make another film. "I was with all these other filmmakers and we were asking the question 'What's next?' Everyone there was so focused on distribution, and when you make a movie you have to beg and scrabble. And then this turned up."

"This" was Amazon Prime, Amazon's streaming service, which makes original films, and, through them, Soloway made the critical smash hit series *Transparent*, starring Jeffrey Tambor as a transgender father. "They don't need everybody to watch something, so I can make something that's very niche-specific, something for women, Jews, intellectuals, queers, not necessarily heterosexual white middle-class men," says Soloway.

The way Soloway sees it, the American entertainment business is now divided in two: "There's old Hollywood, that's owned by traditional corporations. There are your Time Warners and your Viacoms, and all of these organizations where you have the feeling that the people in charge of the decisions are being made on the golf course by old, white golfy men. Then you look up to the north in Silicon Valley and you think the people in charge of these companies have probably all been to Burning Man and maybe aren't so good at golf, but are people of a different generation and are able to see without waiting for their ratings and testing results, because they use their instincts."

Whether or not people at HBO have been to Burning Man, it is clear that TV has become the place for filmmakers and actors who want to tell interesting stories. It is also far more welcoming to women than movies. So many of the actresses who triumphed in film in the eighties, after finding that forty years old was still considered the sell-by date for women by Hollywood studios, have increasingly moved over to TV: Jessica Lange, Kathy Bates, Glenn Close, Sally Field.

"I remember I was in bed, online, watching Twitter and Facebook blow up when *Orange Is the New Black* started, and watching the critical reviews come in," says Soloway. "Here was a show featuring ten women in prison and the only guy was the villain. There was nobody mediating the experience of whether the women were pleasing to men. That felt like such a change."

"Actors are running now to content," says Jeffrey Tambor, the star of *Transparent*. "Amazon Prime has Malcolm McDowell, Gael García Bernal, John Goodman—they're running over there because an actor will always go to a good script. The revolution is here now and those not paying attention will go to the dinosaur area. It used to be the agent saying, 'If everything goes well [in TV] you'll get a movie,' and they don't say that anymore—it's flipped. And that's the big surprise."

This is great, of course. Maybe kids in two generations' time will dress up for Halloween like Walt and Jesse the way adults today still don proton packs for fancy dress parties. But as great as those shows can be at giving depths to characters and layers to plot, there is also an argument to be made for concision over flabbiness, punchiness over pretension. My test of a great movie is to ask myself two questions:

1. Do I want to see this movie again right now?
2. Does it make me view the world a little bit differently?

The eighties movies I've mentioned in this book fulfill both those criteria and then some. I've watched every one so many times they have become part of my mental landscape. But it takes a person with more stamina than me to watch a fifty-hour drama as many times as my generation has watched *Back to the Future*, getting to know its every nook and cranny.

There is something to be said, too, for the collective experience of seeing a movie in a theater with others, as opposed to watching it on your own on a tablet, tweeting to others, like a vision of dislocative solitude from a dystopian sci-fi novel. It is easy to get sentimental about the excitement of a movie (and alarmist about modern technology), and I'm afraid I'm a total sucker for stories about that.

"I remember going to see *Ghostbusters* on opening night and it was like a rock concert on Long Island—the line went down the whole street!" Judd Apatow recalls.

"One of the great movie experiences of my life [was *48 Hours*]," Bill Simmons writes.

> We went on opening weekend in December (me, my mother, my stepfather and a friend) to the old Avon Theater in Stamford, Connecticut. The crowd couldn't have been more jacked up—it was about 70 percent black and 100 percent pro-Eddie. If you remember, Eddie didn't appear onscreen for the first 15 minutes. When he finally showed up (the scene when Nick Nolte's character visits him in jail), there was an electricity within the theater unlike anything I can remember. People were hanging on every line, every joke, everything. At the end of the scene, when Nolte storms off and Eddie screams, "Jack! Jack! (Defiant pause.) FUCK YOU!," someone who had already caught a few showings stood up on cue and screamed "FUCK YOU!" with Eddie. And it went from there. The scene when Eddie rousts the redneck bar practically caused a riot. Bullshit, you're too fucking stupid to have a job. People were doubled over. People were cheering. I've never seen anything like it.

"There's that gag in *Coming to America* about the [black characters'] hair leaving a [grease] mark on the sofa," says John Landis. "If you saw the movie with a white audience, that scene got a little laugh—a scandalized laugh, but a laugh. But if you saw it with a black audience, they went crazy! It was terrific!"

These are collective experiences future generations simply won't have because the kinds of movies that will make it to cinemas won't inspire that same kind of love and excitement. It's fun to talk about box-set series on social media with friends and fellow fans, follow critics who live-tweet the shows. But it's not quite the same. What we've gained in fifty-hour dramas on prestige cable channels, we've lost in ninety minutes of pure pleasure in local cinemas.

But if there's one thing I've learned from eighties movies, it's that you should never end on a downer. And there is nothing to be down about! Even if there is never a Hollywood studio movie that affects people the way *Ghostbusters* or *Back to the Future* did, we still have all these wonderful, hilarious, and deeply formative movies they made in the eighties that we can watch forever. A friend asked when I started writing this book if I was worried that writing about eighties movies would make me sick of the subject. This was a fair question: after all, this friend had been to university with me and saw firsthand how studying for a degree in English literature made me incapable of reading a novel if it wasn't written by Danielle Steele for three years after graduation. With apologies to my university tutors, the same, to my huge relief but not in any way to my surprise, has not happened with this book, which conclusively proves that *Coming to America* has more depths than *To the Lighthouse*. Indeed, writing this book has achieved what I heretofore would have thought was impossible: it has made me love these movies even more.

The man who is lucky enough to share a home with me spent nine months dwelling with a strange creature who lived in a tracksuit and was incapable of fitting conversation with him (or washing herself) into her busy schedule of watching about six hours of eighties films a day, emerging only to bark out some catchphrase from *Three Amigos!* at him (like I said, he is a lucky, lucky man). In fact, just typing "*Three Amigos!*" has made me need to watch that movie again, so excuse me for a few minutes. (This, actually, was a very common problem in writing this book: every time I typed out a film's title, I had to go watch the movie again, which explains why it ended up taking so long to write. Sorry, editor people, but such are the obvious risks when you commission me to write a book that entails the typing of words like "*Tootsie*," "*Ghostbusters*," and "*Moonstruck*" repeatedly.)

But what's been an even more delightful surprise has been the reaction of others to my eighties film binge. I assumed, when I started writing this book, that people of my generation (ages, roughly, thirty to forty-five) might enjoy it and everyone else would shrug, a little bemused. Instead, the more I spoke about it to others, the more I realized these movies still occupy such a huge place in culture today, and for people of all ages. Okay, so the over-fifties in my office looked at me a bit askance when I explained I couldn't possibly work late as I was writing a ten-thousand-word essay on the genius of *Beverly Hills Cop* that evening. But twenty-somethings and teenagers would all happily squeal and tell me how much they love Molly Ringwald, how their favorite film of all time is *Back to the Future*, how much they love *Die Hard*. Often these bursts of excitement would come from teenage girls, expressing their love for Ringwald in *Pretty in Pink*, or Mary Stuart Masterson in *Some Kind of Wonderful*, or Winona Ryder in *Heathers*. And, of course, this thrilled me—there are few things more likely to warm a thirty-something's heart than the realization that the pop culture that shaped you as a teenager is still relevant and adored today. But it also made me a little sad because the fact that young people today feel such a connection to Ringwald et al. underscores the sad lack of brilliant young female characters in movies today. Studios are now too keen to appeal to as many people as possible to include a character like *Pretty in Pink*'s Andie, one who might—maybe, probably not, but who knows—scare young male audiences with her fearlessness in calling Andrew McCarthy and James Spader out for their cowardice.

Damn, there's that downer again. Let's look at the positives here and take reassurance from the fact that, clearly, audiences are a lot more sophisticated than studios think, more than able to enjoy movies about difficult girls, about abortions, about black guys being better than all the white dudes. Maybe we all knew that already, but it's nice for that suspicion to be validated.

The reason I—sorry, WE—love movies such as *Back to the Future*, *Ferris Bueller's Day Off*, *Trading Places*, and *Ghostbusters* is that they are sweetly specific in their references and completely universal in their humor and stories, whether they be about parents, friendship, or money, and that's a key combination and one that won't ever change. One question I did get asked a lot when writing this was why I like eighties movies so freaking much. The simplest answer is also the most honest: because they make me happy. I think—hell, I KNOW—they make other people happy, too. I hope this book has captured some of that.

Obviously, the only way to end this is with an eighties film quote and, when it comes to eighties films, you're spoiled for choice for quotes. Originally I thought I might go for "I guess you guys aren't ready for that yet—but your kids are gonna love it." But it didn't really make sense (not that that has ever stopped me from using an eighties quote before). Then I considered some timeless life advice: "If someone asks if you're a god you say YES!" But then I thought, The hell with it, let's go for the obvious jugular here and use the quote that sums up the message of this book, which is that movies are changing and it's easy not to notice it—with added Ferris: "Life moves pretty fast. If you don't stop and look around once in a while, you could miss it."

Eighties Movies I Didn't Look at Properly in This Book That You Really Need in Your Life

20 Weekend at Bernie's

The second-greatest Andrew McCarthy film, and that is high praise.

19 Little Shop of Horrors

Rick Moranis singing! Of course you want to see this.

18 The Blues Brothers

You probably haven't seen this for a while. You should rectify that.

17 Spaceballs

Lone Star, Dark Helmet, Pizza the Hut—it's a rare day that I don't make some reference to *Spaceballs*, and it's an even rarer day that someone recognizes it.

16   *Gremlins*

Classic eighties setting (suburbs, Christmastime) set against surprisingly black humor. Obviously, it's not a competition* but the gremlins > the ewoks.

15   *Desperately Seeking Susan*

Feminism, fashion, and Madonna.

14   *Three Amigos!*

The Singing Bush! The Invisible Horseman! This film has what its director, John Landis, rightly calls "a real commitment to silliness," and songs by Randy Newman to boot.

13   *A Christmas Story*

A Christmas classic, up there with *It's a Wonderful Life*. Like *Radio Days*, but without the sentiment.

12   *Parenthood*

Cheesy? Off the charts. But it's also really funny, really sweet, and it's got Jason Robards, Tom Hulce, Dianne Wiest, Martha Plimpton, Keanu Reeves,

---

*Everything's a competition.

Rick Moranis, Steve Martin, Mary Steenburgen, and Joaquin (then Leaf) Phoenix all being brilliant in it. Come on. PS: Can someone please cast Tom Hulce in something soon? I miss that guy.

 Young Sherlock Holmes

A truly great teen adventure film and that it isn't better known is definitive proof there is no God.

 The Flamingo Kid

A too-little-known Matt Dillon film, featuring Hector Elizondo as his father, and a truly classic 1960s soundtrack.

 The Goonies

A seminal film for so many people I know. Man, remember when Corey Feldman was one of the most awesome child actors as opposed to the reality TV casualty he is now?

 The 'Burbs

Crazy and dark, in a great way. I miss funny Tom Hanks.

7   *Stand by Me*

It would be too sad to watch poor River Phoenix as a sweet little boy if this film weren't as great as it is.

6   *Bull Durham*

Yeah, I love eighties Costner, but he is acted off the screen here by a young Tim Robbins. A great funny and sexy sports film.

5   *Troop Beverly Hills*

A movie about Girl Scouts, shopping, and the importance of shoulder pads. Shelley Long at her best.

4   *Planes, Trains and Automobiles*

After Molly Ringwald, John Candy became John Hughes's film muse, and this is the pair at their finest. John Candy's speech about liking himself will never not be heartbreaking.

3   *Bill and Ted's Excellent Adventure*

Still hilarious, still adorable. Just thinking about Napoleon going to the water park, called Waterloo, makes me laugh out loud on my own.

Field of Dreams

Best film ever about dead people playing baseball in a cornfield, and the filmmakers are welcome to put that quote on the DVD.

 Lucas

One of my favorite films of all time, albeit starring one of the most cursed casts ever. Go watch it now, it's wonderful.

Notes

Introduction

2 "We're massive fans of John Hughes": "The 1975 Takes Cues From John Hughes for Debut," radio.com, July 12, 2013.

6 "Some of the people who come up to me": Interview with the author.

8 "I still get stopped in the street": Interview with the author.

10 "There are a million reasons": Interview with the author.

10 "The studios had been individually held entities": Interview with the author.

11 The world has changed: Lynda Obst, *Sleepless in Hollywood* (New York: Simon & Schuster, January 2013).

11 But it's less brilliant: P. Nash Jenkins, "How *Transformers 4* Became the No 1 Film in Chinese History," *Time*, July 8, 2014.

11 "I doubt very much": Interview with the author.

12 "Half of my movies": Interview with the author.

12 "would rather spend $250m": *Variety*, June 12, 2013.

13 "It's very much like when television": Interview with the author.

14 Teen actors: As noted by Charlie Lyme, producer of *Beyond Clueless*.

14 "Without a film": Interview with the author.

14   *"Field of Dreams"*: Interview with the author.

15   "What happens in movies": Interview with the author.

Dirty Dancing

19   "to present it in a pleasurable way": Interview with the author.

24   "Vincent Canby": Carrie Rickey, "'Dirty Dancing': Panned as a Dud but Dynamite," *Philadelphia Inquirer,* August 19, 2012.

27   "You can have a movie": Interview with the author.

27   "The subway scene": Interview with the author.

32   What makes the movie industry's: "US Views on Overturning Roe Versus Wade," Gallup poll, January 2013.

32   The 2014 indie film *Obvious Child*: boxofficemojo.com; thanks also to Amanda Hess on medium.com for the comparison.

32   "The entertainment industry has elected": Sandra Kobrin, *"Knocked Up* Bans Abortion From Script," womensenews.org, June 20, 2007.

33   "Anyway, I'm as pro-choice": Hadley Freeman, "Judd Apatow: 'I Still Feel like a Nerd,'" *Guardian*, August 27, 2009.

33   "Any feminist out there": Hadley Freeman, "Diablo Cody: Devil's Advocate," *Guardian*, January 20, 2012.

33   But *Juno's* star: Hadley Freeman, "Ellen Page: 'Why Are People So Reluctant to Say They're Feminists?,'" *Guardian*, July 3, 2013.

34   The *Los Angeles Times*: Laurie Buckland, "The 80s: A Greenhouse for Teen Pregnancy," *Los Angeles Times,* March 14, 1993.

35   This attitude shift is reflected: Planned Parenthood.

36   "American movies have become": Interview with the author.

36   "We're like lobsters": Interview with the author.

36   By 2008, the U.S. government had spent: Guttmacher Institute.

37   Between 2006 and 2008: Planned Parenthood.

37   The Obama administration: Guttmacher Institute.

37   "One big problem": Interview with the author.

38   Thus, the U.S. ratings system: Interview with the author.

The Princess Bride

47 "*The Princess Bride* is a story about love": Interview with the author.

47 "I was absolutely smitten": Cary Elwes, *As You Wish* (New York: Touchstone, 2014).

51 "It's safe to say": Ibid.

51 "four or five entrees": Ibid.

53 "I said to them both": William Goldman, *Which Lie Did I Tell?* (New York: Pantheon, 2000).

53 "Please understand that this": Elwes, *As You Wish.*

54 "Rob unfurled the poster": Interview with the author.

55 "We were in dangerous terrain": Goldman, *Which Lie Did I Tell?*

Pretty in Pink

61 "I was growing up": Interview with the author.

62 "John was frozen in time": Interview with the author.

62 "One of the great wonders": Sean M. Smith, "Teen Days That Shook the World: The Oral History of *The Breakfast Club*," *Premiere,* December 1999.

64 "When we were filming": Interview with the author.

67 "Teenage girl [audiences]": Interview with the author.

69 "bubbly, shallow cinematic creature": Nathan Rabin, "The Bataan Death March of Whimsy Case File #1: Elizabethtown," avclub.com, January 25, 2007.

70 "Rabin is rightly uncomfortable": Ben Beaumont-Thomas, "Why the Manic Pixie Dream Girl Must Never Return," *Guardian,* July 16, 2014.

74 "I didn't want it to be a makeover scene": Smith, "Teen Days That Shook the World."

77 "*Clueless.* That changed everything": Interview with the author.

77 "*Clueless* was never meant to be": Interview with the author.

80 "This is a very different kind of knight": Susannah Gora, *You Couldn't Ignore Me If You Tried* (New York: Crown Archetype, 2010).

81 "John could be very sullen": Ibid.

When Harry Met Sally

86 "RIP Romantic Comedies": *Hollywood Reporter,* September 26, 2013.

86 "Why Are Romantic Comedies So Bad": *Atlantic,* February 20, 2013.

86 "Death of the Romcom": boxofficemojo.com, via *Jezebel,* May 20, 2013.

87 "I was the first": Interview with the author.

88 "Because I think I am an interesting woman": American Film Institute Archives, December 17, 2012.

91 "not *Annie Hall* but a movie": Mark Harris, "When Harry Met Annie," *Grantland,* July 21, 2014.

91 "What *When Harry Met Sally* . . . is really about": Nora Ephron, *The Most of Nora Ephron* (New York: Knopf, 2013).

92 "I realized that I had found a wonderful character": Ibid.

95 "I am over him": Ibid.

96 Ephron "struggled" with the screenplay: Nora Ephron, "My Life as an Heiress," *New Yorker,* October 11, 2010.

97 "I'm a guy": Hadley Freeman, "One Male to Bond Them All," *Guardian,* June 26, 2014.

97 "The reality is, I'm a dude": Tad Friend, "Funny like a Guy," *New Yorker,* April 11, 2011.

98 "Women's films, like weepies": Interview with the author.

98 "There is also a creeping sexualization": Interview with the author.

100 "trickle-down equality": Manohla Dargis, "Women in the Seats, but Not Behind the Camera," *New York Times,* December 10, 2009.

100 In 2013 women constituted: Source: Women Make Movies.

100 "You're talking about a dozen": Friend, "Funny Like a Guy."

100 "Studio executives think": Ibid.

Top Five Rick Moranis Moments

102 "I took a break because": Interview with the author.

Ghostbusters

111 "a series of soundtracks": Charles Fleming, *High Concept: Don Simpson and the Hollywood Culture of Excess* (New York: Bloomsbury Publishing, 1999).

113   "sank to the bottom": Ibid.

114   recruitment went up 400 percent: David Sirota, *Back to Our Future: How the 1980s Explain the World We Live in Now—Our Culture, Our Politics, Our Everything* (New York: Ballantine Books, 2011).

114   "setting up manned tables": Mark Evje, "*Top Gun* Boosting Service Signups," *Los Angeles Times,* July 5, 1986.

115   "hyper-macho": Inkoo Kang, "Tales of the Military-Entertainment Complex: Why the US Navy Produced *Battleship*," *Movieline,* February 6, 2013.

115   "When you know that you're going to need": David Robb, *Operation Hollywood: How the Pentagon Shapes and Censors Movies* (Amherst, NY: Prometheus Books, 2004).

120   "ancient power struggles": Adam Bertocci, "Overthinking *Ghostbusters*," runleirun.com.

120   "totally sexist": Noah Berlatsky, "Newsflash: The Original *Ghostbusters* Was Totally Sexist," ravishly.com, February 3, 2015.

122   "Abbott and Costello": Dan Aykroyd and Harold Ramis, *Making Ghostbusters*, Don Shay, ed., (San Rafael, CA: Insight Editions, 2015).

122   "a well-regarded history": Lesley M. M. Blume, "The Making of *Ghostbusters*: How Dan Aykroyd, Harold Ramis, and 'the Murricaine' Built 'The Perfect Comedy,'" *Vanity Fair,* June 4, 2014.

123   "Bill Murray, who revered": Tom Shales and James Andrew Miller, *Live from New York: An Uncensored History of Saturday Night Live* (New York: Little, Brown, 2014).

123   dead comedian's coffin: Judith Belushi Pisano and Tanner Colby, *Belushi: A Biography* (New York: Rugged Land, 2005).

123   "Belushi's death was the soul": Interview with the author.

123   "My first draft": Aykroyd and Ramis, *Making Ghostbusters*.

124   "For actors, especially": Ibid.

126   "It was trust": Ibid.

126   "My career was completely": Interview with the author.

127   "Sigourney insisted": Aykroyd and Ramis, *Making Ghostbusters*.

128   Katha Pollitt's Smurfette Principle: Katha Pollitt, "A Group of Male Buddies Accented by a Lone Female, Stereotypically Defined," *New York Times,* April 7, 1991.

129 "As soon as I read": Interview with the author.

130 "Murphy was never": Blume, "The Making of *Ghostbusters*."

130 but Aykroyd has said: Jason Matloff, "An Oral History of *Ghostbusters*," *Premiere, n.d.*

130 "As writers, we'd never done": Ibid.

132 "I don't know anyone who wants": Interview with the author.

135 "Tony [Soprano], Walter [White]": A. O. Scott, "The Death of Adulthood in American Culture," *New York Times,* September 11, 2014.

136 "the echt lesson": Peter Biskind, "The Last Crusade," in *Gods and Monsters* (New York: Nation Books, 2009).

138 "It's emphasized in the screenplay": Interview with the author.

Ferris Bueller's Day Off

144 "I remember how upset Crispin": Interview with the author.

145 "The point was that self-confidence": Interview with the author.

146 "Class has always been the central": Interview with the author.

146 "the fidelity of observation": David Thompson, *The Biographical Dictionary of Film* (New York: Knopf, 2010).

148 "John always meant": Interview with the author.

151 "You know how Salieri": Gora, *You Couldn't Ignore Me if You Tried.*

152 Shermer High School: *Ferris Bueller's Day Off, The Breakfast Club.*

152 Hill Valley High School: *Back to the Future.*

152 Westerberg High School: *Heathers.*

152 "a place of refuge": Director's commentary, *Ferris Bueller's Day Off,* DVD.

155 "I thought it was very relevant": Ibid.

156 "There is an avoidance of talk": Interview with the author.

156 "Eighties films were willing to deal": Interview with the author.

157 "Never underestimate Hollywood's eagerness": Interview with the author.

159 "never had the emotional impact": Interview with the author.

Steel Magnolias

165 "The status of women in movies": *Backlash* Book Club, medium.com, August 8, 2014.

165 "Just look at 1983": Interview with the author.

170 "People still talk to me about": Interview with the author.

172 "It was very, very hard": Interview with the author.

174 "I don't think that *Steel Magnolias*": Interview with the author.

174 "the negative sisterhood movie": Wesley Morris, "Poison Candy: *The Other Woman* and the Disastrous State of Female Comedies," *Grantland*, April 25, 2014.

175 "Back in the 80s": Updated introduction to the 15th Anniversary Edition of Susan Faludi, *Backlash* (New York: Broadway Books, 2006).

175 In 2013 women made up only 21.8 percent: Stephen Follows, "Gender Within Film Crews" (blog), http://stephenfollows.com/hg4h4/Gender _Within_Film_Crews-stephenfollows_com.pdf.

176 "I love directing women": Interview with the author.

177 The books website Goodreads: Alison Flood, "Readers Prefer Authors of Their Own Sex, Survey Finds," *Guardian*, November 25, 2014.

178 In fact, Silverstein's *Women and Hollywood* blog: Inkoo Kang, "Suck It Haters: Female-Led Films Make More Money," *Women and Hollywood* (blog), http://blogs.indiewire.com/womenandhollywood/author/ inkoo-kang.

178 "We still don't know whether gender": Amanda Hess, "Women Buy Half of All Movie Tickets. That Won't Mean More Female Characters," *Slate*, March 27, 2014.

179 "*Thelma & Louise* [which came out in 1991]": Interview with the author.

181 In a study of the top five hundred: Dr. Stacy L. Smith, Marc Choueiti, Elizabeth Scofield, and Dr. Katherine Pieper, "Gender Inequality in 500 Popular Films," Annenberg School for Communication and Journalism, University of Southern California.

181 In 2011 women accounted for: Center for the Study of Women in Television and Film.

181 In 2013 one journalist: Linda Holmes, "At the Movies, the Women are Gone," NPR.

181 That year, women made up: Martha Lauzen, "It's a Man's Celluloid World," Center for the Study of Women in Television and Film.

181 And as *New York* magazine: Amanda Dobbins, "Do They Ever Make Movies About Women?," *New York*, July 11, 2013.

182 "We can see that women are not": Interview with the author.

182 "Women have advanced": Dargis, "Women in the Seats but Not Be-
     hind the Camera."

182 After all, according to the latest: Dr. Stacy L. Smith, Marc Choueiti, and Dr.
     Katherine Pieper, "Gender Bias Without Borders: An Investigation of Fe-
     male Characters in Popular Films Across 11 Countries," http://seejane.org/
     wp-content/uploads/gender-bias-without-borders-executive-summary.pdf.

183 "Some of the more profitable": Interview with the author.

Baby Boom

192 "Unfortunately, some men": Carrie Rickey, "Baby Boom Is Her Baby,"
     Philadelphia Inquirer, October 7, 1987.

193 As journalist Megan Reynolds pointed out: Megan Reynolds, "How
     Baby Boom Set the Template for Future Movies About Working Moth-
     ers," vulture.com, July 25 2014.

195 "When Charlie and I interviewed women CEOs": Carrie Rickey, "Baby
     Boom Is Her Baby," *Philadelphia Inquirer,* October 7, 1987.

195 In one instance, Meyers was late: Carrie Rickey, "Baby Boom Is Her
     Baby," *Philadelphia Inquirer,* October 7, 1987.

200 "When Hollywood depicts a prestigious occupation": Walt Hickey,
     "Government Data Agrees: Hollywood Is Even More Sexist than the
     Real Workforce," fivethirtyeight.com, March 12, 2015.

201 Similarly, a 2014 study confirmed: Martha M. Lauzen, "It's a Man's
     (Celluloid) World: Onscreen Representations of Female Characters in
     Top 100 Films in 2014," Center for the Study of Women in Television
     and Film, 2014.

Back to the Future

212 "One afternoon, I was digging": Interview with the author.

214 "*Teen Wolf* was a teen film": Interview with the author.

215 "By the time I was cast": Interview with the author.

216 "Bob Zemeckis pointed out": Interview with the author.

218 "that reflect my psychological": Catherine Shoard, "Crispin Glover:
     Back to the Dissected Snails," *Guardian*, February 9, 2011.

220 "Gosh, we're in a high school": Tom Shone, *Blockbuster* (New York:
     Simon & Schuster, 2004).

220 "The average teen films": *Back to the Future*, DVD extra.

222 "It's in the eighties that": Interview with the author.

Batman

230 "I could add": *Burton on Burton*, Mark Salisbury, ed., (London: Faber & Faber, 1995).

231 "I know people say": Hadley Freeman, "Dark Arts," an interview with Tim Burton, *Guardian*, July 22, 2005.

231 "I was very strange": Salisbury, ed., *Burton on Burton*.

233 "Certain images": Freeman, "Dark Arts."

233 Burton has said: Ibid.

239 "gritty reality": Peter Travers, review of *The Dark Knight*, Rolling Stone, July 9, 2008.

241 "Nearly half of Americans": "More Say Iraq War Hurts Fight Against Terrorism," Pew Research Center, July 21, 2005.

241 "We will destroy innocent": David Brooks, "The Age of Conflict," *Weekly Standard*, November 5, 2001.

241 "a conservative movie": Andrew Klavan, "What Bush and Batman Have in Common," *Wall Street Journal*, July 25, 2008.

242 the cost of the war: Michael Boyle, "How the US Public Was Defrauded by the Cost of the Iraq War," *Guardian*, March 11, 2013.

242 "we need dark knights": Party Ben, "*The Dark Knight* Turns Out to Be a Dick Cheney Fantasy," MotherJones.com, July 23, 2008.

242 "certainly that wasn't": Shawn Adler, "*Dark Knight* Star Aaron Eckhart Downplays Analogy Between Batman, George W Bush," MTV.com.

243 "The president's vows": Susan Faludi, *The Terror Dream* (New York: Metropolitan Books, 2007).

243 "to tear open his shirt": Peggy Noonan, "The Right Man," *Wall Street Journal*, January 30, 2003.

243 "Bush punctuates his rhetoric": Peter Roff, "Analysis: The Return of Evildoers," upi.com, October 15, 2001.

Eddie Murphy's Eighties Movies

257 As Jimmy Early: Brian Hiatt, "Eddie Murphy Speaks," *Rolling Stone*, November 19, 2011.

263 "You know why it worked then": Ibid.

264 "That was very controversial": Interview with the author.

264 "the black guy": Quote by Neil Levy in Shales and Miller, *Live from New York*.

265 "If not for Eddie's talent and popularity": Ibid.

265 "The status of the black person": Interview with the author.

265 "treated horribly": Shales and Miller, *Live from New York*.

266 Lorne Michaels cut it: Doug Hill and Jeff Weingrad, *Saturday Night: A Backstage History of* Saturday Night Live (Untreed Reads at http://www. untreedreads.com, August 2015).

266 "It's too white": Shales and Miller, *Live from New York*.

266 "this weird, Waspy": Ibid.

266 "Eddie never catered": Bill Simmons, "The Career Arc: Eddie Murphy," *Grantland*, November 10, 2011.

267 "I never connected": Richard Pryor, *Pryor Convictions and Other Life Sentences* (New York: Pantheon Books, 1995).

269 "From the very beginning": Hiatt, "Eddie Murphy Speaks."

270 "*Trading Places*, John Landis movies": Ibid.

272 "There's this little box": Ibid.

274 "I know because of the level": Spike Lee, "Eddie," *Spin,* October 1990.

275 "I don't think you can beat": Ibid.

276 "The scariest thing": Ibid.

276 "I am very black": Ibid.

278 "You get these black people": Ibid.

278 "If I was rubbing you": Ibid.

279 "I went back to the house": Ibid.

283 "Hollywood had to be convinced": Interview with the author.

283 "His films introduced": Interview with the author.

284 "Eddie's movies have grossed": Simmons, "The Career Arc."

284 In 2014, for example: "Inequality in 700 Popular Films," Smith, Choueiti, Pieper, Gillig, Lee De Luca, USC Annenberg.

285 "No matter what you do": Hiatt, "Eddie Murphy Speaks."

Epilogue

299 "I was with all these other filmmakers": Interview with the author.

301 "Actors are running": Interview with the author.

302 "I remember going to see *Ghostbusters*": Interview with the author.

302 "One of the great movie": Simmons, "The Career Arc."

302 "There's that gag": Interview with the author.

Acknowledgments

Enormous thanks to the following, for their love, support and advice. You guys can be my posse in an eighties teen film anytime: Andy Bull, Carol Miller, Nell Freeman, India Knight, Catherine Shoard, Tim Robey, Julia Kingsford, Charlie Campbell, Ed Howker, Adam Curtis, Patrick Kennedy, Benedict Cumberbatch, Dixie Chassay, Kamila Shamsie, Michael Hogan, Peter Bradshaw, and Arthur Ferdinand Freeman.

Huge thanks, too, to my editors at the *Guardian*, Catherine Shoard (again), Malik Meer, Tim Lusher, and Nosheen Iqbal for commissioning me to interview various eighties legends for the newspaper during the writing of this book, thereby making it much easier for me to track them down. You guys are nothing like the evil bosses in eighties movies.

Endless gratitude to two people in particular: first, my agent, Georgia "patience of Job" Garrett, who had faith in this book when no one else did, myself very much included (I know that's a terrible cliché for a writer to say about their agent, but it really is the truth here). Next, to my ceaselessly supportive editors in the United Kingdom and United States: Louise Haines at 4th Estate and Emily Graff at Simon & Schuster.

For professional insights and interviews, thank you so much to Celestia Fox, Steven Gaydos at *Variety*, Paul Feig, Judd Apatow, Col Needham at IMDB.com, Jill Soloway, Jeffrey Tambor, Peter Biskind, Mark Cousins, Tom Shone, Mark Kermode, Linda Ruth Williams, Lynda Obst, and Melissa Silverstein. Rebecca Wind and Laura Lindberg at the Guttmacher Institute helped me with research on the history of U.S. sex education while Natika Halal and Bekki Burbidge at the Family Planning Association, Harriet Gill at Brook Advisory, and Lucy Emmerson at the Sex Education Forum provided me with the British perspective. Joan Graves at the MPAA and David Cooke patiently talked me through the ratings systems in their two countries. Dr. Helen Sharpe at the Institute of Psychiatry talked to me about the influence of celebrities' body shape on teenagers' self-image, a subject matter I didn't, in the end, write about in this book but may well return to in another. Eileen Jones at the University of California, Berkeley and Dr. James Russell at De Montfort University were fascinating about the depiction of social class in movies. Professor Mark Anthony Neal at Duke University and Professor Anna Everett at University of California, Santa Barbara very kindly talked to me about African-American pop culture in the 1980s and helped me to place both Eddie Murphy and Spike Lee in context. All of the mistakes in the discussion of these subjects in this book are mine.

Finally, enormous thanks to all my eighties movie interviewees for pretending not to notice that I was and am utterly starstruck by them all: Molly Ringwald, John Landis, Ivan Reitman, Jon Avnet, Matthew Broderick, Amy Heckerling, Andrew McCarthy, Michael J. Fox, Cary Elwes, Nancy Meyers, Tom Hanks, Lea Thompson, Crispin Glover, Howard Deutch, Tim Burton, Rick Moranis, Kathleen Turner, Geena Davis, Eleanor Bergstein, Olympia Dukakis, Bob Harling, Bob Gale, and Ron Howard.

Index

About the Author

HADLEY FREEMAN is a columnist and writer for *The Guardian* newspaper in the UK. She was born in New York and lives in London. Her other books include *The Meaning of Sunglasses* and *Be Awesome*, and her work has appeared in *VOGUE* US and UK, *New York* magazine, *Harper's Bazaar*, and many other publications.